THE POSITION OF WOMEN IN INDIAN LIFE

THE POSITION OF WOMEN IN INDIAN LIFE

SIDDHA MOHANA MITRA

GYAN

Published by

Gyan Publishing House
5, Ansari Road
Daryaganj, New Delhi-110002
Phone: 011-47034999, 9811692060
E-mail: books@gyanbooks.com

Distribution Network
gyanbooks.com
India, USA, Canada, UK, Australia

ISBN: 978-93-6920-281-2 (PB)

First Published, 1911

2nd Impression 2025

Printed at: Gyan Press, Delhi.

THE POSITION OF WOMEN IN INDIAN LIFE
Author: SIDDHA MOHANA MITRA

THE
POSITION OF WOMEN IN INDIAN LIFE

THE MAHARANI OF BARODA

THE POSITION OF WOMEN IN INDIAN LIFE

S. M. MITRA

AUTHOR OF

"LIFE OF SIR JOHN HALL," "INDIAN PROBLEMS," "HINDUPORE," ETC.

1912

TO

INDIAN WOMEN

THIS WORK IS

DEDICATED

"Women must solve the problems of humanity."—IBSEN

PREFACE TO THE SECOND EDITION

In three months the first edition has been exhausted. No alterations have been made in this edition. Some useful suggestions have been received both from this country and India, and I shall be happy to have further hints from various provinces of India which might add to the utility of this book.

S. M. MITRA.

London,
February 1, 1912.

PREFACE

BY HER HIGHNESS THE MAHARANI OF BARODA

During the course of several visits to the West, both to Europe and to America, I was naturally struck by the difference between the position of woman in English and in Indian public life, as represented by her share in the organizations for human welfare in the two countries. The co-operation which exists between Western men and women in public affairs is practically unknown in India. Public matters in India are almost entirely in the hands of men, and the reason is not far to seek, because the useful organizations for human welfare, in which women co-operate with men in the West, hardly exist in India, and where they do technically exist, their influence is scarcely felt. What can be the reason for this great difference? Should the Indian woman continue to be isolated from all public affairs? What is the remedy, and how is it to be applied? These were the questions that each succeeding visit to the West brought with ever-increasing force to my mind, and I often wondered whether I could do anything to awaken my Indian sisters from their lethargy of ages, to enable them to take their proper place in Indian public life. I therefore tried to learn what I could from the Western systems—British, Continental and American—which came under my observation, feeling strongly that I owed it to my sisters in India to give them the benefit of the impressions gathered during my travels on matters peculiarly affecting the position of women. Some of the experience thus gained I was anxious to lay before my countrywomen, with a view to receive opinions and contributions from all parts of India, and with the hope that some of the Western organizations might be adapted to the conditions of my native land. But here I met with a great difficulty, which at first appeared almost insuperable. It is one thing to be impressed with the position of women in Western public life and with their useful organizations, but it is quite another thing to be able to convey such impressions to others who have not been out of India at all. Not only accurate information, direct and collateral, was wanted, but it was necessary to edit such facts carefully and in good style, with a view to Indian requirements and with particular reference to the Hindu caste system. I therefore saw at once that I needed the co-operation of an able and well-informed literary man, who could handle the subject with special knowledge acquired on the spot. The question then naturally arose as to whether I should entrust the work to an Englishman or to one of my own countrymen. To my mind an Englishman, however clever, cannot possibly understand the subtleties of the Hindu caste system, which are factors of great importance in every organization in India. The manners and customs of Indian Mahomedans would also present considerable difficulty to him. For these reasons I decided, during my last visit to England, to confide the task of materializing my views to the distinguished Hindu writer Mr. S. M. Mitra, who is also well acquainted with Moslem ways, having lived for years in the great Mahomedan State of Hyderabad. He at once willingly responded to my suggestion, and on my return to England I found that he had finished editing my impressions, having supplemented them with valuable information, the result of his study of Western sociology during his seven years' residence in England. That is the genesis of this book, which is now being published in the hope that additional contributions and opinions from all parts of India may be collected and carefully edited, with the object of deciding what practical form women's organization should take there. Now in this year of the Coronation, when so many prominent Indian men and women have come to England, let us hope that they have probed deep into the workings of British social government, that they have attempted to find out what are the pillars upon which the great edifice of British institutions rests, and especially what part women take here in the maintenance of this the social and moral system of a nation which owns the greatest Empire ever known in the history of the world.

The ideas put forward in these pages are naturally mere sketches and imperfect suggestions, for volumes could be written on each subject alone, many of which it has been considered necessary to pass over in short paragraphs. Some of the projects dealt with have already been tried in Baroda, though not solely for the benefit or with the co-operation of women. For instance, Co-operative Credit Societies have been taken up by men to a considerable extent, as discussed in the Baroda Administration Report, 1908-9, which showed a total of thirty-two of these societies at the end of the year. Agricultural Banks are also in operation, but progress is admittedly slow in these directions. There is a Model Farm which was started in December, 1908, the head-master being a diploma-holder, capable of instructing his pupils in the comparative merits of Eastern and Western methods. The Borstal System for young criminals, introduced since April, 1908, is employed for boys, and the Thana System of sending certain selected prisoners to work at a Model Farm, as practically free men, was introduced in December, 1908. But these methods are not universal throughout India, and none are as yet in force for the benefit of women or girls. It has therefore been thought expedient to give some short account of their principles and progress in other lands.

The system of providing travelling instructors to teach the people dairy-farming and other agricultural processes has been tried in Baroda, and found of little practical use; hence the abolition of these posts, as recorded in the Baroda Administration Report for 1908-9. Various other schemes attempted in India have not had quite the brilliant success that their promoters hoped. May not the reason of this be that hitherto systematic feminine co-operation has been lacking? With this idea in view, some projects for Indian women have been described which Indian men do not at present regard very favourably, in the hope that the former may step in where, single-handed, their fathers, brothers, or husbands have failed, and show that the co-operation of both sexes is necessary to insure successful organization.

In December last I was present with my husband at the Allahabad Exhibition, and the thought came to me there that every Native State in India should send at least two women scholars to Europe to qualify themselves as teachers of such subjects as are discussed in this book, especially in Chapters II. to XI. My

State is prepared to lead the way in this direction by offering two scholarships to ladies, one to a Hindu and the other to a Mahomedan, to enable and encourage them to carry out my project.

What struck me at the Allahabad Exhibition was the want of women instructors. If there were women lecturers to teach *purda* ladies the advantages of exhibitions and the methods of organizing them, dozens of small exhibitions would spring up in all parts of India, and would do a great deal of good. It is evident that my countrywomen are beginning to take a keen interest in these exhibitions, for at Allahabad I noticed that numbers of *purda* ladies attended at the usual times, and no doubt profited largely by the displays of artistic and industrial work which were on view. Such visits cannot fail to have an immensely educative effect, and their results might be made still more lasting if some system of explaining the various objects and the different processes of manufacture were set on foot. Such operations as sugar-making, juggery-making from the date-palm tree, rosa grass distillation for the manufacture of perfumes, sericulture, the working of a printing press, the making of glass, gold and silver enamels, pencils and nibs, matches, hosiery, carpets, and other textile industries, which were all on view at the Navsari Exhibition, opened last April by the Maharaja of Baroda, would have assuredly acquired an added interest in the eyes of the lady visitors if there had been someone of their own sex to lecture to them on the exhibits. The plan now adopted at the British Museum of sending a lecturer round, when desired, to explain briefly to visitors the history of the objects there displayed, might with advantage be adopted in our agricultural and other exhibitions. In this way a stock of most useful and practical information would be gained, such as could not be acquired from text-books, and the task of lecturing would be a pleasant occupation for educated women.

What appeared as the more striking phases of forward movements affecting feminine interests in England and elsewhere are given in this book, and I leave it to my countrywomen to decide which of them—modified to suit local circumstances—are worthy of a trial. Some of the projects will no doubt appeal to them, but it would nevertheless be well for them to bear in mind the need to guard against too slavish an imitation of Western notions. Every country by intelligent observation can learn something from other lands, but at the same time each should strive to preserve its own racial characteristics, just as each sex should endeavour, not to ape the other, but to make the most of its own peculiar distinctions of character. There should be no hasty adoption of customs essentially foreign to our habits. In the words of Bacon, the great English philosopher: "It were good that men in their innovations would follow the example of Time itself, which, indeed, innovateth greatly, but quietly, and by degrees scarce to be perceived. . . . It is good also not to try experiments in States, except the necessity be urgent, or the utility evident." Experience has shown in some cases that Western ideas transplanted to Eastern soil have not been wholly successful, and certain questions, particularly labour problems, differ totally in England and India. But it is also possible to lean too much to the ultra-conservative side, a phase of which the same philosopher speaks thus: "A froward retention of custom is as turbulent a thing as an innovation; and they that reverence too much old times are but a scorn to the new."

So, proceeding with circumspection, I hope that something tangible may be effected to raise woman's position in Indian public life. I trust, however, that it has been made quite clear throughout this little volume that what is required is not antagonism, but co-operation between the sexes; that woman needs the guidance of man to enable her to achieve the highest of which she is capable, as man needs woman's help and sympathy to aid him on his path through life. Feminine individuality is essentially distinct from the masculine. The characteristic features of both are deeply rooted, and any effort to coerce them would probably mean not evolution but revolution. The great organic distinctions between man and woman will always tend to produce different characteristics in each. Such differences should be fostered, not checked; that development may proceed on natural lines, following the guidance of those fundamental dissimilarities which through long ages have been the distinguishing marks of the sexes.

In addition to British institutions, it has been thought advisable to give an account of some of the projects that have been tried for the benefit of women in other countries, especially in France, Germany, and America, as representing the other foremost nations of the world. It is hoped that the chapter on Japan will be read with special interest. My visit to that country convinced me that Japanese women have not made progress in comparison with the advance of their men.

In conclusion, I thank Mr. Mitra for his pains-taking labour, which has enabled me to bring my ideas to maturity, and for the hearty co-operation which he has accorded to the work from its first conception to the final revision of the proofs.

LONDON,
July 22, 1911.

NOTE

WHEN I wrote a few years ago, "India must learn Western ways and keep pace with the West, or she must go to the wall. India must assimilate Western ways. Blind imitation will not do. The Indian must try to harmonize Eastern practice with Western civilization,"* I had no idea that the thoughts of the most prominent Hindu Princess were turning in the same direction. I need hardly say, therefore, that I was much gratified when, last year, the Maharani of Baroda made known her views to me, and desired my humble co-operation in a work which Her Highness wished to project on those lines for the benefit of our countrywomen. The result is now laid before the public in the present volume, "The Position of Women in Indian Life," which gives an account, not of the present status of the female sex in India, but of some Western feminine institutions, the adaptation of which to suit Eastern requirements is likely to help Indian women to achieve a higher

* "Indian Problems," p. 393. John Murray, 1908.

position in public life than they at present hold. When the Hindus were a great nation, there was more practical sympathy between the sexes in matters of public utility than is to be found in India at the present day. There is no more useful work than the promotion of such harmonious co-operation between man and woman, for on that the peace and welfare of the world depend. To the Maharani I therefore tender my grateful thanks for affording me this opportunity of collaborating in Her Highness's most excellent and noble project, which has been conceived in the hope of furthering the interests of our motherland.

It is impossible to enumerate all the books into which I have dipped during the years of my residence in England in which I have studied this subject, but the annexed bibliography gives the titles of some of the works consulted, to the authors of which I am much indebted for valuable information, and to whom my best thanks are due. I also wish to express my obligation to several English ladies and gentlemen who have helped me with useful information, and have very kindly promised their assistance in building up women's associations in India.

S. M. MITRA.

LONDON,
July 31, 1911.

BIBLIOGRAPHY

ABRAHAM, MAY E., and A. LLEWELYN DAVIES. *The Law relating to Factories and Workshops.*

ALDEN, MRS. PERCY. *Child Life and Labour.*

ARIGA, DR. *Japanese Red Cross Society and the Japanese War.*

ASTON, W. G. *History of Japanese Literature.*

AVES, ERNEST. *Report on Wages Board, etc., of Australia and New Zealand.*

BACON, ALICE MABEL. *Japanese Girls and Women.*

BEBEL, AUGUST. *Woman in the Past, Present, and Future.*

BLACK, CLEMENTINA. *Sweated Industry.*

BOOTH, CHARLES. *Life and Labour of the People in London.*

BRABROOK, SIR E. W. *Provident Societies and Industrial Welfare.*

BRINKLEY, CAPTAIN F. *Japan and China.*

CADBURY, EDWARD, M. CÉCILE MATHESON, AND GEORGE SHANN. *Women's Work and Wages.*

CHAMBERLAIN, B. H. *Things Japanese.*

CLEVELAND, A. R. *Women under English Law.*

COBBE, FRANCES POWER. *The Duties of Women.*

COLLET, CLARA E.

1. *Educated Working Women.*
2. *Report on Changes in the Employment of Women and Girls in Industrial Centres.*
3. *Report on the Statistics of Employment of Women and Girls.*

D'AUTREMER, J. *Japanese Empire.*

DIÓSY, ARTHUR. *The New Far East.*

DUTT, R. C. *The Peasantry of Bengal.*

ELLIS, HAVELOCK. *Man and Woman.*

FRASER, SIR ANDREW. *Among Indian Rajahs and Ryots.*

GILMAN, N. P. *Profit Sharing between Employer and Employee.*

GORST, SIR JOHN E. *The Children of the Nation.*

HAGGARD, H. RIDER. *Regeneration.*

HEARN, LAFCADIO. *Japan : an Interpretation.*

HIGGS, MARY and EDWARD E. HAYWARD. *Where Shall She Live?*

HOLYOAKE, GEORGE JACOB. *History of Co-operation.*

HUTCHINS, B. L., and AMY HARRISON. *The History of Factory Legislation.*

KAKUZO, O. *Awakening of Japan.*

KEELING, FREDERIC. *The Labour Exchange in Relation to Boy and Girl Labour.*

KRUKENBERG, ELSBETH. *Die Frauenbewegung.*

LANESSAN, J. L. DE. *L'Éducation de la Femme Moderne.*

LAWSON, LADY. *Highways and Homes of Japan.*

LOCH, C. S. *Charity Organisation.*

LOMBROSO. *The Man of Genius.*

LYTTELTON, HON. MRS. ARTHUR. *Women and Their Work.*

MACDONALD, J. R. *Women in the Printing Trades.*

MACKAY, THOMAS. *The State and Charity.*

,, ,, *Methods of Social Reform.*

MADDISON, ARTHUR J. S. *Hints on Rescue Work.*

MASON, PROFESSOR OTIS. *Woman's Share in Primitive Culture.*

MCKENZIE, F. A. *Waste Humanity.*

MEAKIN, BUDGETT. *Model Factories and Villages.*

MILL, J. S. *Subjection of Women.*

MOCHIZUKI, KOTARO. *Japan To-Day.*

MORISON, SIR THEODORE. *Industrial Organization of an Indian Province.*

MORSE, PROFESSOR. *Japanese Homes.*

NORMAN, H. *Real Japan.*

OKUMA, COUNT. *Fifty Years of New Japan.*

POOL, JOHN J. *Woman's Influence in the East.*

Pratt, Edwin A. *Pioneer Women in Queen Victoria's Reign.*

Reich, Emil. *Woman through the Ages.*

Sainte-Croix, A. de. *Le Feminisme.*
Scherer, J. *Young Japan.*
Smith, Constance. *The Case for Wages Boards.*
Stopes, M. C. *A Journal from Japan.*
Swiney, Frances. *The Awakening of Women.*

Takaishi, Shingoro. Introduction to *Women and Wisdom of Japan.*
Tuckwell, Gertrude M., and others. *Women in Industry.*
Tyndale, W. *Japan and the Japanese.*

Webb, Catherine. *Industrial Co-operation.*
Webb, Mrs. Sidney. *The Case for the Factory Acts.*
White, Arnold. *The Great Idea.*
Wilson. *Poultry-keeping for Women.*
Wolseley, Hon. Frances. *Gardening for Women.*

Zimmern, Alice. *Renaissance of Girls' Education in England.*

REPORTS, PAMPHLETS, ETC.

Apprenticeship and Skilled Employment Association. Reports.

Baroda Administration Reports, 1907-8, 1908-9.

Charity Organization Society. Pamphlets and Leaflets.
Christian Social Union Reports.
Co-Education. Edited by Alice Woods.
Conferences of Rescue Workers, convened by the National Union of Women Workers. Reports.

Deuxième Congrès International des Œuvres et Institutions Féminines (1900). Compte Rendu des Travaux. 4 Vols.

East India Co-operative Credit Societies Return. (97.)
East Indian Factory Labour Commission, 1908. 2 Vols.
East India (Textile Factories). Cd. 3617.
Encyclopædia Britannica (11th Edition).

English Poor Law Commission. Report (1909).

Englishwoman's Review of Social, Industrial, and Educational Questions affecting Women.

Englishwoman's Year Book.

Fingerpost. Published by the Central Bureau for the Employment of Women.

Friendly Societies. Reports of the Chief Registrar for year ending December 31, 1909. Part A. (171.)

Guide to Sanitary Inspectors (P. S. King and Son).

International Association for Labour Legislation. Reports and Papers.

Japan Year Book (1911).

Local Government Board. Reports.

London County Council. The Apprenticeship Question, 1906.

Metropolitan Association for Befriending Young Servants Reports and Leaflets.

National Society for the Prevention of Cruelty to Children. Reports and Papers.

National Union of Women Workers. Reports and Pamphlets.

Position of Woman, Actual and Ideal. Preface by Sir Oliver Lodge.

Report of the London County Council on Technical Instruction for Women, 1903.

Salvation Army. Pamphlets.

Scottish Council for Women's Trades. Leaflets and Pamphlets.

Special Reports on Educational Subjects (Wyman).

Statistik der Frauenorganizationen im Deutschen Reiche (1909).

Technical Education for Women and Girls at Home and Abroad. The Women's Industrial Council.

Women's Industrial Council. Reports and Papers.

CONTENTS

CHAPTER I

THE WOMAN MOVEMENT

CHAPTER II

PROFESSIONS FOR WOMEN

CHAPTER III

AGRICULTURE

CHAPTER IX

DOMESTIC SCIENCE

CHAPTER X

WOMEN INSPECTORS

CHAPTER XI

MATRONS AND SUPERINTENDENTS

CHAPTER XII

CO-OPERATION

CHAPTER XIII

MONEY-LENDING

CHAPTER XIV

CHARITABLE ORGANIZATIONS

CHAPTER XV

THRIFT

CHAPTER XVI

ANTI-SWEATING

CHAPTER XIX

WOMEN IN JAPAN

THE POSITION OF WOMEN IN INDIAN LIFE

CHAPTER I

THE WOMAN MOVEMENT

WHEN the final chronicle of the twentieth century comes to be written, probably the most remarkable feature in its annals will be the history of the development of woman. Far and wide throughout the world to-day a new energy is spreading amid the ranks of women of every class. Rich and poor, educated and ignorant, all alike feel the dawning of an era of fresh usefulness for their sex. From North and South, East and West the active impulse comes, and women of every land call to one another to join hands for the enlightenment and betterment of their sisters, that they all may help in the great forward movement of the world. This activity among women is a sign of good, for it is at one with an inclination towards a more universal brotherhood that is sweeping over mankind. Over the Atlantic the women of America recognized the same impulse as the women of Europe. Through England, France, and Germany, across the Continent it passed, gathering force as it sped, till the women of the East felt its summons, and are taking their part also in the fresh life which is dawning in this second decade of the twentieth century.

So widespread a feeling must be taken seriously. Above the strife and noisy extravagance of the public champions of the cause of women, there is a true and earnest endeavour which the thoughtful mind of either sex acknowledges and approves. Therefore, since no one can ignore the progress or the sincerity of the movement, we propose to give a very brief account of the history of woman throughout the world, to remind the women of India of the position in public affairs which their sex occupies to-day. Some of the actions of their sisters in other lands may seem to them worthy of adaptation; others may be pitfalls to be avoided. In either case the subject is one full of importance, alike to East and West.

In the earliest times of which we have any historical knowledge men and women were grouped together in hordes, and seem to have led a nomadic life, holding all their possessions in common. The primitive ancestors of Indo-European stock probably had their home in Asia, near the Hindu Kush Mountains, though later critics have assigned North-East Europe as their dwelling-place. There they spoke the same language and venerated the same gods. In primitive times woman would appear to have been fully equal, both mentally and physically, to man, and observations made among savage races of the present day, who are presumably at a similar stage of civilization, also point to this conclusion, since we find among them little or no difference between the male and female, either in physique or brain-power. The next step in the advance of civilization was the banding together of hordes into tribes, and gradually the separate tribes, migrating in different directions, developed into various nations of the earth. Their common characteristics disappeared in time to a great extent, under the influence of changed surroundings, of which climate is the most important feature in the evolution of distinct nationality.

In the most primitive stage of human life there was no permanent union between man and woman. Afterwards the custom of marriage arose, out of which developed in turn the home, the family, the tribe, the nation. It was woman who reared the children, built the rude hut or tent in which the family lived, made what scanty clothing they possessed, fed the household, in short, performed the general domestic labour, and left man to do most of the work outside the home. Later on, when, the human race increasing, it was found incumbent to sow and plant, it was chiefly woman who at harvest-time gathered in the crops. Subsequently the nomadic life of the tent was abandoned for that of a fixed home, and her position improved, but she still remained the property of her husband, who had absolute right over her in every way. Such was woman's condition in primitive times.

But a gleam of brightness breaks upon the pages of her early history. Strangely enough, amid the bygone civilizations of the world, an era of glory dawned for woman, and we find in most nations a heroic age, when woman was worshipped and set in the highest place of honour. In the ancient literature of India, dating from centuries before European culture began, in the great epics of the Ramayana and Mahabharata, woman took distinguished part in her husband's work, aiding him with her love and counsel, accompanying him, like Sita and Draupadi, even into exile. She shared in the public ceremonies, and was accorded the highest rank and dignity.

This heroic age of woman differed considerably in date among the various nations. Earliest among the Egyptians, Hindus, and Hebrews, it did not reach Europe till about the Christian Era. Judæa had its golden age for women in the days of Miriam; also about the twelfth century B.C., when Deborah, the prophetess, arose, "a mother in Israel," who "dwelt under the palm-tree between Rama and Bethel in Mount Ephraim: and the children of Israel came up to her for judgment." To this woman-judge of the Hebrews is due what is assuredly one of the most exultant battle-songs in all literature, the hymn of victory chanted by Deborah after Jael's slaughter of Sisera. So we find in ancient Judæa women as rulers, prophetesses, judges, warriors.

In early ages the Musalman woman of Arabia was permitted equal instruction with men. The social position she occupied when the power of Islam reached its meridian proves that she possessed rights similar to those enjoyed by men. The Prophet's own women-folk were very far from leading lives of idle seclusion. On the contrary, they were allowed great freedom. His first wife, Khadija, shared the changes and chances of his career for twenty-five years, and, after her death, Ayesha, his young wife, took prominent part as an active combatant at the "Battle of the Camel." His daughter Fatima gained high distinction in political debate. His granddaughter Zainab was noted for her attainments both in public and private life. A life of empty idleness was no part of the Prophet's scheme of feminine existence. Moslem women held positions as sovereigns, teachers, theologians, and superintendents of religious communities, and, like Hindu women, were famous for learning, eloquence, and capacity to impart instruction. In the reign of the Sultan Bayazid I., women gave lectures in the mosques and schools to students of either sex, and in those days girls and boys were educated together. In the days of the Ommayads and of the first Abbasids, until the reign of Kadir b'Illah (A.D. 921), when progress in the Musalman world began to decline, women took prominent part in public life. Under Mansur, two of his women cousins went forth to the Byzantine Wars, clad in coats of mail. In the reign of Rashid-el-Mamun, ladies took part in poetic contests and learned discussions, while young Arab maidens fought on horseback and commanded regiments. The Empress Zubeida wife of Harun-al-Rashid, was renowned as a poetess, and with her money the great aqueduct at Mecca was constructed and the town of Alexandria rebuilt after its destruction by the Greeks. The category of Musalman women who similarly distinguished themselves in almost every art of peace and war is too long for quotation. It only ceases when the invasions of Tartar hordes and religious or dynastic struggles checked the onward march of civilization in the East, and in the general retrogression the cause of the Mahomedan woman suffered wellnigh total eclipse. In ancient Egypt women were the equals and comrades of their men-folk; the law conferred like privileges upon them; they were eligible for the priesthood and the throne.

Greece, too, from her Homeric Age has handed down types of noble, honoured womanhood, such as will live for ever in the pages of her literature.

Penelope, Andromache, Clytemnestra, are names that will keep her memory green in the history of the world's women. Italy, also, in the early days of the Republic, has given mankind an ideal of the Roman matron, steadfast, brave, resolute as her husband, yet tender and loving withal. Among the Germans we find a time when, according to Tacitus, women were the chieftains of certain tribes, and excelled the men in valour and wisdom, so that, speaking of the Teutonic conception of women, he says: "They hold that there is in her something Divine." Nor can Britain be omitted from the category of the lands that, thus early, honoured women, since she, too, had her Boadicea, that warlike Queen of ancient Britain, who herself drove her chariot against the invading Romans.

Yet this early liberty was but a phantom dawn of freedom for woman. It passed, and a period in each case followed when her progress was checked. Among the upper classes a frivolous, or purely passive existence, now fell to her lot: among the lower ranks, a degrading, soulless toil.

Not until mediæval times does a fresh glimpse of sunshine flood her path. Through Europe, generally, the Middle Ages brought a revival of the honour formerly paid to woman. This was the time of chivalry, when the Knight-at-Arms devoted himself to the service of the poor and weak, when, under the influence of woman, the old love of brute force gave way before the nobler standard of right and duty. Every warrior, in taking upon himself the sacred vows of knighthood, swore, at the same time, an oath of allegiance to his Lady, and in his devotion to her there mingled the dim and holy adoration of the worshipper for his God. Surely never had European woman more power than in those centuries of chivalry!

Intellectually, woman had high distinction in the so-called Dark Ages, for we find lady-professors and doctors abounding on the Continent of Europe, and lecturing to students of both sexes. Various towns in Germany admitted women to trades, on a footing of perfect equality with men, and in France there were corporations of women-workers who had the monopoly of certain callings suitable to their sex. In the latter country, men and women voted equally in the management of the affairs of the different municipalities, and, after the Crusades, when wars for the protection of the Holy Sepulchre had decimated the ranks of the male population in France, women took up the administration of their lords' estates, proving themselves just and efficient in the highest degree. Thus, woman was the light of the Dark Ages of Europe.

But the inevitable reaction set in; for no sooner do we find a period of enlightenment, than, within a few centuries, we see her dejected again. This time it was due to the Renaissance, that passionate love of beauty in art, in literature, and above all in woman, which, spreading from Italy, infected France, England, and the larger part of Europe with its young enthusiasm. It was a great intellectual movement, this Revival of Learning, as men also named it, but the mad desire for freedom led to excess in all things, and woman, though outwardly deferred to as before, was no longer the inspirer of the purer worship of the Knights of the Middle Ages. Alongside intellectual refinement there grew up unbridled licentiousness, and in the sixteenth century we find the Court of Marguérite de Valois, sister of Francis I., one of the most immoral in history. In the seventeenth century, in France, woman was pre-eminent in intellectual culture, and we find her, as in Madame de Maintenon, the adviser of Kings and the educator of the young; in Mademoiselle de Scudéry and Madame de Sévigné, the personification of feminine intelligence.

In England, in the reign of Charles II., the reaction after the Reformation swung the pendulum over to the opposite extreme. As the old reverence for women departed, a frivolous, light, and inconsequent side of feminine nature developed, against which the satire of the time, in the epigram of Pope, directed its lash. In his second Epistle, dedicated "To a Lady," those who will may read his opinion of the society woman of the day. Meantime, in spite of culture in the higher ranks, the lower classes, engaged solely in the deadening round of domestic toil, were still sunk in ignorance and apathy. "Home-keeping youths have ever homely wits," and so it proved with the majority of women of lower rank in the eighteenth century in Europe. Not till the latter half of the nineteenth century, when again light dawned, in the shape of higher education, did woman once more lift up her head, and she seems now on the highroad to permanent freedom of development. It is to be noted that most of the Western nations, which have formally granted her the greatest liberty, are not (except America and Russia) of foremost rank as world-powers. In Finland, Norway, Sweden, Iceland, she is legally most emancipated. Finnish women may vote and sit in Parliament. In Norway women municipal franchise holders possess the parliamentary franchise. In Russia, which it has been said should be called the most Western of Eastern, instead of the most Eastern of Western nations, women have made marvellous progress, and have distinguished themselves in the political world. The Zemstvo and all the progressive political parties acknowledge the principle of absolute equality for men and women, and the latter are practising in most of the liberal professions. Many are doctors, several are engineers, while the number of literary aspirants increases daily at an almost alarming rate, for at the present time to be an authoress who has published a book is a hall-mark for the Russian literary woman.

Each country has its own peculiar phase of the woman question. In England woman's general condition since feudal days has been one of social freedom, but where she has had to enter the labour-market in competition with men, she has sometimes suffered disadvantage. By degrees she has won her way through, till now most of the liberal professions, except the Law and the Church, are open to her, and the majority of other callings, except those for which her physical limitations manifestly unfit her. A few of the stages marking the Englishwoman's progress may be briefly noted. In 1870 the Married Women's Property Act was passed (amended 1882), by which a married woman is capable of acquiring, holding, and disposing, by will or otherwise, of any real or personal property, and may enter into any contract or carry on a trade. The Hindu woman has enjoyed these rights since the days of Manu, probably before the Christian Era. In 1894 qualified Englishwomen were granted permission to vote for District Councils, Boards of Guardians, London County Council, and Parish Council elections. They can be elected on County and Borough Councils, Education Committees, Boards of Guardians, District and Parish Councils. In 1907 women were allowed the privilege of being Aldermen and Mayors, but they cannot act as Justices of the Peace nor can they sit on juries, as they may do in America, Norway, and Finland, where it is said that they fulfil their duties with extreme conscientiousness and impartiality.

During the latter half of the nineteenth century a great educational wave overflowed England and bore woman upwards on its crest. One of the chief reasons for this increased culture lay in the growing preponderance of the female sex, both in England and throughout Europe, which made it necessary for some to come forth from the more secluded life of the home to take their part in the struggle for existence. The rise of the middle classes was now an established fact. Industry was expanding on a wonderful scale. New machinery, novel modes of communication, were introduced; the whole face of the world underwent a marvellous transformation during the nineteenth century. Such a change in the methods of production as was brought about by inventions for spinning and weaving, and for the manufacture of the countless objects of daily use, now made by mechanical skill instead of by hand, left woman freer from domestic duties than she had ever been before, and gave her liberty to turn her energies to different pursuits. So she has progressed, little by little, till now she claims the right to stand by the side of man and earn her moral and material independence. Englishwomen have not yet been admitted to the suffrage, and the attainment of this privilege a certain section of the female population is agitating to secure.

Though not permitted to play an immediate part in English politics, women here, even without the vote, are, as they can be if they choose in all countries of the world, a great indirect power. Particularly in English society do we find ladies taking up the cause of their husbands, fathers, and brothers, helping them to win their election-fights, charming the hearts of the constituents by their enthusiastic championship, and promoting the welfare of the poor and suffering by their appearance on public platforms. In England they have peculiarly ample opportunities for such influence, since there for many centuries social and political functions have been harmoniously interwoven. Those who would form an idea of the wide influence exercised by ladies of highest rank in England, will find a very thoughtful and interesting account of this phase of political life in some of Mrs. Humphry Ward's novels, and, in lighter vein, in Lady Randolph Churchill's witty and amusing "Reminiscences."

But how has it fared with the woman of India through the long centuries since civilization dawned upon her land? We have seen that in the early ages of the world, while Northern Europe was yet steeped in barbarism, she enjoyed the highest public honour, and was a participant in all the wisdom and activities of her day. Neither should we omit to recall the fact that in ancient India the laws of Manu and of other Hindu lawgivers touching women's property rights, known as Stridhana, though introduced about 2,000 years ago, have hardly yet been excelled by any laws in any country in the West. Mahomedan women also have long enjoyed their share in the property of their male relations, which is granted to them by their laws. But succeeding years in India checked woman's glory. Our land became a prey to external invasion and internal strife, and in the ceaseless struggle that was waged, the cause of learning, and with it that of woman, was forced to the wall. The arts of peace had no room to expand, and, with the constant warfare that devastated India in the seventeenth and eighteenth centuries, woman's interests and education fell into a depth of miserable neglect and suppression, from which they are only now recovering.

Fortunately there is no longer need to ask by what means woman may rise to a higher and nobler position. The woman of the East, like the woman of the West, may depend on this, that in the proper use of education lies the salvation of her sex. As long as she is ignorant, so long will she remain dejected, oppressed, incapable of sharing man's pursuits and ideals. But educate her, help her to organize her efforts, and she will respond to the changed environment. It is education and useful organizations that alone can give true freedom and enlightenment.

By means of women's Associations woman has gained in Europe and America, and should acquire in the East, a broader outlook, wider interests, a brighter, more generally useful attitude to life than she has had in the past. High and low, rich and poor, all are shaking themselves free to a great extent from the lethargy and indifference which seemed in past ages to envelop them. The movement is confined to no one rank or creed, country or continent; its professed aim is the uplifting of the feminine mental and public status throughout the world. In this matter there can be no separation of the interests of the sexes. The good of woman is the good of man. Many famous men have recognized the importance to the race of the well-being of its womenkind, and have agreed that it is by the character of its women that the standard of a nation's civilization is judged. In the word of Sheridan, the well-known dramatist: "Women govern us; let us render them perfect: the more they are enlightened, so much the more shall we be. On the cultivation of the mind of women depends the wisdom of men."

Only by education can a woman fit herself to be the companion and inspiring helpmate of her husband. Only by information can she gain the ability to direct her children's course and follow their careers with loving, intelligent sympathy. Therefore the women of every country should feel it their duty to seek the highest culture within their reach, that they may be in truth the moral and intellectual mothers of their children. The mother whose sons "get beyond her" in information generally loses a certain amount of influence over them. The bond between her and them cannot be so close and tender, unless she, by her training, has fitted herself to be their true comrade in things spiritual and mental, as well as things material.

That there is a dearth of female teachers in India no one can deny. At a meeting of the Legislative Council of the United Provinces, held in April last, Mr. De La Fosse, speaking on behalf of the Government as to the insufficiency of female teachers, said that the difficulty lay with the people themselves, who thought it beneath the dignity of the better class of Indian women to earn their living as teachers. We for our part have no hesitation in endorsing this view. No Government in the world is perfect, and we do not for a moment say that either the British Indian Government or that of any Native State is perfect. But it must be admitted that no Government, either native or foreign, can make improvements without the hearty co-operation of the people. Therefore, we appeal to the women of India, whether British subjects or subjects of Native Rulers, to help the cause of progress as much as lies in their power.

"It is through good education," says Kant, "that all the good in the world arises." An ideal feminine education, leading to a wider, freer life, is difficult to realize. It must be one that will prepare its pupils for all human duties—those of the household, as mother, daughter, wife, and those of the State, as useful members of the community. It must be practical as well as theoretical, physiological as well as psychological. India, with her long centuries of philosophic teaching, may find her methods somewhat prone to abstractions, but she should remember that pure intellect is not all. The education that unfits a girl for the practical duties of the home is a progression on totally wrong lines, since the majority of women will always be called upon to direct household tasks. Here, from the experience of England, the women of India may glean a warning. Beware of too literary an education! In Europe many women have directed their energies so zealously to the intellectual side, that the practical part of life is in danger of being neglected, and the result is the overcrowding of certain careers. There are many manual occupations affording light, pleasant, skilled employment for women, which we shall discuss in later chapters, but which at present are disregarded in favour of exclusively mental pursuits. Yet such callings, demanding the supple manipulation and refinement of taste which are woman's innate attributes, would be eminently suited to her. Moreover, some women are of a distinctly practical bent. They do not all incline to mental work, and would often be more happily engaged in something of an active tendency. Till lately, the fault in the average higher education of Englishwomen has been its unpractical nature, its failure to inculcate the organizing spirit, its neglect of physiology, its small care for imparting the principles of hygiene. Its success has arisen from the fact that the mental development, though advancing by leaps and bounds, has not been allowed to interfere with the physical well-being of the girl. The stature of the gentler sex has been increasing latterly in England to a noticeable extent, and the physique of the highly educated woman leaves little to be desired. The woman question in Europe and America differs fundamentally from the Indian one, because in Europe and America the surplus population of single women has rendered it imperative for many widows and unmarried women of the middle and lower classes to bestir themselves, and cease to be a burden upon their male relatives. The desire for a wider sphere of usefulness shows itself also among the well-to-do, for never was there a time when larger charitable schemes were set on foot, or more done to relieve the lot of the poor and suffering than now. What gentleness, pity, kindness there is in the world to-day, is due largely to woman, who has had the greatest share in stimulating the progress of humanity in this direction. Under her guidance the homeless are sheltered, the sick made whole, the weak ones strengthened, the fallen raised and cheered. The amount of honorary philanthropic work performed now is larger than it has ever been before. All this is the result of the broader education of women, and of their organizations.

The question may be asked, "Is woman equal to the efforts required of her? Is she mentally and physically capable of profiting by an education as wide as that given to men?" Here the women of India, if the experience of their own clever countrywomen be insufficient for them, may accept certain of the conclusions arrived at regarding their sex in Europe and America, where it is more and more acknowledged that the peculiarities of woman need prove no obstacle to her advance in most branches requiring intellect or manual skill. Woman's brain is not proportionately smaller than man's at birth, and observations among races at a low stage of civilization show that the female brain differs in size and weight far less from that of the male than it does among nations of higher culture, the deducible conclusion being that the long centuries of carelessness and ignorance through which woman has passed, may have prevented the normal evolution of her mental faculties. Though the average female brain is actually smaller than that of the male, yet, if it be compared with the total weight of the body, the female brain will be found relatively heavier. As the case stands, however, woman is generally inferior to man in mental capacity. Lombroso accords her only a small place in the history of genius, but it must not be forgotten that her peculiar training, in which the faculties of feeling and sentiment, rather than those of the understanding, have been fostered, has probably made her yield the foremost rank to man in science, poetry, philosophy, and the fine arts. Similarly, woman's physical education has been neglected through long centuries, and the laws of evolution have produced their inevitable result in the comparative inferiority of the feminine physique.

Those women who have been called upon to rule have proved themselves equal to the noble task. In India Razia Begum, daughter of the Sultan Altamsh, reigned at Delhi after the dethronement of her brother. Nurjehan, wife of Jehangir, was so admired by her husband that he made her the virtual ruler, and struck a coinage in her image. This Queen was not Lalla Rookh celebrated by Thomas Moore, as sometimes supposed. The present Begum of Bhopal may be cited as another successful Moslem lady-ruler. Ahalya Bai, who ruled over Holkar's State in the eighteenth century, may be taken as a model Hindu Queen. In England the greatest Empire the world has ever known has expanded beneath a woman's sway. Indeed, the number of successful Queens all over the world is quite remarkable, so that it cannot be urged that women have no talent for responsible work.

Most of the great agitations for the bettering of humanity have had a woman as their primary mover. In America, for instance, Harriet Beecher Stowe was the organizer of the famous struggle which ended in the abolition of slavery. In England Elizabeth Fry devoted years of unselfish toil to the improvement of the pestilential prisons in which her countrymen and women languished. Therefore women must be granted a capacity for social reform.

Where women have hitherto failed is in organization. This is as much the fault of their training as of their false pride, which prevents their seeking the co-operation of man. A woman's household duties call for an independence of action which develops individuality, but does not foster unity of spirit, to acquire which, at least during some generations to come, she must needs have man's co-operation.

Inaccuracy as to technical and scientific detail is another defect in women, which militates against their conduct of social and moral reform movements. Too much sentiment, too, is another weakness; a woman reasons from her heart, not from her head; hence many of her errors and difficulties. Energy misdirected by enthusiasm leads her to extremes, so that we find in her the noblest heights of virtue, and, on the other hand, as in the French Revolution, the most appalling depths of vice. Her energy, moreover, is apt to be of an evanescent quality. "A woman's fitness comes by fits," says Shakespeare. These characteristics are, however, such as a practical, broad education may with time eradicate, and then, with her noble gifts of intuition, sympathy, earnestness, moral instinct, unselfishness, and tact, woman would seem to have a glorious prospect of usefulness and happiness before her. But in the meantime she cannot afford to do without the aid of man's business capacity.

The difficulty with regard to woman's education is how to construct a scheme by which she may, if called upon to do so, earn her livelihood or contribute actively to the betterment of her fellow-creatures, without unfitting herself for the all-important duties of wifehood and motherhood. This is a problem which is recognized as difficult of solution by modern scientists and educationalists, who see clearly that to employ woman in manual, or even intellectual, labour unsuited to her sex is a terribly wasteful method of carrying out the world's work. The ideal seems to be that women should seek out lines of development in which they may make the most of the special characteristics of their sex. They should abandon the old idea of following men along the beaten tracks marked out in the past, and they should try to devise occupations in which their own peculiar excellences may have full scope for exercise. The differences between the faculties of the sexes are fundamental. In some qualities man excels woman; in others woman surpasses man. "The special qualities," says Dr. T. S. Clouston, "are complementary." There is no question of comparison of worth; both are requisite for the welfare of the world. Eminent scientists declare that the past history of woman and the experience of the race should be taken into account before rushing blindly into any advanced scheme of feminine development; and, above all, it should be kept well in mind that to encourage the professional career to the exclusion of the domestic life is a movement on wrong lines. No doubt, it is a hard case to decide, and would appear to impose on woman the duties of a twofold education, the one fitting her for wifehood and motherhood, and the other rendering her capable, in case of necessity, of earning her livelihood outside the home circle. The only conclusion that can at present be arrived at is that extremes are dangerous, that no general rules can safely be laid down for woman's education, but that the needs of the individual should be carefully studied, and changes imposed only after diligent observation, and in a scientific spirit. There would appear, according to European and American educational authorities, no reason why girls' education should not at first proceed on a plan identical with that of boys, but only for a certain time. Afterwards it should be continued on a different system, which would take into account the psychological peculiarities of their sex.

In the State of Baroda there is compulsory primary education, with mixed vernacular schools, which both sexes attend up to a certain age. As stated in the Baroda Administration Report for 1908-9, the people of the Antyaj, or depressed classes, have derived considerable benefit from the compulsory primary education system. In the other higher girls' schools in Baroda such subjects as embroidery, drawing, cooking, plain needlework, etc., are taught, in addition to the usual curriculum. A boarding-house for girl-students in connection with the Female Training College has also been started, and a number of scholars have taken advantage of it.

The education of women is a cause which the Maharaja of Baroda has particularly at heart. At the annual general meeting of the Bombay Sanitary Association, held last April, the Maharaja spoke of the share that the people themselves, and especially the women, must take in their own uplifting, and he emphasized the fact that the training of women was the all-important object after which to strive. He said: "Our only weapon is education—education of women, because it is their part to influence home-life, and to fashion future generations; and education of our ignorant masses in the simple teachings of elementary sanitation and hygiene. . . . It is insufficient to teach boys and girls how to read, write, and cipher. We must deal with their lives in their homes. For that purpose I appeal to the educated portion of the community, and to the natural leaders of the people, to set the example, and, by personal practice and precept, teach their backward neighbours how to lead hygienic lives. I advocate education."

The practical trend which education should take if it is to be of any real good to the nation is fully recognized by Queen Mary who believes firmly that the moral and physical well-being of her country is dependent on the proper education of its children, a task which is mainly in the hands of women. Her Majesty thinks that every girl's education ought to include some study of domestic science and domestic arts, by which a trained and experienced head of the household would take the place of the now often inefficient mistress. Women are too apt to proceed simply by "rule of thumb," but it is hoped that the establishment of an institution, with the express purpose of training them in the science of the household, will do much to change old, irregular, traditional methods. A sum of £100,000 is being subscribed to endow a University of Domestic Science, which is to be provided with a staff of professors and lecturers on such subjects as chemistry, hygiene, economics, physiology. It is to be a residential University for women students, and its many influential patrons hope that Queen Mary's Hostel, as it is to be called, will prove one of the most effective monuments of this Coronation year.

The important rôle that Englishwomen have played in the furtherance of female education in India has perhaps been scarcely emphasized so strongly as it deserves. It is acknowledged that the largest number of lady graduates in India come from Bengal, and it is interesting to note that the earliest attempt to educate Hindu women in Bengal was not made by the State, but the entire credit is due to two Englishwomen, who, in 1819, more than a generation before the Indian Universities were established, first tried to elevate the condition of Indian women. The names of these ladies, Lady Amherst and Miss Cook, the two pioneers of female education in India, show what women can do to benefit members of their own sex, even though differing from them in religion, race, and language.

The Indian ideal of womanhood differs from that prevalent in Europe and America, and, therefore, the methods of education to be adopted for our countrywomen will naturally differ accordingly. But the aim of all education should be to teach the pupil to apply her acquired knowledge to the pursuits of daily life, to *fit* her, not *unfit* her, for the position she will have to fill. It is systematic training alone—training begun in the most elementary stages of her development—which can accomplish this. The ideal which many Western thinkers now set before them, and the all-powerful factor which they hold education to be, are well and concisely set forth in the following words of one of England's most progressive writers, Mr. H. G. Wells:

"We want to invigorate and reinvigorate education. We want to create a sustained effort to the perpetual tendency of all educational organizations towards classicalism, secondary issues, and the evasion of life.

"We want to stimulate the expression of life through art and literature, and its exploration through research.

"We want to make the best and finest thought accessible to every one, and more particularly to create and sustain an enormous free criticism, without which art, literature, and research alike degenerate into tradition or imposture.

"Then all the other problems which are now so insoluble—destitution, disease, the difficulty of maintaining international peace—the scarcely faced possibility of making life generally and continually beautiful—become . . . *easy* . . ."

In some of the following chapters we propose to deal with a few professions in which it would appear from the experience of England that women by better organization might carve out a future for themselves in particular and for their sex in general. In this there need be no question of actual comparison with man, no thought of surpassing, or even of equalling, him. The highest aim of woman's education should be to fit her to work freely and bravely *with man*; or if not with him, then alongside him, for the benefit of the human race. The spiritual side of woman's nature is the complement of the material side of man's. Hitherto these faculties have often been separate, or even at variance. Who can tell what the combination of the two, working together in perfect harmony, may not achieve? Likewise in the adaptation of certain Western organizations to Eastern requirements the abstract nature of India may find the leaven of the practical nature of England prove beneficial to her people, and the coming age may see in their happy union the dawn of a brighter day. It would raise the position of Indian women in public life, and thus help the great forward movement in India which most cultured men and women there have at heart.

CHAPTER II

PROFESSIONS FOR WOMEN

"He that hath a trade hath an estate, and he that hath a calling hath a place of profit and honour. A ploughman on his legs is higher than a gentleman on his knees."—FRANKLIN.

WHEN so many callings are now attracting women's attention, it might not be amiss, before considering in detail the chief of the more novel professions open to them, to note briefly the general conclusions arrived at concerning their success or failure in such occupations as engage their activities at present.

First of all, it should be observed that the task of improving woman's position must be undertaken by woman herself. If she desires a higher and securer condition, she must work out her own salvation. So far women, even in the West, have not been resourceful enough in seeking out special lines for themselves. They have been too content to follow one track, so that Europe and America are swamped with poorly paid governesses and half-educated girl-clerks. For such want of originality their education is partly to blame. Their training has been far too abstract, too intellectual; it moves on a uniform plane, forgetting that feminine character is as diverse as the masculine, that some girls have a practical bent, others an artistic or intellectual tendency, which, if fostered, would produce good results. Even for the sake of the added enthusiasm with which anything off the beaten track can be pursued, it is worth while to look about for fresh spheres of action. Therefore, in our detailed discussion of the various professions we shall omit practically all account of the stereotyped ways in which an Indian woman may get a living, and pass on to consider other callings which she, by means of organization, might divert partially or entirely to her own profit.

In this connection, a great aid to women's work in India would be the establishment of a Central Society, with the object of studying the fluctuation of supply and demand in different occupations in various Indian Provinces, to collect information as to new and interesting lines available for women, and to raise the general level of efficiency, by giving precise details as to how a special training could be obtained by those who are unqualified. Such a Society could also use every effort to raise the standard of women's salaries, and might, in addition, act as a Registry to bring its clients into touch with suitable employers. Certain Associations in London give gratuitous advice about women's work, and even have loan funds for apprentices or training-fees, which are granted under conditions to those who desire to enter on a course of professional education, for which they have not the necessary means at their disposal. After employment has been obtained, these loans are repaid in instalments by the recipients. Another society for promoting the employment of gentlewomen has, as well as a free registry, a central depot for the sale of work, including garden and dairy produce of all kinds, and even jams, cakes, sweets, etc.

There is a quaint old Western saying, applicable alike to either sex of all nations, "There are no foolish trades, only foolish people," and this brings us to the question of woman's capacity in the various branches in which she is engaged. Hitherto, for reasons not altogether due to her own fault, she has frequently been lacking in efficiency, the main cause being that the majority of women are not educated with any earnest intention of gaining a livelihood. In India matrimony is the goal of all, for which no serious preparation is deemed necessary. Even in the West, only a small minority expend any ingenuity in choosing out an original career for themselves, and pursue their training with the same zeal as that which the boy devotes to his apprenticeship, or to his course of professional study. This want of definite purpose in women is the rock on which they have hitherto split. In England many methods have been adopted to remedy the evil, and to fit girls for their several walks in life. Such are Science and Art Classes; Technical Art Schools; classes of instruction in manual training, cookery, needlework, dressmaking, basket-making, lace-making, gardening, wood-carving, metal-work; lectures on such subjects as bee-keeping and poultry-rearing; Domestic Economy Schools; Day Trade Schools, where girls are taught the latest method in dressmaking, upholstery, photography, etc. In the latter schools the system resembles an apprenticeship, and, after a two years' course, the pupils are supposed to be capable of taking a beginner's post, and commencing to earn a salary. Various scholarships are offered at these classes to assist the cleverer students. To the learner the result of the scientific method adopted in teaching the trades, is a thorough and more speedy mastery of the subject.

The question of salaries is a much-vexed theme, for there is no doubt that women's wages are, as a rule, smaller than would be paid to men for the same quality of work. The remedy, perhaps, lies in efficiency and proper organization, by which women may get the control of certain industries more in their own hands than they have ever done, or tried to do, before. Women have not as yet the faculty of banding together for the protection of their interests. They are more apt to work individually, and accept the present conditions as incapable of improvement. But when it is found that they are able to execute really good work, and able also to combine to prevent the undue exploitation of their services, it is more likely that the higher salaries will be forthcoming.

Education, organization, specialization—the women of India who purpose entering on any career of usefulness, will find these three points essential to their success in life.

CHAPTER III

AGRICULTURE

"And he gave it for his opinion that whoever could make two ears of corn or two blades of grass to grow upon a spot of ground where only one grew before would deserve better of mankind, and do more essential service to his country, than the whole race of politicians put together."—SWIFT.

As in India about 70 per cent. of the population live by agriculture, we take up this calling first for consideration. Can women be employed in agriculture? Women will probably never be efficient substitutes for men in the hard manual labour necessary on a farm, and many of the duties connected with management of live stock are manifestly unsuited to them; but if they have had the proper theoretical and practical training, there are numerous other ways in which their services are invaluable. They can aid with counsel and ideas, and, if orderly and competent, would be capable of undertaking the entire superintendence and commercial direction, including book-keeping, distribution of produce, etc. In few other callings is there greater scope for a woman possessed of practical business instincts.

The advantages of agriculture as a profession for women are mainly two:

1. The healthy nature of the life; and
2. The fact that its adoption need be no hindrance to carrying on the duties of wife and mother.

In this calling, as in all others, efficiency depends on well-systematized instruction. To succeed, a technical education, practical as well as scientific, is essential, and naturally those who in childhood have been accustomed to life on a farm will have a great advantage over city-dwellers. To aid those who wish to take up this profession, schools of agriculture have been formed in England, where the various subjects, such as rearing of cattle and game, dairying, veterinary science, study of the soil, horticulture, and domestic economy in general are taught. Poultry-keeping and bee-keeping are also included among the subjects studied, and the scientific methods adopted in such work have met with wonderful success. But before considering these colleges proper, it might be well to make some suggestions as to the advisability of awakening a love of rural occupations at a much earlier age than that reached by the students of such colleges. It is among school children, first of all, that the love of agriculture should be fostered, especially in the country districts. If young girls were taught the love of country life, the benefits to health of labour on the land, they would be less prone to turn their thoughts to exclusively intellectual pursuits, and would think of work connected with the soil as strengthening and ennobling, not degrading. If in the elementary teaching in rural districts the subject-matter of the reading, writing-lessons, etc., could be of an agricultural nature, the pupils would naturally from childhood imbibe an inclination towards that form of life, and would acquire information in easy fashion. In many schools in England the subject of horticulture is made a part of the usual routine. Each girl has a garden, varying in shape and size, in which she cultivates, under a teacher's direction, whatever plants, flowers, fruits, vegetables, she chooses. Once a year a horticultural exhibition is organized, and prizes are given for the best displays.

A good scheme has already been adopted in the Primary Schools in the Central Provinces of India. In the rural schools there is now in practice a half-time system under which pupils are only taught from 7 to 10 a.m., so that during the remainder of the day they may assist their parents in field-work. The course of study embraces reading, writing, arithmetic, accounts, geography (taught in a practical manner, beginning with the village where the pupil lives), simple land measurements, and agriculture. Each school has a garden, and the reading-books employed deal chiefly with agricultural subjects.

A similar plan might be adopted throughout India as a means of furthering agricultural training among girls. There might be (1) a theoretic course, consisting of lectures, dictation, essays on essential points, the subjects varying according to the district. For instance, in a part where dairy produce was a prominent local feature, particular attention might be given to that section; in another where grapes abounded, the culture of the vine might be made a speciality.

(2) A practical course, given in a school-garden, on the culture of vegetables and other kitchen-garden produce, on the use of chemical manures, etc.

(3) To foster the business faculty so necessary to run a farm successfully, the older pupils might be taught to keep an inventory each term of the entire expenses, profit and loss. Such training would be of the highest possible benefit.

In France, near Biarritz, vast farms are cultivated to some profit entirely by women. On some, young girls are employed, who have been sent there from various reformatories or charitable institutions, and the moral effect upon their character has been found to be excellent.

For those women who aspire to become proprietors or managers of a large farm advanced knowledge is necessary. The duties of this post are exceedingly varied, including direction of the labourers, oversight of the cooking and domestic arrangements, and management of the financial part of the business. To be a first-rate superintendent a woman should, therefore, in addition to a knowledge of agriculture proper and of dairying, possess a thorough grasp of the principles of hygiene, of the construction and internal organization of the dwelling, and a knowledge of first aid in case of wounds or accident. The subject of hygiene is one of the highest importance, and one of which great ignorance prevails among certain classes in India. Cleanliness cannot be too strongly urged, both with regard to the animals, where the want of it is one of the most frequent causes of failure, and also with regard to the persons of the workers, their clothes, food and habits. In the dwelling the principles of hygiene, with reference to pure air and cleanliness, are absolutely necessary to success. In matters of this nature a woman's surveillance need not be inferior to a man's.

Dairying of course can be taken up separately and run at a profit entirely by women. Men's assistance in the roughest part of the labour would be desirable, but in the manufacture of butter and of ghee (clarified butter), in the milking and distribution of the milk, the control can rest wholly in the hands of women. Butter is most profitable when undertaken on quite a large scale, as in the large creameries of Great

Britain. That this industry is remarkably suited to women is proved by the example of Denmark, essentially a butter-producing country, which employs women in a large majority to carry on its dairy-work.

The method of disposing and packing of dairy produce is the crucial test of good management. One of the best modes of running a dairy and poultry farm at a profit is to work up a regular clientèle by post. The Value Payable system of the Indian Postal Department gives the Indian dairy-keeper better facility than in England. An energetic Hindu mistress of a large farm, situated not too far from a town, could thus create quite a wide demand for hampers containing butter, ghee and honey, and in time might find herself the head of an extensive and flourishing source of supply. The Mahomedan mistress might add fowl and eggs to this list of supplies. Farms even on a limited scale can be made to pay to an appreciable extent, but though the beginning may be modest, it is by quantity that profits are made. The small farm will bring in a living, but fortunes can only be achieved if industries are established on a wider footing.

A co-operative scheme for transporting the produce of small farms to the consumers would be an enterprise well worth considering. Such an organization would require to be of vast dimensions, but would be an inestimable boon to the small landowner. Another project which would benefit the isolated woman-farmer is that adopted by the English County Councils, which send women into the country districts to teach the farmers' wives the best and newest systems of butter-making at no cost to those instructed. Competitions for prizes are held among them, and are keenly contested.

In England there are various dairy-schools, where everything connected with dairying is taught. University College, Reading, is an agricultural college, which has in connection with it the British Dairy Institute, where courses of three months, six months, one year, or two years may be taken in dairying, the latter course being necessary to gain the College Diploma in dairying, and to prepare students as dairy teachers and managers of dairy-farms or creameries. The subjects usually studied in agricultural courses include agriculture, botany, chemistry, zoology, geology, meteorology, physics, mensuration, surveying, and book-keeping. After the termination of their professional training, students are advised to join an agricultural union, which has a paper, a library, lectures, and other means of instruction, to keep them abreast of the times. Such a union is the "Women's Agricultural and Horticultural International Union," an international league for women engaged in agriculture and horticulture, and affiliated to the National Union of Women Workers. The aim of this union, as set forth in the Report of the

Second International Congress on Women's Work and Institutions,* is:

1. To form a link between women of all countries who are engaged, as professionals or amateurs, in farming, dairying, rearing of poultry, bee-keeping, culture of flowers and fruit, development of land, forests, and management of estates.

2. To publish useful information, and to compare the methods of different countries and districts.

3. To give advice as to how to dispose of the produce, and to bring members into touch with suitable employers or employees. Members may consult each other, and valuable advice may thus be obtained from persons residing in quite another country as to the prospects of starting there.

4. To endeavour to maintain a proper standard of women's wages in this branch of work.

POULTRY-KEEPING is another section of farming which can be made to pay if worked on thoroughly business lines. At first, advertisement is the only method of working up a large connection; afterwards, when success has been achieved, recommendation partly takes the place of advertisement. This calling has for women the same advantage as that of farming or dairying—*i.e.*, it need not take them from the duties of their own home.

* Vol. iii., p. 605.

Horticulture is an allied branch of farming to which women might devote their attention on a larger scale. To increase the profits, several women might unite and combine the business of kitchen and nursery gardens with that of poultry- and bee-keeping, dairying, the manufacture of chutneys, bottling of fruits, pickles, etc. Such an enterprise, if started in a favourable locality, might develop into a huge store for the delivery of dairy and garden produce.

Horticulture requires an all-round practical training of at least two years' duration, such as may be obtained in England at Swanley Horticultural College, Kent. In this institution a knowledge of business routine is imparted, as well as a scientific education—instruction in botany, agriculture, chemistry, geology, horticulture, poultry- and bee-keeping, dairy-work, land-surveying, entomology, and book-keeping. There would seem to be an opening for women of artistic sense and organizing capacity as landscape gardeners. In this most interesting domain a knowledge of architecture is useful, to insure that the garden shall be laid out in a style conformable to the house. Also an acquaintance with the growth and management of trees is desirable. A woman who has been through the proper training would have to plan the garden and carry out the entire scheme from start to finish. When a connection with the leading architects was once obtained, it is probable that the woman landscape-gardener would find herself able to employ a staff of assistants under her to execute her projects. She might open an extensive nursery business in connection with the work of consultation, and herself supply the plants and labour required.

Women could also start jobbing-gardening on a considerable scale. With a nursery garden as a basis from which to furnish the necessary plants, they could undertake the keeping in order of fruit, flower, and vegetable gardens, and would probably be found a great improvement on the ordinary labourer. By co-operating in numbers the business might be made to pay better than it otherwise would.

In connection with nursery gardening, a profitable trade could be organized as florist in adjacent towns. In this calling a woman's deft fingers and taste in the fashioning of bouquets and flower-garlands, *malas*, etc., are unrivalled. Moreover, a fresh branch of this industry might be opened up in the shape of floral table and house decoration for weddings and festivities of all kinds. To the business of florist could in time be added that of seed merchant, which is clean, light, healthy, and exceedingly suited to women. If all these allied lines were grouped together—market and nursery gardening, landscape and jobbing gardening, florist, seed merchant, also jam- and pickle-making, fruit-bottling, vegetable-preserving, etc.—in one large concern under one proprietress or manageress, with each department organized by a capable head, the result would probably be much more satisfactory than if each section were worked separately by individual owners. Considerable capital would be necessary for the start, possibly sufficient to maintain the originators for two, or even three, years until the scheme was fairly launched as a going concern; after that, if conducted on business lines, a good profit and a practical monopoly of the work of the district might reasonably be expected.

To show the means by which capital for such an enterprise might be obtained, and the value of co-operation in farming projects, we may quote a passage from Sir Theodore Morison's "Industrial Organization of an Indian Province":

"The co-operative movement can hardly be said to have yet begun in India. At present the Indian cultivator does not see the desirability of the objects for which European peasants usually associate. . . . Most of all, he is ignorant of the superior efficiency of co-operation in industrial or commercial operations. When once the co-operative spirit has taken root, it is very probable that the Indian villager will realize that he may develop the trade in *ghi* (clarified butter) with great advantage to himself. Pure *ghi* is difficult to get in Indian towns; it is for the most part scandalously adulterated by means most offensive to high caste Hindus. In the manufacture of good *ghi* on co-operative principles, there is an opening for co-operative dairying which has in Europe often proved to be the beginning of a far-reaching co-operative movement. But these openings are not likely to be used until the Indian cultivator has learned by experience the value of association. . . . It is, therefore, to co-operative village banks that we must look to teach the cultivator the virtue of co-operation. . . . It is reported that Sir Horace Plunkett has declared that if he had to begin his economic work in Ireland over again he would begin with village banks. In India the ground is already prepared for the foundation of small co-operative banks; the villager is fully conscious of his need for capital to buy bullocks or seed, and he is painfully aware of the burden imposed upon him by the village moneylender. If he can be got to realize that by association he may borrow, not perhaps as much as he wants, but as much as his fellow-villagers think good for him, the foundation may be laid of a genuine co-operative movement, which will easily extend to co-operative buying and the maintenance of co-operative industries. At present the obstacles to this movement are not either legal or economic, but moral, and the great virtue of the co-operative movement is that it educates in thrift and self-reliance at the same time as it provides the desired capital. At the heart of every economic problem lies a moral problem, and the surest cure of economic evils is one which gives the people the means of overcoming their troubles themselves. The experience of Europe seems to show that co-operative banks are such a means, and there is, therefore, no nobler or more genuinely patriotic work to be done in India than to teach the people to organize village associations upon the principle of mutual credit."* The women of India, who propose to adopt agriculture as a profession, would do well to note these hints on the value of co-operation.

* Edition 1906, pp. 170-1.

CHAPTER IV

HOME PROFESSIONS

"Is the liking for outside ornaments—for pictures, or statues, or furniture, or architecture—a moral quality? Yes, most surely, if a rightly set liking. Taste for *any* pictures or statues is not a moral quality, but taste for good ones is. . . . To teach taste is inevitably to form character."—RUSKIN.

AMONG the callings open now to women in India, scarcely any are entirely under feminine control. The result is that woman, as a rule, seldom gets a chance to show her business capacity. Men are at the head of all branches of industry which employ women, and therefore, if even a small proportion of the 160,000,000 women in India are to earn a livelihood, which is to be anything more than a mere pittance, the key to success will lie in taking energetic measures to qualify Indian women, so as to enable them to co-operate with their fathers, brothers, and husbands. As long as man has the monopoly of the direction of every concern, it is only natural that woman's interests should not receive as much attention as they ought. But there is no reason why women should always be unable to co-operate with men. There are several branches of employment which would seem peculiarly their work. Their aim, then, should be to seek out those callings for which by nature and training they feel themselves best adapted, so that by combination and organization with men they may, in time, be so qualified as to be at least co-directors with them.

Why, for example, should the many branches of work connected with the home rest so largely in the hands of men? It was not always thus, for in primitive migratory times it was woman's task to carry the tent from place to place, and, later on, to build the hut in which the family dwelt. It seems a strange thing that nowadays only when the house is finished, when the architect has designed the plan, when the builders and workmen have done their part, when an army of upholsterers and other operatives have had their say, and the house is fully equipped from floor to ceiling, does woman step in and do her best to render it habitable. Granted that a man must build the house, but it is only the deft touch of a woman that can make that house a home. "Taste," says W. R. Lowell, "is the next gift to genius." We may go even farther and say that in many women it amounts to genius. Why, then, when her ingenuity and artistic skill in such domestic matters have been always admittedly superior to man's, should she not endeavour to push her way in this direction, and make an effort to get at least the decoration and furnishing of the home under her control? To promote such a scheme on a large scale would require considerable organization and capital. The technical and scientific knowledge possessed by Indian women would have to undergo a vast improvement, but the field affords great scope for their artistic and practical talent, and an almost unlimited outlet for labour of feminine brain and hand.

To start at the very beginning—the profession of DOMESTIC ARCHITECT is itself exceedingly interesting, and one which Indian women might, in part, very well take up. The oversight of the workmen would have to be left to men, nor could women very well climb the scaffolding to superintend the progress of the building, but the drawing of the plans and the details could easily be done by our women if they made it the subject of a course of professional study. There is, however, no need for women to undertake the entire architecture of the house. There is ample room for their talent in designing portions of the interior—such as useful wall-cupboards, mouldings, friezes, ornamental designs for doors and windows, and the general decorative details of construction. Such training as the architectural profession affords would also be invaluable to them in the decoration of public buildings—a department which might be left to a great extent in their hands. It is highly improbable that women will for a long time enjoy the public confidence sufficiently to succeed as architects, but there would seem to be no reason whatever to prevent them from prospering in some of the sections of this most interesting profession. In buildings devoted to charitable purposes, round Hindu temples and Moslem mosques, there is ample scope for women's talent. The artistic decoration of temples during great fairs is a business which in India would employ thousands of women.

In the trade of HOUSE DECORATING and FURNISHING a number of women should unite, each taking up a separate section. This is absolutely necessary to insure thoroughness, as the scope is so vast that no one woman could possibly master all its branches. Here, as in most other callings, *specialization* is the secret of success. The head of such an enterprise must be a person possessed of thorough business principles in combination with a knowledge and love of art. It is no easy thing to deal with the countless array of workpeople whose services are necessary to equip the "House Beautiful," nor is it a simple matter to please the idiosyncrasies of the clients, who in affairs relating to household furnishing are notoriously hard to manage. A woman, "to be excellent in this way, requires a great knowledge of character, with that exquisite tact which feels unerringly the right moment when to act." The possession of such tact, however, has always been one of woman's chief assets, therefore this side of business ought to prove one in which she will be *facile princeps*.

The next general requisite, after business principles, is a training in the theoretical part of the work, in the history of architecture, and of furniture and design. For this there should be classes and lectures as well as private study. An artistic training in the various branches of textile design is in itself a separate career, and would employ thousands of women. When one looks at the infinite variety of design required for carpets, rugs, tapestries, linen, and house furnishings of all kinds, it is easy to recognize the vast field open to those women who are possessed of artistic talent and originality. Even in England the greater part of this work is at present executed by men; in India woman's share leaves much room for improvement.

Furniture-designing and carving is a trade in which there is a good opening for the skilled woman-worker. It is one in which both brain and hand are kept busy; and those who have a love of art will find it a most congenial employment. Much carving is of course done now by machinery, but hand-work is still highly prized, and, as an artistic product, is naturally far superior. The practical part of the upholstery trade is also highly suitable for women's fingers.

House-decorating is by no means an easy trade. There are many things to be learnt before even the elements of the business can be carried through successfully, but it is an occupation which has the charm of infinite variety, and one in which business capacity has wonderful room for exercise. Customers require good work as well as economical work; therefore the woman who can combine sharp commercial instincts with an artistic sense and the power of managing operatives is the one to prosper in house-decoration.

As regards the sale of upholstery and furniture, it is a branch eminently adapted to women, and one which, like house-decoration, requires considerable experience before proficiency can be attained. The different styles and periods of furniture must all be familiar, and, as has been said before, a knowledge of the history of architecture is necessary to carry out high-class work. Connected with this section there is the trade in antique furniture, which might very well be added to the list of the woman-furnisher's enterprises. There is a rising demand, not for the brand-new products of the modern workshop, but for objects that have been mellowed by the hand of time. To make money in this line one must be able to recognize a genuine article when one sees it, and must have the faculty of striking a good bargain. Thus, many valuable old pieces of carving, silver, furniture, prints, coins, lace, crockery, intaglios, bronzes, engravings, etc., may be secured and sold at a handsome profit. The restoring and renovating of antique furniture is a very paying side of the trade, but great care should be taken not to encourage in any way the too prevalent practice of "faking." To start a business in antiques, a woman would do best to take up one or two special lines only, which would teach her the details of the trade, the methods of treating with both seller and customer, and the policy of disposing quickly of the goods purchased. In this way, by gradually adding other classes of goods to the list, she might become an expert in art-dealing—a business in which large fortunes are to be gained. A peculiar temperament is necessary for such work, and a training not of one, two, or even three years, but constant, unceasing study of art-values in the particular branch which she may elect to take up. Here, again, specialization is recommended, though, of course, several branches may be combined. A woman art-dealer might work in several ways. She might buy generally to sell at a profit, or she might sell the work of artists on commission; or, having formed a connection among purchasers, she might obtain for them to order articles to suit their individual requirements. It is readily comprehensible that a keen critical faculty is absolutely indispensable in this profession; but, given the true collector's temperament, the occupation is most congenial, and indeed, often of enthralling interest. Like most things connected with the artistic side of the home, it requires a hard business head as well as a love of the beautiful. Capital, of course, is a *sine qua non*, but to make a living a large business house is not necessary. A small establishment can be made to realize handsome profits. It is a pursuit which may be taken up as a hobby, and continued to great pecuniary advantage.

To descend from the decoration of the home to the less artistic sphere of culinary matters, there is one most striking fact which confronts us—that whereas it is woman who spends the greater part of her life in the kitchen, yet man, who is ignorant of most of the processes and occupations of that domain of housekeeping, is the very one who has to design the appliances for carrying out her work. The fault must have lain with woman herself. She has not hitherto shown much inventive faculty. But it is a subject well worth her consideration. The man who first thought of inserting a small piece of indiarubber at the end of a tin case round a lead-pencil amassed a fortune. There is a golden harvest awaiting the clever housewife who can invent little labour-saving contrivances for the household, which may look so simple, yet have never before been put into practice.

Furniture-removing might also be undertaken as a department of the trade of house-furnishing, and other branches might be incorporated, as experience showed their suitability. If women combined to run an establishment such as this, providing all things connected with the equipment of the home, they might either work it as a private concern, or it might be turned into a large co-operative store, similar to the English Societies registered on the Co-operative Union, in which the shares bear a fixed rate of interest, and the net profits, with a few reservations for bonuses to employees, contributions to reserve funds, etc., are divided among members and customers in proportion to the amount of goods purchased at the store.

Yet another pursuit may be included with all the foregoing—that of HOUSE AND ESTATE AGENT. This is a calling which, though scarcely touched as yet by women, even in England, affords great possibilities for the exercise of the tact and talent of Indian women, and is certainly one in which their intimate knowledge of the working of the home will stand them in good stead. The first branch, in which a woman must enlist masculine co-operation, in order to gain experience, is that of rent-collecting. She must see that rents are collected regularly every month, choose new tenants, dismiss the old, keep houses in repair, pay rates and taxes for the landlord, and look after the entire interests of the property. To complete these duties efficiently, she must have a considerable knowledge of valuations, of book-keeping, of the laws referring to house-property, especially such as deal with the sale of estates, leases of houses and ground, agreements between landlord and tenant, etc. She must be able to keep a register of houses and estates, must be acquainted with the work of building and decorating, that she may be able to keep a businesslike eye upon the repairs which may be necessary, and she must also know the value of furniture and fittings. This latter qualification is necessary in case of the letting of furnished houses, when she would have to estimate the value of the damage, if any, done by the temporary tenant.

In the work of rent-collecting the educated woman has a great opportunity of introducing improvements in housing and hygiene. If she has the entire control of a large property, she will find ample room to exercise her scientific knowledge of sanitation; and in her intercourse with the tenants, when these are of the poorer classes, she can do much to instil into them the principles of hygiene. To this end a course of study in sanitation is most helpful, and there is abundant information to be had nowadays in books and pamphlets on sanitary appliances.

The occupation is one that has the manifest advantage of requiring little capital for a start. Business initiative and tact in dealing with clients are the main requisites. There are dozens of Indian lady graduates who cannot possibly all expect to find posts as teachers and companions. In a country of *purda* our University women might with great advantage try their abilities in this direction. The illiterate Ghataki (female negotiator of Hindu marriages) has fairly ousted her male rival (Ghatak) by taking advantage of the *purda* system at Calcutta. The Ghataki now brings about more Hindu matrimonial alliances at the Indian capital than the Ghatak, who, until twenty years ago, had held for centuries the monopoly as agent of Cupid. If this proves anything, it shows that there is ample room for all sorts of women-workers behind the *purda*.

CHAPTER V

ARTS AND CRAFTS

"In the life of the artist there need be no hour without its pleasure. No other business offers a man his daily bread upon such joyful terms. Suppose it ill-paid: the wonder is it should be paid at all. Other men pay, and pay dearly, for pleasures less desirable."

So wrote R. L. Stevenson of the fine arts, but his words apply to other callings. They are true of anything into which artistic skill enters, and it is the business of the woman who takes up the arts and crafts for a living, to see that the scanty pittance hitherto earned by her sex in these lines shall be substantially increased. In this busy age, when machinery and science would seem to have rudely brushed grace, and romance, and sentiment aside, one might expect that there would be no time for the careful workmanship required in hand-wrought arts and crafts. Yet it is found that there is a genuine demand for the excellent quality of hand-made goods, for delicate laces, beautiful enamel and jewellery work, or the exquisite designs of the skilful wood-carver.

Moreover, these industries ought to be encouraged, since in them the true artistic spirit is revealed, and the craftswoman, watching the design grow beneath her deft fingers, can derive the same deep delight from the beauty of form and line, as the artisans of Cutch and Cuttack take in the creations of their clever hands. "The true epic of our times," said Carlyle, "is not arms and the man, but tools and the man." We would expand this saying, and make it include as well "tools and the woman," for there are many crafts nowadays to which women of artistic talent may devote their energies, and with the labour enjoy the peculiar pleasure which falls to the lot of the creative artist, in seeing the inventions of his brain take shape before his eyes. Chief among the crafts are the several branches of ART METAL WORK of India, in gold, silver, copper, and brass. But "he that sips of many arts drinks of none," and so numerous are the various metals from which beautiful articles can be fashioned, that it is necessary to make a special study of one branch alone, as, for instance, silver, or brass. The requisite qualities for such work are an artistic sense, a capacity for designing and modelling, and a certain deftness of manipulation. A clumsy worker could never hope for success. In the delicate repoussé-work and fine tracery of jewellery there is a great field for woman's slender fingers.

She who hopes to secure distinction in this domain, must lose no opportunity of studying beautiful specimens of her art, so that in time the spirit of those masterpieces will imperceptibly animate her work. Such beauty of design and execution in things of daily use gives constant pleasure. The time has gone by when these handicrafts were considered beneath the dignity of anyone possessed of real artistic faculty, and it is now thought better to produce a good practical design than a second- or third-rate picture. For those whose taste inclines to the useful, rather than the purely ornamental, there is abundant scope for the fashioning of all kinds of household fittings—door-plates, handles, mantelpiece-carving, etc., and in such labours they will find their toil not mere mechanical drudgery, but of real interest and charm. As the European and American purchaser pays a much higher price for works of Indian art than do the Indian nobility, it is time that the Indian exporters paid more attention to Western requirements.

It would take too long to deal in detail with all the sections of Art Metal Work. We shall therefore only treat of one, which should especially attract Indian women, since it is known to have existed in India at a very remote age—namely, ENAMELLING. Persia and Japan also excelled in the culture of this fascinating art; it was familiar to the Romans, and attained its highest perfection in Europe in the Middle Ages. Of late years it has been revived in England, and has been exceedingly popular when transformed into articles of jewellery, or employed to decorate spoons, vases, caskets, ecclesiastical ornaments, etc. Working with enamel is particularly pleasing because of the beauty of the colouring. With enamel, too, there is a greater freedom of design than can be used in handling precious stones, and it thus affords more scope for originality than does the exceedingly conventional pattern of most of the modern jewellery. Enamels are made of fusible glass, which is given its varying colour by an admixture of metallic oxides. In the raw state they look merely like lumps of coloured glass. The first stage is to grind the enamel with water in a mortar; this renders it easy to transfer on a brush to the metal—copper, silver, or gold—which is to form the basis of the ornament. Such metal is washed in acid, and then in water; the enamel is applied in a coating and the object put in a furnace, which fuses the coating and causes it to adhere to the metal. The length of time required for the firing process varies; the colour changes, too, under the action of heat, and differs according to the metal—gold, silver, or copper—used as a foundation. Some enamels are transparent, others opaque. The Japanese enamels, known as "cloisonné," are wrought in different colours, and each little section of colour is separated in the design by means of thin gold wire. There are numerous other methods of enamelling. In one kind the design is carved deep in the metal, leaving a thin ridge of metal to keep the different colours apart. Another variety has copper for a background, on which silver lines separate the colours; after the firing and hardening stages are past, the copper foundation is taken away, leaving only the enamel. The result is one of the most exquisite effects that can be produced in enamelling, and is known as "appliqué à jour."

Bookbinding is another craft which requires both deftness of workmanship and artistic talent. An acquaintance with drawing and design is necessary, and a certain amount of capital, if a woman aims at setting up as a bookbinder on her own account. At present there would seem to be few opportunities of money-making in this most interesting profession, and to do fine work a great amount of patient effort is indispensable. Good prices are obtained for specially choice bindings, with some tooling of the leather on the cover, and it is this class of work—not the ordinary bookbinding—for which women are advised to enter. The first requisite to commercial success is to obtain some sort of connection with the trade, and by means of numerous specimens of choice bindings to display one's art to private individuals. The time required for training is about a year. This is a craft which has been chiefly followed by men, therefore women will have to make an effort if they wish to co-operate with them. Enterprising women who take to bookbinding, might with advantage specialize in binding the sacred Scriptures of the Hindus and Mahomedans. We need not tell our Hindu readers that no leather of any kind—except deer-skin in certain forms—may be used in binding the holy books of the Hindus. The religious susceptibility of the Mahomedans must also be studied in binding works of theirs which are of a religious nature. A very large number of manuscripts, both Sanskrit and Arabic, are left unbound to the present day all over India, simply on account of the difficulty experienced in finding binders with establishments where regard is paid to Indian religious susceptibility.

Lace-making is an industry which, if carried on by the poor alone without the aid of the artist, is apt to degenerate as far as both design and execution are concerned. Therefore it is a trade which affords ample scope for the co-operation which is becoming a feature of modern times. An educated woman who is a skilled lace-artist could easily, with capital, get into touch with the scattered workers of a village or district, appoint local collecting-agents, or travelling buyers, and form a central depot for the disposal of the work. Capital would be necessary for such a scheme, since orders take time to execute and workers must be paid. A woman who undertook this project would have to devote her attention to several matters connected with the business organization. She would have to institute classes to maintain a suitable standard of design and workmanship; she would have to revive old designs and originate new ones; and she would have to possess a knowledge of the commercial worth of the lace, to enable her to give estimates and to value the specimens sent forward for sale. In agricultural districts a fostering of lace-making among the poor would be a great aid to the household revenues. It would also help to improve the condition of the home as far as cleanliness is concerned, since dirty needlework will find no market. Practice early in life is essential, and to acquire speed the craft should be begun in childhood. It is, however, only by organization that any tangible gain can be secured to the workers. The woman who, with a moderate capital, financed such a scheme, would probably find that she could make a comfortable living for herself, while at the same time she would be conferring a boon on the isolated Indian cottager who does not know how to find a market for her goods.

Pottery Manufacture is another industry which women might organize and turn to profit. In districts where the right kinds of clay abound, women might institute on a large scale such industries as the manufacture of earthenware cookery utensils, flower-pots, ornamental terra-cotta work, and all the various other articles made of the humble but useful clay. Among other enterprises, in the county of Dorset in England, Lady Baker has promoted a co-operative scheme for pottery-making, and as soon as the industry has achieved independence, she proposes to set aside 75 per cent. of the profits for further development of the trade, while the remaining 25 per cent. is to be divided among the operatives. By experiments in this line different processes may be discovered and products patented which in time might prove valuable sources of revenue.

WEAVING is another craft which among the villagers and also among women of higher rank might be developed by means of co-operation. Schools have been started in England to promote the textile crafts among women, and by their agency it is hoped that instruction may be given to cottagers, ladies in straitened circumstances who require to increase their income by some extra employment, and even among the blind, deaf and dumb, to whom spinning and weaving would be a pleasant and profitable occupation. Rug-making is also a suitable industry for women, and silk-weaving (the manufacture of the richest silks, satins, velvets, etc.) is a skilled trade for which ladies and women-workers generally are very well qualified. In all these crafts it is of the utmost importance that the designing should be in the hands of an educated, artistic woman, otherwise it will degenerate, and from the artistic point of view the work will be worthless.

Fortunately, it is not altogether necessary for our countrywomen to leave their native land in order to see what British organization can do to revive an interest in weaving and kindred employments among the scattered villagers, since something is already being done in India by the Salvation Army to further that end, and to promote the development of cottage industries generally. *The Times of India* (June 10, 1911) contains the following paragraph concerning the Army's work among handloom weavers, showing how a handloom factory and weaving schools have been set on foot, and four silk farms established to give a fresh impetus to the manufacture of silk:

"This class [handloom weavers] numbers about 11,000,000 of the population, and is next in importance to the agriculturists. Owing to the severe competition of mill-made and foreign goods, and to their lack of organization, the condition of the weaving community has steadily declined from one of great prosperity to comparative poverty. During the last five or six years the Army has been enabled to inaugurate a movement which has largely restored hope and confidence to these classes. A handloom has been invented by one of the Salvation Army officers, which, while being a marvel of simplicity, can work in the finest and coarsest counts, in silk, wool, or cotton, at a rate scarcely less rapid than that of the power loom. About 800 of these looms have been already manufactured and sold, and they are steadily increasing in popularity. Gold and silver medals and first prizes have been taken year after year at the principal exhibitions, and the loom has recently been patented in Europe. Warping machines have also been made of a very simple pattern, and at a price well within the reach of the weaving community. Weaving schools have been established, where master weavers have been trained and sent out as teachers of the use of improved looms and methods.

"Mr. Booth-Tucker is of opinion that the weaver will be able to compete permanently and successfully with the power looms and mills for five reasons: (1) he has the unpaid labour of his family; (2) he has skill acquired by generations of practice; (3) he is abstemious, and has few expenses; (4) what he lacks can be easily supplied; he can be taught improved methods; (5) he can be supplied with capital by the Co-operative Credit Societies, which can also purchase his yarn for him in the cheapest markets, and sell in the dearest.

"But, in addition to helping the handloom weaver in his struggle for existence by introducing improved machines and methods, the Salvation Army is also engaged in calling his attention, and that of the depressed classes generally, to other lucrative forms of cottage industry, including the rearing of the silk-worm, the reeling, and spinning, and weaving of the silk, and the provision of those agricultural products on which the silk-worm subsists. By their natural habits, the weaving community would be admirably suited for taking up this pursuit, and the Salvation Army is actively engaged in fostering and encouraging what has for some years been a somewhat decadent industry so far as India is concerned, while being a source of such immense wealth and prosperity to China and Japan."

The systematic organization of these schemes by the Salvation Army, and the co-operation aimed at between British and Indians in the labours connected with the promotion of village industries, might serve as a suggestion for Indian ladies, many of whom must feel that they have ample time, money, and—it is to be hoped—inclination to originate such a good work. The village worker has frequently been enabled, by the Salvation Army's aid, to maintain his family in their little cottage home, which otherwise would have had to be broken up for lack of suitable local employment. As well as weaving, needlework of various kinds is taught to the Indian women and children, including lace-making and drawn-thread work.

There are many other departments that might be developed. Basket-making, though not one of the most lucrative industries, is a very pleasant occupation, and an addition to the list of those callings which are suited for the blind, deaf and dumb. Many women, too, who may be too delicate to undertake any strenuous labour, will find it attractive, light, and easy work. Like everything else it requires to be properly taught, and when skilled hands perform the task, many beautiful specimens of wicker-ware can be produced. At present there is a craze for hand-made straw trimmings for English millinery, and this would prove a more lucrative pursuit for poor Indian women if they could be put in touch with the British market.

The many branches of decorative needlework are valuable as affording pleasant home-work to women. Hand-embroidery, lace-making, spinning, leather-work, wood-carving, decorative painting, design, metal-work of all kinds, book illustration, illumination, pottery, basket-making —all these industries only require a central organizer in every Indian District to work them up into profitable pursuits. Such organizations can best be started by women of leisure, who have time and means at their disposal to direct the concern, and consider both the purchaser's and producer's interests. In the large towns depots should be established, and exhibitions and sales promoted periodically to popularize the hand-made goods. With reference to a similar scheme in England, it has been suggested that a shop containing choice specimens of the various handicrafts might become one of the most alluring of the city, and when the discriminating purchaser discovered the superior quality of hand-workmanship over the machine-made goods, the articles would probably not languish long in the shop-window or in the depot, but would find speedy custom. The fate of such a co-operative scheme would depend upon the business capacity of its chief manageress. As we explained with regard to the organization of lace-making, each industry in India would have to employ its special travelling buyers to collect the goods. Each group of these would be responsible to a special head, over whom the central manageress would have control, and she, in her turn, would work under the direction of a small committee. Such an enterprise would call into play both the business and artistic faculties, and as a philanthropic scheme it is worthy of every encouragement, for it would do much to decrease poverty and brighten the lives of the industrious poor, whose talents now are often wasted for lack of time and energy to organize them. So far, we have only dealt with the crafts. Now we will consider one or two of the arts which hold out a tempting prospect for the woman of originality.

POSTER-DESIGNING is one which is most paying, when one is lucky enough to possess the gift of arresting attention by some striking quality in the drawing. A sense of humour is a valuable asset, and above all, one must have had a training in art, and in black-and-white design. Posters may be executed in black and white or in colour. The variety of subject is of course infinite, but the aspirant should bear in mind that originality, and suitability to the district or the subject, are the only things that count. A poster that might be humorous in one neighbourhood, might not elicit the vestige of a smile in another. In India great attention should be paid to religious susceptibility. A Mahomedan lady once stated that she refused to purchase a gramophone because the portrait of a dog was used in advertising it—the advertiser did not know that the Mahomedan regarded the dog as an unclean animal. If the designer had studied the tastes of the probable purchasers such a result would not have occurred. A design should be calculated to catch the public eye; it need not be elaborate, but there must be a certain freshness about it to capture attention, and it must always be practical from the commercial point of view. Some work is confined to border-drawing, simply to set off the advertisement; some consists of border-drawing and artistic lettering; some is of the comic figure order; some comprises artistic figure-drawing.

To make a beginning in this calling, the free-lance must carefully study the specimens of work done for advertisers by successful artists. Then she should endeavour to execute some original designs suitable for particular advertising firms, and submit these to them on approval. Gradually in this way she may work up a connection, and may afterwards be able to work on commission, without submitting the finished sketch for approval. The income derived from free-lance work is, of course, exceedingly variable. A connection with various advertising agents may be formed, and so regular employment secured; but the only way in which any really lucrative position could be obtained would be by organizing an independent agency for advertisement design, and working up a large clientèle among enterprising advertising firms. One point that is of great importance in connection with all advertisement design is a knowledge of the cost of reproduction. The possession of such business information will prevent excessive elaboration either in colour or in line, and will secure the acceptance of work when a novice might fail through ignorance of the processes of reproduction.

As well as for posters, designs are needed for calendars, book-plates, title-pages, book-covers, business catalogues, show-cards, etc. These may be combined with poster-work, and book and magazine illustration may also be added. The latter has been somewhat displaced by photography, but is still in considerable demand, and in its higher forms will probably develop. Specimens of illustration should be sent to leading journals and publishing firms. When a connection has once been formed, it will be found quite a profitable employment, and there is always a market for original design.

ILLUMINATING is another branch of art that is in request for presentation addresses and choice editions of books. It is a very dainty, delicate art, and the artist requires to be a good draughtswoman, designer, and letterer. A long training is necessary, but when proficient, a steady income may be earned. It is an ideal profession for women, yet has been little studied by them. Miniature-painting is also well paid, and for this a complete art-training is essential.

An effective method has been tried in England for focussing into one centre the productions of isolated women-workers by means of a journal, some of whose pages are occupied with descriptions and private advertisements of work done by ladies for their living. All the work thus advertised has been examined by a committee, so that purchasers have a guarantee of its quality.

In conclusion, none should attempt to earn a living by any of these artistic callings who are not filled with keen enthusiasm for their work. The beginner will not always find it easy going on pleasant paths; a large stock of energy, perseverance, and business initiative is essential to success. Yet, if these qualities are present, the pursuit of art in any shape or form will prove an absorbingly delightful vocation, and one on which a woman may enter not merely as a means of supplying the needful daily bread for the body, but as a joyous work into which she can throw her whole heart and soul. Only let her never forget the words of Sir J. Reynolds: "If you have great talents, industry will improve them; if moderate abilities, industry will supply their deficiency. Nothing is ever denied to well-directed labour; *nothing is ever to be attained without it.*"

CHAPTER VI

INTELLECTUAL CALLINGS

"God has placed no limits to the exercise of the intellect He has given us on this side the grave."—BACON.

THERE are countless ways now in which a woman may exercise the powers of her busy brain. She may go in for chemistry, and, like Madame Curie, give to the world some fresh discovery—such as radium—as the result of her scientific research. As a woman doctor she may perform skilful operations with unflinching nerve. She may enter the realm of literature and win distinction as authoress or journalist. Or she may follow a path in which she is universally admitted to stand unrivalled—the teaching of the young. All these main roads with their many side-tracks are open to her; but as the secrets of success in these callings have been publicly discussed so often, we propose to pass them over and to treat of only one or two in which the women of India will be perhaps on less familiar ground. The first of these is LECTURING—a field which might prove highly interesting for the intellectual woman who has a gift for speaking and a love of imparting information. Here, as elsewhere, the cardinal rule is specialization, but specialization on top of a broad general knowledge. Choose a special topic, one for which you have a particular love, make yourself thoroughly mistress of it, and your enthusiasm will communicate itself to the audience. In England the University Extension Societies do much to encourage lecturing by organizing courses on different subjects at various centres, and, by applying to these bodies, a woman who possesses a university degree or its equivalent, and some testimonials as to qualifications for lecturing, may be appointed on their list of lecturers. She is required to give a test lecture before the University authorities before her application can meet with success.

In connection with art, music, literature, nursing, hygiene, domestic science, social schemes, there is an infinite variety of subjects to choose from, and if lecturing-tours on an extended scale were organized and carried out by eloquent speakers, they might become a feature of women's life in India which would do much to broaden their mental outlook. Science is a subject of which women of all classes are mostly very ignorant. Physiology, too, is a domain in which they badly need instruction. The woman lecturer who organized a series of interesting addresses on such themes would probably meet with an enthusiastic reception, and her audience would find the facts of science put in attractive fashion even more enthralling and much more practical than most general literature. A popular lecturer on art, science, etc., could earn a considerable sum, while those who undertake the work merely for love of it will find it a valuable intellectual training. The effort necessary to systematize one's information, to present it in the clearest and most pleasing form to the audience, is a splendid method of mental culture for the lecturer herself. Immediately after a University Extension Lecture is finished there is a certain time set apart for answering any questions the listeners may like to put, also for returning papers which they have written on the subject-matter of the previous lecture. Such discussion is most helpful in bringing different points of view before the notice of both lecturer and audience. Anyone who wishes to become a good public speaker should take every opportunity of practising the art of addressing others, so as to gain confidence and ease of delivery, not forgetting that simplicity and earnestness are the secrets of eloquence.

The profession of lecturer has the advantage of not monopolizing the whole time of the woman who devotes herself to it. It can be carried on in addition to her household duties, and so need entail no sacrifice of home interests. Undertaken as a social work, it is a valuable means of imparting knowledge on medicine, cookery, etc., to the poor. Even to take one branch, hygiene, and institute a course of lectures throughout the country districts, would do a great deal to awaken a sense of the necessity of fresh air, light, and pure food among the crowded dwellings of the lower classes. To the poor the spoken word always comes with greater force than the written message, and in a country like India, where so large a proportion of the population is illiterate, it seems absolutely the only expedient to reach them at all. In this way, viewed as a philanthropic work, as well as a paying profession, lecturing by women to women might achieve great results.

In England the Women's Imperial Health Association has already done much good work by its health caravan-tours, during which lectures are given to children and adult women in poor districts which would otherwise be out of reach of medical addresses. At present this society is organizing a national crusade to promote the care of the teeth among school-children, and is arranging a series of "talks" with children at various centres, when an eminent dental surgeon will demonstrate to the young people the importance of the subject from the point of view of health. Such "tooth-talks," as they are called, will doubtless do much to impress and interest the children, and the idea is capable of being developed.

The next profession which we shall deal with is Advertisement Writing: and as this has scarcely been touched as yet by women, even in England, the best thing will be to show Indian women the method by which their masculine predecessors in the field have gone to work to climb the ladder of success.

Advertising is not a modern art. It was known to ancient Rome. Our primitive ancestors, too, had recourse to various methods in order to make a fact known to their neighbours. In England the muffin-man's bell was perhaps the first advertising medium used by the forefathers of the present Briton. In our own country, the blowing of a conch-shell announced to the neighbours that they were expected to divert their attention to something unusual that was taking place. It may be noted here that both the muffin-man's bell and the conch-shell have survived the inroads of the more elaborate contrivances of civilization, both in the East and in the West. But although advertising is of such ancient origin, yet the systematic employment of advertisement writing as a means of earning a livelihood is quite a recent development. An enormous amount is now spent yearly by the public in advertisement, and the placing of these sums of money with the different newspapers and other advertising media affords occupation to a large number of advertising agents.

Before starting anything so ambitious as an

agency, it is necessary to have a thorough knowledge of the principles that govern advertisement writing, which in itself would constitute a lucrative profession for women. Good advertisement writers are badly wanted, but one must have a gift for the subject, so that the advertisement may catch the public eye and pay the advertiser well by bringing increase of custom. Originality is essential, also a knowledge of trade, and the power to look at things from the purchaser's point of view. The writer must have the faculty of making the commonplace interesting, he must have a literary style, concise and to the point, a knowledge of printing processes, of the costs of reproduction, of the nature of the different magazines, newspapers, etc., and of the various classes of advertisement which will appeal to them. In a word, the more general his knowledge, the greater his chance of success. Training for such a post is best attained by studying the style of successful advertisements, always bearing in mind that originality is the goal after which to strive. Those who take up a magazine of, say, twenty years back, cannot fail to notice the difference between past and present modes of advertising. The way in which the modern advertisement writer seems to take the public into his confidence and address the reader individually is a feature of present-day publicity.

As well as newspaper advertising, there are pamphlets, circulars, and other advertising matter to be studied. Sometimes such examination may suggest innovations, and novel ideas may be submitted to the firm in question, who will probably be quite willing to pay for a new suggestion. Thus a connection may be formed, and the foundation laid of a more ambitious career as advertising-consultant or advertisement agent. Advertising-consultants are experts whose advice is sought as to the best methods of conducting huge publicity schemes. Naturally it would take a long time before a woman could hope to command sufficient confidence to direct such large undertakings; but everything has a beginning, and she might start by first acquiring a practical knowledge of advertisement writing, advertisement illustration, typesetting, and proof reading. Then by degrees she might set up an office with a small staff under her. She will have to possess a thorough acquaintance with all the journals, and their methods of doing business; she must know the cost of advertisement in each, and the public among whom they circulate. She will have to be a thoroughly practical woman, proficient in accountancy, with a clear head when it comes to entering into contracts with advertisers or papers. At first she would probably have to be a general factotum, and supervise all sections of the office routine.

Advertising agents usually buy a certain amount of space in various leading journals, which they then fill to their own advantage. The custom in

England is for the newspapers to give the agent a percentage on the worth of the advertisement sent in to them, but of this commission the advertiser in his turn usually expects a certain proportion to be restored to him. The buying of space alone and then the passing on of the advertisements as they are secured to the newspaper will not bring any very great prosperity to the agent. If she acts on a more ambitious scale and organizes the whole scheme of advertising for her clients, she will naturally be able to command a much higher rate of remuneration for these advertisement campaigns than when merely acting as a broker between the advertising public and the publisher.

After taking an office, a connection is worked up by means of public advertising, private issue of circulars, by letters, and by diligent canvassing. Much, of course, depends on the personality of the aspirant, and push is indispensable. An advertisement writer in India must pay special attention to caste rules. She must keep herself quite familiar with the Hindu and Moslem almanac, for religious fairs regulate the demand for particular articles. Nor should the "wedding seasons" be forgotten. To make the most of occasions such as these and to be alive to every opportunity is the only way to succeed.

CHAPTER VII

PHILANTHROPIC WORK

"Woman has this in common with the angels, that suffering beings belong especially to her."—BALZAC.

THE aim of all social and philanthropic work is the same, whether it be undertaken as honorary employment, or for a fixed salary. Many women have the temperament for such a life of usefulness, but sometimes the means are lacking which would enable them to give their services to the cause they have at heart. Yet they need not be debarred on that account from choosing a path for which they feel they have a vocation, for nowadays the necessity for their help is recognized, and many salaried appointments are open in philanthropic undertakings, which formerly would have been closed to them for want of funds. To relieve suffering humanity, to bridge the gulf between the classes, to remedy the evils of our social system—in these things lies woman's great sphere. In woman the religious spirit is more highly developed than in man; likewise her bent towards charitable work is stronger than his. In the past the ignorance and helplessness of women have often been the cause of poverty and illness. Now, in the twentieth century, it is the cultured woman's great privilege to help her poorer sister to understand the all-important principles of hygiene, the value of self-reliance, the rights conferred upon her by the laws of her country, her responsibility as a human being and as a citizen. Indian ladies in the past have done much good and charitable work, but their efforts would have been more successful if properly organized. Let us see what great attempts European women are making in charitable organization, and to urge forward that happy day when "Peace on earth, goodwill towards men," will be the guiding principle of this world of ours.

The work of the WOMAN DOCTOR is a great social profession, and one in which there is a brilliant future for her sex. It seems strange that an office which in earliest ages was woman's prerogative should ever have been considered unsuited to her. For it is probable that women were doctors before men. The "wise women" of the primitive tribes existed before the wise men. Woman's skill in nursing is incontestable, but some wonder whether as operator she will have the same success as her masculine rival. Yet doctors themselves are loud in their praise of their feminine colleagues, who undertake cases requiring surgical skill, and there is no doubt that women doctors are, especially in India, a wonderful boon to their sex. Lady Dufferin's scheme for female medical aid in India, has earned for her the gratitude of millions. Women's lack of physiological knowledge is often lamentable, and this ignorance the advent of the woman doctor will go far to dissipate.

Further details need not be given here concerning the social aspects of medical work, as various philanthropic schemes connected with medical attendance and nursing will be treated in subsequent chapters. We shall, therefore, proceed to discuss a more novel calling for women, which combines in a striking fashion, social, philanthropic, and medical work among the poor. The office of ALMONER to the large London hospitals, is one that would appeal to the Indian woman interested in the social condition of the patients who visit the outdoor departments of those institutions. The almoner's duties are varied. The chief is to interview those who come for treatment, to select the cases most deserving of urgent aid, to visit the patients in their homes and see that the doctor's instructions are properly executed, to note the patients' circumstances, and find out whether they are making fair use of the hospital treatment, to inquire into such cases as need surgical instruments or special medical appliances. So the almoner acts as an intermediary between the patients and the hospital authorities. In her visits to the homes of the poor, she has every opportunity of tactfully giving information concerning the laws of hygiene, the importance of a wholesome diet, the better organization of the household, the promotion of thrift, and other similar matters of which the lower classes are often so careless or ignorant. But she must, of course, proceed in such affairs with a wise discretion, not like the society lady in a modern play, who, on being asked if she is fond of work among the poor, replies enthusiastically, "Oh, yes! I *love* interfering with other people's business! And the poor are the only persons who cannot actively resent it!" This is hardly the spirit in which to succeed with the working classes.

It is evident that people who undertake this calling must be bright, strong, of a cheerful temperament, tactful, energetic, and fond of social work. They should be young, at any rate at the beginning, and must have a knowledge of nursing and the various laws that govern health. In London, training as an almoner can be obtained practically free of cost by likely candidates. They are appointed by the Hospital Almoners' Council, which selects its nominees by sending each girl for a few days to a hospital to gain a little practical insight into her proposed career. If she seems suitable and feels drawn to the work, she enters upon her course of instruction, which should last about eighteen months. During this time she will, in addition to the duties already mentioned, have to make personal acquaintance with the working of different charitable organizations; she must also learn to conduct her business in a methodical manner, to keep accounts and detailed lists of the patients, and to manage the sometimes considerable correspondence arising out of the cases. She must improve her knowledge of sanitation, nursing, etc., by attending lectures, and in London she may obtain theoretical and practical instruction from the School of Sociology that will greatly aid her in the social side of her work. The London School of Sociology gives courses of training both practical and theoretical in all sociological subjects, and in connection with several universities and colleges there are courses of teaching which are most helpful, not only to almoners, but to anyone who purposes entering on a career of social usefulness. Lectures are given on such matters as local government, industrial history, economics, sanitation, hygiene; and sometimes practical work is done in rent-collecting, in organizing dwellings for the extreme poor, playrooms for the children, clubs for factory girls, holiday funds for destitute children, and similar objects.

In connection with charitable societies there is abundant room for the paid woman worker. With regard to factory girls, too, there has arisen of late years a novel calling which has been a marvellous influence for good in the life of the workers. At the head of several large factories where women are employed is placed a WELFARE SECRETARY, whose duty it is to look after the comfort and general well-being of the employees. There are countless ways in which a capable woman can ameliorate the girls' circumstances. The Welfare Manager has generally an office where she interviews new applicants for situations, choosing the healthiest and fittest. She explains to each fresh candidate the rules of her employment, and informs her of any clubs, societies, etc., which she may join in connection with the company or firm for which she is working. Then the Welfare Secretary has to superintend the arrangements in the dining-rooms, where such are provided, to see that the meals are organized in the most simple, wholesome, and attractive style, so that the operatives may get the best possible value for their money. In some large factories in England the employees can purchase their dinner at a very low cost, and have the option of doing so or of going home for the meal. Often when good wholesome food is provided for them in the factories, they find it cheaper and better than anything they could obtain outside. The organization of this meal is one of the Welfare Secretary's duties. Sometimes at the dinner-hour music and games are instituted to brighten the leisure time. Occasionally meetings are held, and the girls listen to an address on hygiene, temperance, or some other social or religious subject. Occasionally the larger firms have also set up Savings Banks for their workpeople in which interest at 5 per cent. is allowed on the deposits, and the girls are thus encouraged to cultivate thrift. In some factories there is a Hospital Fund, which at the end of the year distributes its collections among different hospitals, receiving in return recommendation forms that admit to the hospital in case of illness, and which are used of course for the benefit of the factory hands. If there should be a garden attached to the factory for their use at the dinner-hour, it is the duty of the Welfare Secretary to superintend its management, and generally to do all she can for the comfort of the workers. Sometimes she may have to run a library and issue books to the applicants. One company has a lady doctor and a dentist who attend regularly and do their work free of cost to the patient. Medicines are paid for, but otherwise the attention is gratis. All such business is under the direction of the Welfare Secretary. Should any employees absent themselves through illness, the Welfare Secretary hunts them up and investigates the cases.

It has been abundantly proved that in all instances where trouble is taken to brighten the lives of the workers, it is quite as much to the interests of the employers as of the employed, since the quality of work done is far superior. Girls need to be taught the truth of Martial's epigram, "Life is not to live only, but to be well," and these Welfare Secretaries are the very people to help both them and their employers to understand it. Serving as a medium between the factory hand and the employer, the former, if she have a grievance, can approach the latter through the Welfare Manager, and so much friction may be avoided. One firm may not be large enough to require the entire services of such an agent, but in that case it might combine with one or two others to share the expense. The Welfare Secretary could then give a proportionate amount of her time to each.

In philanthropic projects connected with working girls there are numerous openings for the educated woman. Most of them, it is true, are undertaken as honorary work. There are the various girls' clubs, which members may attend on one or two nights of the week, and where sewing, games, drill, etc., are the order of the evening. In Birmingham there is a general union of all such clubs under a central committee, which holds competitions annually, and offers prizes for work executed by the members. The first prize in each section of work is a shield, which is retained for a year by the winning club, when it is again put up for competition, but it remains the property of any club which carries it off three years in succession. The head of such clubs is generally a purely philanthropic, honorary manager, but there are other schemes for the benefit of working girls, the directors of which receive a salary. One of these is the institution of holiday homes, where, under a co-operative scheme in connection with their clubs, girls are sent for a holiday to the country or to the seaside, to houses under the superintendence of a capable manager. To run an establishment of this kind well is a most useful occupation, whether it be done as pure philanthropy or for a fixed salary.

Then there is the organization of what is known in England as "Evening Continuation Classes," in which instruction is given in the evenings to workers who are busy all day long, but who wish to improve themselves in their spare time. Most of these are under the direction of some public body, but some are private organizations, and all afford opportunities for women as teachers and lecturers. Some are for advanced women students, others for working women, to help them to advance to greater technical skill in their callings.

In Germany there thrives a unique institution which might very well be adopted by other nations—public consultations for women with women lawyers. In India there is only one woman lawyer, Miss Sorabji, who is now employed by the Bengal Government. But there is ample room for others. In Germany in certain towns at appointed hours, and in some places at any time, women may seek legal advice from one of their own sex. Most Indian women, especially *purda* ladies, are terribly helpless as far as legal matters are concerned. When it comes to a question of property management, many are content to let man have the entire control, and so women have been swindled out of considerable fortunes solely through their own ignorance of legal matters. Some hesitate to consult a male practitioner, either by reason of *purda*, or because a busy lawyer has no time to enter into detailed explanation of the intricacies of the legal system. But if a clever woman made a thorough study of the laws affecting her sex, especially those dealing with property, her professional advice might be a great boon to her more uncertain, helpless sisters. This institution in Germany acts in two ways: (1) by means of bureaux, which, as we have described, help women in cases of legal difficulty; (2) by public meetings, in which general attention is drawn to any legal disabilities under which women are suffering. Thus grievances with reference both to woman's position in the family and her rights as a citizen, are voiced by competent exponents. A proof that such consultations are appreciated in Germany is given by the fact that in the first year of its establishment 628 women made use of the bureau, and in each of the five following years over 900 availed themselves of the privilege.* In difficult cases a solicitor's aid is called in, but in most instances the matters are settled by ladies of tried knowledge and experience, who have fulfilled their office with great tact and success. Where women's interests are concerned, they probably bring a more unbiassed mind to bear upon the subjects in hand. In America, New Zealand, Australia, Belgium, Sweden, Norway, France, Holland, and Finland women may practise law in some form, but this permission is not granted them in either Germany or England.

* "Deuxième Congrès International des Œuvres et Institutions Féminines," vol. ii., p. 724.

CHAPTER VIII

HOTELS, TEA-SHOPS, ETC.

"Good cheer is no hindrance to a good life."—ARISTIPPUS.

IT is an extraordinary thing, that though women have so much to do with the preparation and ordering of food-stuffs, they have seldom or never—even in England—attempted any large catering enterprise. The best cooks are man cooks. The kitchens of the large restaurants are all supervised by men. Men are the proprietors and organizers of all the big hotels. Yet here is a field in which woman, one might suppose, could largely co-operate.

Her backwardness in catering may, perhaps, be partly accounted for, by the fact that she has always possessed a less sensitive palate than man. Men are endowed with acuteness of taste in a much higher degree than most women, few of whom, in the opinion of the practised *gourmet*, understand the art of ordering a decent dinner. The greatest epicures have always been of the masculine persuasion; men are universally acknowledged to be the best judges of the chef's art, and tea-tasters are without exception appointed from among men. As a set-off to the lack of this faculty, women may claim that the physical appetite is, after all, a grosser part of human nature, in which man may be allowed to excel.

However this may be, the organization of hotels, tea-shops, etc., is no sinecure. Some idea of the amount of management necessary to run the catering side of a large luxurious club may be gathered from the following scheme for carrying out the culinary work of the new Automobile Club, in Pall Mall, London. The Committee, aided by four of the best restaurant managers and chefs in London, select the host of servants required. The kitchen is divided into ten sections, for each of which a separate room is provided, communicating with a central chamber, from which the manager and the chef direct the work of all departments. The ten departments are (1) meat, (2) game, (3) oysters, (4) fish, (5) hors d'œuvres, (6) ices, (7) fruit, (8) pastry, (9) bread, and (10) vegetables. Besides these, there are five service rooms: one to contain knives, another china, another glass, another plate, etc. All this is essential solely for the regulation of the food-supply, to say nothing of the array of helpers required for the other parts of the establishment.

With regard to the organization of workers, a most practical principle is set forth in a remarkable article in an American magazine, *The Century*, for last March, showing how the management of working men can be reduced to a science. By this means men are scientifically trained instead of sweated, and the result to the employer and the public is far better labour and far healthier workers. Some years ago the experiment was tried by Mr. Taylor, a graduate of Exeter and of Stevens Institute (America), who, forced to abandon his professional career through failing eyesight, conceived the project, while acting as foreman of some large steel works, of studying the methods by which the men performed their tasks, with a view to increase their speed by means of the adoption of better methods. At first he chose two ordinary labourers, who for two months went through the processes of pushing, pulling, fetching, and carrying, while all the time their rate was being accurately timed by two men with stop watches. The discovery was made that the usual period of rest was not properly calculated, and by working out a formula to regulate the rest period and the period of work, it was found that each man's labour capacity was increased *four times* without any over-exertion on his part. In the same way he investigated the process of shovelling, and found out what shape and species of shovel was best adapted to remove each kind of stuff—also what weight on a shovel enabled the men to shovel the largest quantity during the day's work. As a result of the experiment, 140 men were able to perform the work of 600. In like manner he set to work with experiments on the various machines, and found that by careful observation and calculation he was able to raise the labour capacity of a worker from twice to nine times its former power.

Similarly, a New York employer of labour experimented with bricklaying, and, by sundry changes in tools and methods, he reduced the number of motions in the process of laying a brick from eighteen to five or six. As the writer of the article says: "Under the new system the management is working from below—lifting up the workman. Under the old system one foreman directed perhaps twenty workmen. Under this system one 'teacher' helps every four or five. Under these conditions, fewer men—on a salary-roll increased slightly, if at all—double, treble, and quadruple the output. This is not 'slave-driving.' A cardinal principle of scientific management is to work the man within his permanent strength. It is not cutting the wages of the workroom to increase the salaries of the office. Regular increase of wages, as a reward for applying the system, is part of the plan."

The principle of scientific management in business enterprise is felt to be necessary nowadays to success. One of London's largest catering firms has proved by its prosperity the truth of this essential point. Beginning with one small tea-room, it gradually increased its sphere of action till now there is scarcely a street of importance in the metropolis that is without a branch of the firm, which has even extended into adjacent towns. The vast number of these restaurants and tea-rooms, all under one management, cannot fail to strike the traveller; but a fact which the casual passer-by might lose sight of is that the direction of this monster catering enterprise is carried out entirely on the principle of scientific control—*i.e.*, from a central office where the smallest details of each branch are arranged. The method adopted is the same as the American system just quoted—viz., to study every particular, in order to discover the best and speediest way of working; then that way is made the standard to be adopted in all the branches alike. It is said that even such an apparent trifle as the mode of laying a table has been experimented and decided on; the mode which has been found to be the best and quickest being made the rule in every establishment, so that if a waiter or waitress is required to change from one branch to another, he or she is at once familiar with every detail of the work. The same principle runs through the organization of everything connected with the business, and thereby time, which means money, is saved. This is a most valuable hint to women who contemplate the organization of similar undertakings.

What projects in the catering line would be feasible for Indian women? They might undertake the management of tea-shops and restaurants for different castes and creeds. They might also run women's restaurants, some of a better class, others with a very moderate tariff, where women could enjoy a pleasant meal, pleasantly served. These women's restaurants exist in Paris, and those for the working classes, shop-girls, etc., have been a great success. The first was established about 1893, and was considered an extremely bold innovation, since nothing of the kind had hitherto been attempted. At first it was aided financially by some rich patrons, but soon became independent. The idea spread. Spacious restaurants sprang up in various parts of Paris, and the gratifying results of the scheme were acknowledged as chiefly due to the wise direction of its foundress and manager. Now, numbers of young girls come each day to the principal restaurant to partake of an appetizing meal served in cleanliness and comfort, and there they have the pleasure each day of meeting their friends. A reading- and music-room is attached to the restaurant, and once a fortnight the habituées have a social evening and make merry together.

Residential hotels for women are considered in England as a promising enterprise: likely to prove profitable both for the promoters and for those who avail themselves of their accommodation.

Nowadays the tendency is to gain cheapness by running everything on a larger basis, and there is no doubt that a number of women might live together in far greater comfort by employing common kitchens, common washing apartments, and proportionately fewer servants than is possible for them when each has her own house to maintain. Notwithstanding the caste difficulty in India, advantage can be taken of the common kitchen system. Of course each caste will have to be given a separate kitchen. The idea of common kitchens for the supply of a number of families has already been tried in England, and on a larger scale in Germany and America. Huge co-operative cooking establishments are organized there, where machinery does most of the work that used to be laboriously performed by each individual. The humbler families especially have found this plan most effective, for their food costs them one-third less than it did, while at the same time they get it better and more palatably cooked. When it is managed on a small scale for a few poorer women, the latter take it in turns to cook, thus saving both labour, time, and firing. Every housekeeper knows that to prepare a meal for six is very little additional trouble than for four. It seems a pity, then, that the extra energy, time, and money should so often be expended needlessly, when it might be turned to different purposes. Instead of ten kitchens, taking caste into consideration, perhaps four would suffice; instead of ten cooks, four only would be needed; instead of ten small fires, four large ones. The co-operative doctrine here again comes in, for food could be purchased in large quantities at wholesale prices instead of at the usual high retail rates. Hindu officers of the Indian Army have, during their recent visit to England during the Coronation, found the same principle work successfully at their camp at Hampton Court Park. Why should it not be considered practicable in private Hindu establishments?

When women begin to take a larger share in public life than they do at present in India, they may possibly, like a few of their sisters in other parts of the world, find it expedient to make some alteration in the culinary arrangements of their households. Those who have tried it maintain that family privacy would in no way be interfered with if a little care and ingenuity were devoted to producing a workable scheme by which the labour of ten or more families might be combined and minimized. It might be objected, they say, that the particular gastronomic idiosyncrasies of each individual could not be consulted under such circumstances, and in the case of the poorer families that is probably true, but the well-to-do could no doubt obtain dishes to suit their particular fancy, just as they can in any well-organized hotel. The *Kachchi* and *Pakki* Hindu food do not offer insurmountable difficulties in the way of partial co-operation at least. The other sides of domestic life would continue as usual. There need be no break up of home interests or home ties because all the family meals are not cooked in a private kitchen. On the contrary, it is considered in Europe and America that this art of saving time would free the mother from much harassing responsibility, and leave her at liberty to devote more leisure to her children's education; that it would enable her to be more completely the friend and ally of her husband, a more interested partner in his life-work; that it would give her more opportunity for the intelligent cultivation of truer friendships with her sex. When her children are grown up, they are no longer in need of her services to the same extent as in their early youth, so that, if rid of the unnecessary task of directing the kitchen, she would have a considerable amount of extra leisure at her disposal to turn to public service or to the management of some of those private and lucrative enterprises which are discussed in several chapters of this book. Many may look upon this step as an undesirable innovation, but it may be remarked that according to European and American notions it is only another attempt to accommodate ourselves to the keen competition around us. Years ago the good English housewife would have held up her hands in horror at the idea of bread baked anywhere but in her own ovens. Now she buys it unconcernedly from the baker. She used to do all her own sweetmeat-making, washing and ironing, dressmaking, spinning, weaving, yet now she finds it more economical to employ the services of outsiders for the purpose. Why, say the pioneers of the new movement, should she not do the same with the kitchen arrangements? The organizing of such co-operative kitchens, with due regard to caste peculiarities, would provide a new occupation for the Indian widow or married woman who is obliged to earn her living, and whose experience as wife and mother would be invaluable in their management.

The advocates of the co-operative scheme further assert that if a woman has the sorrow of losing her husband, then by the comparative remission of house-keeping cares, afforded by such a system, she would be able to follow some profitable calling and save herself from the humiliating position of a dependant; or if her lot be cast among the affluent ones of earth, she would still have the greater opportunities of public and private service. There will always be a large number of women who will choose from preference or sense of duty to direct personally their own households, but there will probably also arise a minority to whom such ties are not an essential obligation, and it is to them that such a plan would appeal.

For the young childless widow, with her way

to make in the world, a scheme by which she could club together and live in common with other women similarly circumstanced would bring a flood of sunshine into her grey existence. The organizing of a women's residential hotel with restaurant attached is an enterprise which has met with much approbation in Europe and America from those who are obliged to enter actively into the arena of toil. The woman who embarks on professional life has to live for her work. The cares of house-keeping should be taken off her shoulders. Co-operative residences of this kind have actually made a beginning in London, as will be seen by the following extract from a letter written to the London Press last March, by Eda Berlon, the Honòrary Organizing Secretary of the undertaking:

"With regard to our recent letter of appeal in connection with the scheme for co-operative dwellings for educated working women, I beg to state that the response was most cordial, and the greatest interest has been shown from many quarters. In consequence of the support guaranteed we are now financially strong enough to open a house of residence for wage-earning ladies. . . . It is proposed that each resident shall have a share in the profits when it is possible, always keeping in view the ultimate object of building self-contained flats of one to four rooms, with central restaurant and service as required."

The idea of co-operative cookery is not a new one: many extraordinary projects have been put forward, not the least stupendous of which was that of the French Socialists, who seized upon the notion with such avidity that in their hands it assumed colossal proportions. An amusing account is given in Mr. C. J. Holyoake's "History of Co-operation" of their suggestion that the whole city of Paris should be supplied by one immense *restaurateur*. The huge kitchens were to be graced with Greek statues holding frying-pans, with portraits of Lucullus, of Rabelais's Gargantua, of Vatel, Carême, and all the celebrated French epicures. Mighty omnibuses were to run through the city to distribute the food—the soup omnibus, the fish omnibus, the entrée omnibus, the meat omnibus, then the toothpick omnibus, and, lastly, the omnibus with the bill! Such a mammoth plan is manifestly unworkable, even in Europe; in India it is simply out of the question. But, taken on a small scale, the proposed common kitchen and common washing systems have great possibilities in India.

CHAPTER IX

DOMESTIC SCIENCE

"Let all things be done decently and in order."—BIBLE.

TILL a few years ago the one calling for which woman was supposed to require no training was household management. Knowledge of the subject was presumed to be inborn in her, and she entered cheerfully on her duties as house-keeper without any fixed notion of how to carry out her task, or without possessing even a definite idea of the work in front of her. Men have always had a certain discipline in the special lines they have undertaken. Poor woman alone, to whose lot falls the difficult business of organizing the household, has, until lately, been left to "muddle through" without any instruction, and has in consequence often suffered harassing failures in her special domestic domain.

Yet it is with home affairs as with everything else. They need method; they must be managed on scientific principles. "Science," says Professor Huxley, "is nothing but trained and organized common sense, differing from the latter only as a veteran may differ from a raw recruit." It is exactly this training and organizing of common sense on scientific principles that will produce the ideal housewife.

Latterly in England it has been fully recognized that something is required to make the wheels of household management run easily and smoothly. To meet this want, domestic science schools and courses of training have been established. In the elementary schools, at evening continuation classes, practical and theoretical instruction is given in cookery, laundry-work, sewing, home dressmaking, home millinery, hygiene, and housewifery. In connection with the higher education of women, as at Bedford College, a women's college affiliated to the University of London, there is a programme of scientific instruction in hygiene designed to furnish training for teachers of hygiene, and also for women factory and sanitary inspectors. The prominence given to the subject of domestic science has caused a great demand for teachers, and special training colleges have been started to fit women for this very useful profession, where, after a course of study, they may obtain diplomas qualifying them to teach. For women and girls who wish to prepare themselves for home-life there are courses of instruction in the entire care and management of the house, cookery, needlework, hygiene, laundry, duties of servants, care of linen, plate, glass, china, and management of business affairs. At the present time there is hardly a county in the United Kingdom where some or all of these subjects are not taught, so that all, rich and poor alike, can, if they choose, avail themselves of the instruction.

Now as to the advantages of a knowledge of Domestic Science. Firstly, whether for those who intend to make a profession of it, or for those who look forward to a life of conjugal happiness, such training is invaluable. It is also a great aid to a woman in philanthropic work among the poor. Moreover, many women are left widows and unprovided for, and if they had undergone a course of such training, either before or after marriage, they would find it of immense use to them in helping them to earn their own living when death has deprived them of their husband's support. It is a profession that may be begun earlier and continued longer than almost any other, as if a woman be practical, she can more readily keep herself abreast of the times in it than in most other callings. It is, too, an ideal womanly profession, one which entails no exclusion of intellectual culture or refinement, nor any loss of feminine charm. Finally, if any additional argument were needed in its favour, it is the *duty* of women of all classes to be good housekeepers. The woman who can pay to have her household managed for her requires instruction that she may know if those under her are fulfilling their duties properly; the woman who manages her own household or who works for herself must know the best methods and proceed on business lines; and lastly, the working classes, those who have to do work for others, need the most instruction of all. Domestic Science, therefore, should be taught in every school. If it were better understood, it would do much to increase the sum total of happiness in this world. How many homes of the better classes are made miserable by an incapable mistress! How often in the household of the poor the wife's bad management drives the husband to distractions which prove his ruin! The spiritual and material are inextricably interwoven in this world of ours, and good cooking and cleanliness have a wonderful effect on human nature. So great is the effect of cleanliness upon man, that it extends even to his moral character!

The need for knowledge of the advantages of pure air, cleanliness, of the simple processes of cooking food, of the principles of economy, cannot be too strongly impressed upon those in India who are in charge of the educational system of the country. It is a notable opportunity for the Indian woman of good education to improve the circumstances of her poorer, more ignorant, sisters. The teaching of Domestic Science in India is a great social work and a much needed form of enterprise.

The poor especially seem to know nothing of

the relative value of foods. They should be taught their properties, their special uses, and the means of preserving them. They should be told the simple scientific reasons for fresh air and personal cleanliness. Young girls should be instructed in the management of children. To this latter end the French have advocated the institution of crèches, or children's nurseries, in connection with the school, where the babies of the working poor are kept and tended while their mothers are out at work for the day. It has been suggested that the older scholars should for an hour each day be taught the care of these children. A lady superintendent of the crèche would be in constant attendance, and each older girl might have a special child as her particular care. So the principles of the management of children might be imparted to girls while at school.

More elaborate instruction in the management of children is given at several colleges in England to those ladies who wish to take up children's nursing as a profession. As an occupation for gentlewomen it is coming to the fore, and for those who are interested in the mental and physical development of children it forms a most congenial pursuit. In the training colleges, where the care of infants and children is taught, the programme comprises lectures in hygiene, first aid and sick nursing, the study of the psychology of childhood, the preparation of food for the nursery. There is no doubt that nurses of a superior class are infinitely more reliable, and can command quite a good salary. Therefore the organization of such colleges would be a great boon to the mothers of India.

For those who have left school, lectures on the subject of the hygiene of the family and of the child could be given. To organize them on any extensive scale, a committee might be formed, and women doctors and women professors appointed to go through the country and teach the elementary laws of hygiene to adult women. Hygiene is, or should be, woman's special care, since it is she who presides over all the offices of the household. Thousands die every year of preventible diseases; but if the laws of health were better understood by the poor, such diseases might be checked and much needless suffering removed.

The need for the realization of the benefits conferred by a knowledge of the laws of hygiene was dwelt upon by the Maharaja of Baroda in his speech at the annual general meeting of the Bombay Sanitary Association last April. In the course of his address he said:

"As society progresses, the question of the prevention of sickness and disease claims an ever-increasing amount of anxious thought in the minds of humanitarians and statesmen. Fatalism has given way before the march of civilization, and the preservation of health and conservation of national resources form part of all State programmes; for those nations which develop their vital resources, with the help of preventive medicine and science, are those which are enabled to reach the highest standard of efficiency and economic superiority. The influence of sanitary methods on the length of life has been most marked in European countries during the last three centuries. This is a most important point for us to remember in India, where the expectation of life is but slightly more than twenty-three years, and has remained at this figure for the past half-century. Compare the rate of progress in Prussia, where the most modern systems of hygiene are studied and used. In that happy State life has lengthened at the rate of twenty-seven years in a century. This fact, which could be supplemented by many others, should convince the most sceptical of the pressing need of enforcing sanitation in India. For to the extent that disease prevails, national and individual efficiency will be hampered. More than half the causes of death are preventible. This we know with certainty. Experts have estimated that fifteen years, at least, could be added to the mean of human life by the application of preventive medicines. This expert estimate has been based on the average expectation of life throughout the world, and, were we in India able to neglect plague, cholera, and malaria as factors in the death-rate—a happy condition already arrived at in the West—then the estimate of fifteen years would have to be considerably increased. With our present knowledge, we may safely assert that an application of scientific preventive medicine to Indian conditions would be followed by an increase in the mean duration of life of thirty years—the rate of mortality would be lessened by one-half—and, together with the reduction in mortality, would come a twofold reduction in the numbers of those who are annually incapacitated by sickness. To express this in figures, we may say that the Indian death-roll could be diminished by more than four million a year, and the number on the sick list would be lessened by eight million. . . . We must remember that all this preventible mortality and sickness involves a preventible loss of potential earning, amounting to crores of rupees. When this fact is better understood by the people, motives both of economy and of humanity should prompt the initiation of a generous financial policy toward the improvement of the air we breathe, the water we drink, and the food we eat. . . . The preservation of health presents itself under different aspects; put as briefly as possible, these may be grouped under the two heads of public hygiene and personal hygiene. These two are inseparable, and must go hand in hand, for it is obvious, for instance, that the efforts of the State to provide a pure supply of water and milk may be completely nullified if the domestic hygiene which uses it is faulty, and permits contamination in the home. . . . When we come to deal with social customs and personal habits, baneful prejudices of caste and religion, and the inveterate ignorance of the masses, then the State is confronted by the obstacle of public opposition, an obstacle it cannot hope to overcome before the people themselves have arrived at a realization that their own welfare depends on progress, and on a willing co-operation with the benevolent intentions of the State."*

It is in inculcating principles such as these that the influence of women, and especially of cultured women, might find a large field for work among the poor of India.

Germany has long instituted classes in connection with the village schools, where the older pupils come in turns from 8 to 12 a.m. to learn the management of a household, the routine of the kitchen, and the cultivation of a vegetable garden. Sometimes the scholars during their last year of school attendance are taught to prepare simple cookery, which is either consumed by the schoolmistresses, or sold at a low rate to work-people. In Berlin, after their general education has reached a certain stage, girls devote themselves in many cases to special courses, which have a particular profession as their object, and one of these courses is housekeeping. Another very general method there of

* *The Times of India,* April 8, 1911.

instructing young girls of the upper and middle classes in household management, is to send them for a year on completion of their studies to board with a private family, where the ladies of the household teach them every practical domestic duty, and make a livelihood for themselves by receiving these girl-boarders. German parents consider that such instruction can be more thoroughly given away from home.

Without entering for the entire curriculum comprised under the term "Domestic Science," it is a great help to take up even one of its branches, as, for instance, cookery. At the technical schools in England (among which the National Training School in London and the Edinburgh School of Cookery are famous), certificates of proficiency may be obtained, and a professional diploma acquired. The former includes scullery-work, plain and high-class cookery, with practice lessons as well as theoretical instruction. The professional diploma is more difficult of attainment. It requires a training of a year or more, and comprises a minute study of the methods of cookery and domestic management, a strict examination in hygiene and chemistry, and the candidate must also be fully capable of delivering a good lecture on her subject before an audience. In the chapter on catering enterprises, it is shown how such cookery training can be utilized to run co-operative kitchens, hotels, restaurants, tea-rooms, etc.

The above are a few of the best known means by which it has been attempted in England, France, and Germany, to introduce an organized system of domestic science teaching throughout the country. In India, where Provinces differ so essentially from each other, where the people speak different languages, follow different pursuits, have different manners and customs, a general scheme of organization would be manifestly unworkable. It would have to be carried out with due consideration for the special needs of each particular Province, and would be a good opportunity to elevate both the moral and material conditions of the poor.

In the organization of LAUNDRIES, the actual work of which is part of a training in Domestic Science, Indian women might find a lucrative occupation. As laundry-work is considered a "low" profession, in which only the Dhoby caste is at present engaged, there is all the more reason that dignity of labour should be recognized, by improving the organization of laundry-work as a calling for women.

It is a profitable one in many ways. Firstly, laundry-work is a necessity, and there will soon be a demand in India for skilled superintendents, or manageresses and forewomen of departments. Secondly, women can carry on the work of directing a laundry for a considerable number of years, after many other professions are closed to them. In England most laundries are in the hands of women, though, as usual, women are rarely found as sole proprietors. If the concern is a private one, the manageress is under the direction of the owners. If it is run by a syndicate, she has to comply with the instructions of the Board of Directors. The workers are divided into different sections: washers, calenderers, manglers, starchers, ironers, folders, packers, sorters, etc. Over each department is a forewoman ; over the head of all a manageress ; and a clever woman may, after taking charge of a laundry for some time, be appointed superintendent of several establishments under the same management. It can readily be seen that there is ample room for anyone with organizing spirit to exercise her gifts to the full. It is a laborious post, entailing long hours, constant pressure, and responsibility, and it calls for smart business acumen, since the success of the whole enterprise practically depends on the person at its head. Laundry supervision should offer ample scope at present for Native Christian and other women to whom caste is no barrier.

Each steam laundry requires an engineer, but otherwise the whole inside work can be done by women. To organize laundries on hygienic principles at reasonable rates in India would be a financial venture for women that, if properly controlled, ought to prove a most satisfactory investment. The best way to train for such work is to go as pupil to the manageress of some well-directed laundry. The practical part may be learned in a few months; the business part depends on the character of the candidate herself.

After some months' general training, the pupil should act as a forewoman to one or more of the different sections of workers. Then after a month or two in each department has elapsed, and if she have the proper business ability, she may proceed to fill the post of general manageress. Sometimes in the large laundries one manageress is required to direct the work inside the laundry, while there is another to take charge of the financial part of the concern. In a small laundry the former will find it absolutely essential to understand the operation of each machine, as she may often be called upon to instruct individual workers in their tasks. Moreover, the superintendent has the entire disposing of the hands in each department, and one of her duties is to see that the best and most economical division of labour is effected. She must have tact in dealing with the operatives, and must know how to get the best amount of expert work out of each. "Method," said Lord Burleigh, "is like packing things in a box: a good packer will get in half as much again as a bad one." And so it is with those who direct the work of others. A capable organizer will be able to get half as much work again out of the people under her, who will be none the worse themselves, since it only means that they are properly handled.

After a few years' experience as superintendent, the next step for a smart woman possessed of financial means will be to instal herself as proprietress of a small laundry. A woman who has been through the training above described has the best possible chance of making a success of the business.

The larger a laundry is, the greater the opportunity for the superintendent to initiate reforms —such as a slight shortening of the hours, which has often been tried and found to act beneficially both on the quality of the labour and the health of the assistants. The hours are long and the countless details of management that fall to the lot of the directress make it perhaps a harassing calling; but it is not at all unhealthy, and affords a fairly secure means of making a considerable income. The methodical, hard-headed business woman will find it an occupation in which she will be in her element, and may taste the pleasure, of which so far men have had practically the monopoly, of running a big commercial enterprise with success.

CHAPTER X

WOMEN INSPECTORS

> "She who did this thing was born
> To do it, claims her licence in her work."
>
> E. B. Browning.

The post of Sanitary Inspector is one which women have only held a very short time in England—the first was appointed in 1892—and yet they have plainly shown that they have come to stay. All authorities who have a knowledge of the work of women inspectors are unanimous in their praise. In "Women and their Work," the author, the Hon. Mrs. A. Lyttelton, quotes from the speech of Mrs. Tennant, formerly Her Majesty's Inspector of Factories, as follows:

"If the work is to be done not merely effectively, but if it is to be done at all, every Board should have at least one woman sanitary inspector. In large places like Sheffield, where there is now one woman working, there should be, I would suggest, ten women working. . . . No woman of judgment or enlightenment, or of the most common sympathy, could be five minutes on Boards concerning themselves with these matters without realizing that women sanitary inspectors are necessary. It is a point on which I can speak with knowledge. We have to remember that the life of a factory worker or a workshop worker is spent most largely in her factory or workshop, starting at six in the morning and ending at six, or even as late as eight, in the evening; therefore the surroundings of her working life have far more influence upon her condition than can the surroundings of her home; and it is important to secure for her a healthy, moral life in the factory and in the workshop."

Again, on the same subject Clementina Black reports:

"There is perhaps no point upon which the influence of women inspectors has been more beneficial";* and she goes on to comment upon "the criminal negligence shown by some employers in carrying out those precautions prescribed by the law." To obviate such abuses is the work of the sanitary inspector.

The duties of the English woman sanitary inspector are: to inspect the premises of laundries, shops, and workrooms where women are employed; to visit the houses where the inmates take in work from the factory, or bring it home from the factory to do after working hours ("outworkers" is the

* "Sweated Industry and the Minimum Wage," p. 33.

technical term); to inspect tenements and lodging-houses; to visit houses where infectious diseases have been present; to inspect the kitchens of certain hotels and restaurants; to superintend the condition of public lavatories for women; to investigate cases of deaths from diarrhœa of infants under one year; to see that the provisions of the Shop Hours Acts, regulating the time an assistant can be employed daily, are observed, and to enforce the Seats for Shop Assistants Act, by which an employer is bound to provide a certain number of seats for his employees. The qualifications necessary in London for these posts are usually a Government examination by the Sanitary Inspectors' Examination Board, in English, arithmetic with mensuration, elementary statistical methods, elementary physics and chemistry, municipal hygiene, and in the provisions of the Local Government Board in force in London. We quote this curriculum in order to give some idea of the scope of the knowledge requisite for these posts. In addition, those who wish to take the Diploma of the National Health Society have to attend lectures on anatomy, physiology, nursing, first-aid, and elocution. Thus, it will be gathered that only women possessed of plenty of energy, brains, tact, health and strength, need cherish the notion of entering this profession. To prove, however, that it is clearly a sphere for women, an account may be given, in somewhat fuller detail, of the sanitary inspector's work in each section of her labours. With regard to her inspection of the workrooms generally where women and girls are employed, she has to report on the cleanliness, ventilation, number employed in each room (to obviate overcrowding), and on the sanitary accommodation. Should she discover any violation of the law with respect to these particulars, she has to send a notice to the owner informing him of the fact, and requesting its cessation. In case he should refuse to comply with this demand, legal proceedings can be taken against him. It is obvious that such details as the investigation of the sanitary arrangements of rooms where women are employed are best left in the hands of a woman. Women can explain their complaints better to one of their own sex, and, if anything is wrong, a lady inspector is much more likely to be informed of it than a man.

In factory inspection there are many suggestions which the sanitary inspector may make to the employers to improve the conditions under which the girls work. Depressing surroundings often continue because there is no one to voice the grievance, and the employees put up with dirt, noise, and bad ventilation for lack of an efficient spokeswoman. In most cases the employers are perfectly willing to remedy the abuse once it is pointed out to them, recognizing that good conditions mean good quality of labour. The sanitary inspectors also examine the dining-rooms of workshops, and see that the meals, if taken in the factory, are up to the proper standard. The holidays, overtime work, the special rules referring to dangerous trades, and other regulations which affect the employment of women and children in factories, are all under the superintendence of women inspectors in many parts of England. Factory inspectors are appointed by the Home Secretary. They have to pass a preliminary examination, which is not a very severe test, but after this preliminary, a two years' trial is appointed, to see if the candidates be suited for the character of the work in hand. In this profession the personality of the inspector is of greater value than mere book-learning, and a thoroughly capable person is by no means easy to meet with. A factory inspector has often to travel about from place to place, and she has to devote her entire time to her work. She must be possessed of a keen interest in her fellow-beings, of a desire to improve the condition of the workers without undue unfairness to either employers or employed, and she must have decision of character to resort to legal action when necessary.

Conditions of labour differ in England and India, but women factory inspectors would doubtless prove as great a blessing there as women workers have found them in England. The need for factory inspection in India is clearly shown by the following extracts from the Report of the Textile Factories Labour Committee (1906), appointed by the Government of India to inquire into the conditions of factory labour in India:

"The Committee are of opinion that a number of Medical Officers should be assigned to separate areas, these to depend on the number of works and the facilities for reaching them, and that their whole time should be devoted to the work of Factory Inspection. . . .

"Some of the duties to be assigned to the Medical Inspectors may be enumerated as follows, attention to—

1. Water supply.
2. Ventilation, including the carrying-off of dust and noxious fumes. . . .
3. The purity of air and amount of humidity.
4. Temperature.
5. Cubic space.
6. Cleanliness and lime-washing.
7. The drainage of floors.
8. Sanitary accommodation.
9. Investigation and reports on accidents in conjunction with Special Factory Inspectors.
10. Diseases of occupation, such as anthrax, lead-, arsenic-, and phosphorous-poisoning; disease of respiratory organs, etc., and also

11. To satisfy themselves that women and children are physically fit for the work they are called upon to perform."*

It will be seen how closely these duties approximate to those undertaken by women factory inspectors in England. Since in India women factory hands usually work together apart from the men, it would appear that they would derive the same benefit from inspectors of their own sex as English operatives have enjoyed. Against those who would urge that the present system of factory inspection in India is adequate, we might quote the statement made as to the administration of the Factory Act, found in the Report of the Indian Factory Labour Commission, 1908:

"When we find that in Calcutta, the headquarters of a special factory inspector, from 30 to 40 per cent. of the children employed half-time in jute factories, are under the legal age of nine years, and 25 per cent. of the young full-timers are under the legal age of fourteen years; that in seventeen out of the twenty-nine cotton factories visited by us outside the Bombay Presidency, all the children under fourteen years of age are regularly worked the same hours as adults; that factory inspectors admit that they knew of the existence of these abuses, and took no steps to stop them; and that in many fac-

* East India (Textile Factories), 1906 (Cd. 3617), p. 10

tories the provisions of the law for a midday interval, and an entire stoppage of work on Sunday, are more or less ignored—it is evident that, except at a few centres, the present system of factory inspection has proved a failure. The reason seems to us to be that Government has not appointed a sufficient number of full-time factory inspectors, and has depended too much on a number of *ex-officio* inspectors, who have neither the time nor the special knowledge necessary for the work."* This statement clearly proves that there is ample room for women to do good work there among their own sex. Men appointed as factory inspectors in India are recommended to receive a portion of their training in Europe, and probably Indian women would have, at the outset, to do the same.

The sanitation of some of the mills is acknowledged to require looking into. Over and over again the sanitary accommodation is pronounced deficient. Compare the statement made in the 1907 Report of the Textile Labour Committee, that "in many mills there is room for much improvement, and it is believed that there will be no unwillingness on the part of owners and occupiers to carry out improvements, if any suggestions of a practical kind are made."†

Again, in the Report of the Indian Factory

* East India (Factory Labour Commission, 1908) (Cd. 4292), vol. i., p. 66.

† East India (Textile Factories), 1906 (Cd. 3617), p. 21.

Labour Commission, 1908, attention is drawn to the fact, that "in several classes of factories, more particularly cotton-presses, rice-mills, flour-mills, and paper-mills, the amount of solid impurities in the atmosphere is so large as to cause serious danger to the health of the operatives. In many cases the dust was so bad that we could hardly enter the workrooms. In some of the better managed factories mechanical appliances have been used, which entirely obviate this danger, and there is no reason why such appliances should not be insisted on wherever they are needed."* Sir Bhalchandra Krishna "thinks that there is physical deterioration among the mill-hands, . . . due to bad ventilation in the mills, and to the alcoholic habits of the operatives."† "After the Commission paid a surprise visit at 7.45 p.m. to mill No. 27 (Inspection Notes), the following note was recorded: 'The carding and preparation rooms (the only part of the mill at work) were badly lit, and there was no ventilation, all windows were closed, and the air was hot and oppressive: the perspiring workers looked dull, listless, and exhausted, and the few children half-dazed.' "‡

The same necessity seems to exist in India as in England, for the inspection of the dwellings of

* East India (Factory Labour Commission, 1908), vol. i., p. 62.

† *Ibid.*, p. 87.

‡ *Ibid.*, p. 90.

the workers. This task is one in which women as inspectors would excel. The importance which the Committee of the 1906 Commission attached to this question, is evinced by the following extract from their Report :—

"It was felt by the Committee that however efficient might be the administration, or however well considered the laws relating to Factories, no real or permanent good would follow unless in many instances serious attention is paid to the homes and surroundings of the mill-hands."*

A description is given in the Report of the 1908 Indian Factory Labour Commission of the dwellings where the workers live:

"In Bombay, on the other hand, where available land is scarce, little has been done by the mills in this direction, and the operatives as a rule herd together, for the sake of economy, into large, many-storied, barrack-like buildings called *chawls*, which are provided by private enterprise. The rooms occupied by the mill-hands are in general much over-crowded; there is little privacy, and no home life."† Although in Calcutta and several places in Upper India, most of the textile mills have built commodious settlements near the mill premises for large numbers of their operatives, yet enough has been said to show the great need of sanitary inspection that exists.

* P. 6.

† Vol. i., p. 22.

In English laundries women inspectors have to investigate hygienic conditions in general, and they have also already been of some service in the prevention of accidents from the machinery in these places and others where dangerous tools are employed. Carelessness is probably the cause of most mishaps, but it has been shown by figures compiled by women inspectors that the majority of accidents usually occur at certain hours of the day, from 11 a.m. to 12 noon, and from 4 p.m. to 6 p.m.: the conclusion drawn being that in the former case the girls are tired towards the end of a long period of work and so grow careless, and in the interval from 4 p.m. to 6 p.m. the growing dusk or the replacing of daylight by artificial illumination also leads to accidents. In the face of such statistics an employer might be urged to shorten the hours somewhat to prevent over-fatigue, or to adopt some special plan to insure the safety of his workers. The drainage of the floors of the laundry is one particular care of the woman inspector, also such matters as the prohibition of the use of gas-irons which emit unpleasant fumes.

The need for inspection of tenements and common lodging-houses can scarcely be exaggerated. From the hygienic point of view and from the standpoint of morality, these lower-class dwellings require investigation. The law in England regulates the number of lodgers to be received, provides for the separation of the sexes, for cleanliness and ventilation, insists on notice of infectious diseases being given, and on the proper conduct of such houses. There are by-laws which set down detailed rules for the proper ventilation and the sanitary accommodation of the rooms. These lodging-houses are registered in England, and the licence may be withdrawn if it be proved that the by-laws have three times been broken. It has lately been proposed that the licence should have to be renewed annually, and only on condition of proper accommodation being provided. Most of these lodging-houses are inspected by men, but in any where women are housed it would seem advisable to employ women sanitary inspectors. It is the duty of every nation to see that the homes—even the casual dwelling-places—of its women are sanitary and such as a decent woman can avail herself of, and this duty cannot be fulfilled by any so well as by one of her own sex. The evils of over-crowding, bad ventilation and immorality exist in this class of dwelling in all countries. It is time that Indian women took in hand the improvement of existing conditions.

In the inspection of shops, sanitary inspectors have to report on the condition of the rooms where the assistants take their meals; on the sufficiency of the sleeping accommodation where they "live in"; on the observance of the regulation number of hours during which they can be worked; the observance of the Truck Act, which limits fines and enacts that full wages must be paid unconditionally in coin, not partly in board and lodging provided by the employers; of the Seats for Shop Assistants Act, to insure that there be at least one seat for every two assistants in each room in retail places of business. The work of the sanitary inspectors of both sexes has done much in these directions.

As well as factory and sanitary inspectors there are also women SCHOOL INSPECTORS appointed by the Board of Education to visit and report on the teaching and hygiene of the elementary and secondary schools, of technical schools and training colleges. A few women are thus employed, and, like factory and other Government inspectors, they are entitled to a pension at the age of sixty-five. The pensionable age in India is fifty-five, since in a hot country it would be unfair to make men work till they were sixty-five, as is possible in a cold country like England. Factory inspectors in England receive a good salary; the chief lady inspector holds quite a responsible position, and draws a commensurate rate of pay.

As will be seen in connection with the boarding-out of children under the Poor Law (in the chapter on Charitable Organizations), there are women inspectors to supervise the system under which these poor children are placed in the houses of women of the working classes to be brought up amid home-like surroundings. There is a Woman Inspector of Reformatories and Industrial Schools, one of the London Maternity Wards and Infirmaries, and another of Prisons. The latter lady holds a medical degree, the benefit of which in such social work can be readily imagined.

There is a post somewhat similar to that of the sanitary inspector, which is held by women: that of HEALTH VISITOR, which is often taken up as a preparation for the more difficult work of sanitary inspector. The health visitor's special duty is the investigation of the hygienic conditions of the children of the poorer classes. An acquaintance with nursing is a great advantage. The health visitor is not empowered to set the law in motion against offenders. Her mission is to give advice on the proper care of the children and the cleanliness of the home. The importance of this advice to poor mothers has been so keenly felt by the authorities in England, that they have arranged for a course of lectures in connection with the Royal Sanitary Institute, followed by an examination which qualifies for a position as health visitor. Bedford College for Women (University of London) has also a special course in practical and scientific hygiene, lasting for one year, for women students who wish to prepare for factory and sanitary inspectorships, or for work as health visitors. Several other colleges and societies offer a similar training, proving the growing interest that Englishwomen are taking in this most responsible social labour.

The post of school inspector deals with what is, or ought to be, one of the most interesting subjects in the world—the education of the children of the country. It is a domain in which woman's qualities as supervisor are most valuable, for, as regards the moral tone of the school, the hygiene and personal health of the pupils, as well as the actual methods of imparting instruction to girls, a woman is a better judge than a man can possibly be.

The duties of inspector are admirably adapted to the Indian widow without family, or to someone who can devote her whole time and energy to them. The married woman with home ties could not afford the leisure to undertake what is, in fact, an arduous, though absorbing, life-work.

CHAPTER XI

MATRONS AND SUPERINTENDENTS

"For many things the world gropes and stumbles, because it has not enough of women's hands to guide it."—JOHN BOYD KINNEAR.

THE power to manage others is inborn. A woman either possesses it or she has it not, and if she lacks it, it is a quality almost impossible to acquire. To be a successful superintendent, ability to control and organize is essential, otherwise chaos will reign supreme, and the poor matron will be like Defoe's sheep, "at the head of an army of lions."

There are numerous posts—such as matrons of schools, charitable institutions, hospitals, asylums, prisons, reformatories, industrial schools—which, however, are not highly paid. As a rule, salaries in England are not large. For instance, the Prime Minister of England gets a smaller salary than the Governor of an Indian Province. For the matron of a hospital three or four years' training in nursing is requisite, and great powers of administration. She must be strong both in mind and body.

The matrons of reformatories and industrial schools in England play a great part in the material and moral direction of these institutions. Even if the school be for boys and if a man be appointed director, his wife generally acts as matron, overseeing the housekeeping, the food, clothes, etc., of the children, and exercising a beneficial influence upon them. The share of the matron in the good results accruing from such institutions is universally acknowledged. There are so many ways in which woman's gentler sway can make itself felt, that in these corrective establishments there seems to be clearly marked out a place for women to work alongside and hand-in-hand with men. For married people who have no children of their own, and for those whose children are already grown up, there is a great opportunity of social service. A father and daughter, or mother and son, or brother and sister, might be associated in the work, as was suggested some years ago by Mme. H. Rollet, in her report on "Women's Rôle in Boys' Reformatories," read before the Second International Congress of Women's Work and Institutions, held in Paris in 1900. To place only a male student over young boys in reformatory schools is to give them a father, but not a mother. Most of such children are the offspring of unworthy, incapable parents, and the heads of such establishments should strive to recompense them in some degree for the guiding influence which their natural parents have been unable to supply. An efficient matron must, as we have said before, have at heart both the moral and material welfare of her charges. The material side may not be neglected, though frequently the diet in such institutions is far from being either attractive or even sufficient to maintain growing boys and girls. The directress must look to it that the food-supply is varied, and suitably prepared. She must have a knowledge of food values, to see that the inmates partake of the various food-substances in proper proportion. She must superintend the clothing and deportment of the children, the hygiene of the building, the petty ailments to which the young are liable, the treatment of the sick in the infirmary; in short, she must have the essential qualities of mother, housekeeper, and nurse. As regards her moral influence, she must possess a combination of firmness and tenderness: firmness to insure that her orders are obeyed, and tenderness to make the obeying of them a pleasure. In the education of the more youthful members, too, a woman's maternal instinct makes her a greater success than a man, especially with the lower and more depraved portion of humanity. The most incorrigible youth has been known to yield to a woman's persuasion when the master's threats had been unavailing.

It is a matter of the highest importance that positions such as these should be filled by women of good education, and not by those of inferior rank. Candidates should not be chosen from among the incompetents, but from school-mistresses and capable, cultivated women who are willing to devote themselves to the work as to a great cause. In Switzerland the matrons of these correctional houses do not disdain, we understand, to teach their pupils gardening and the management of cattle, while at the same time they are most intelligent women, speaking several languages and possessing a good knowledge of music. The system under such matrons and teachers would thus be formative and educational, not repressive. Many of the children have not actively criminal tendencies. They are merely weaklings, the sons of drunkards or of degenerate parents. For such as these a woman's influence—especially if she has been a wife and mother—is exactly what is wanted.

Women as police matrons in institutions, though the post is not usually a lucrative one, play a very necessary part in this essential, if somewhat unattractive work. They are generally appointed from among the prison wardresses. English prisons for either sex have assistant matrons to help in the catering, clothing, and general domestic superintendence. Such posts are filled by single women or widows without children, and it is considered desirable that candidates should be acquainted with some trade which they may impart to the women under their care. As a proof of the power possessed by women to deal with criminals of their own sex, it was reported at the same International Congress of Women's Work previously quoted that at Indianapolis in America there is a prison entirely managed by women, except for two male warders. The director is a woman and her staff is exclusively feminine. The two warders are there to afford help in case of need, but the matron asserts that such aid has scarcely ever been required, the wardresses having been quite competent to do all that is necessary. The wall which surrounds this prison is not more than a yard high! Another lady was also directress of a prison in Massachusetts in America, and did very useful work among the inmates by her gentleness, discretion, and high moral standard, proving that the coarse natures of criminals are not impervious to the higher influences. Her charges never were unmanageable. A Resolution was put forward at this same Congress that there should be women doctors for prisons as well as women directresses: doctors who would not limit their care to the cure of the body, but would try to gain the confidence of the women and raise their moral level.

Then there are posts as matrons to asylums, which are responsible appointments with good salaries attached. In the large towns in the United Kingdom there are ambulance stations which have horse-ambulances and hand-stretchers ready in case of accidents. Such stations are usually in charge of a superintendent, and his wife, if she be a trained hospital nurse, receives a fixed salary in addition to board, lodging, uniform, coal, gas, and laundry, for attending to the patients when they are brought in.

The post of matron to a large school is a busy, active, and interesting work, requiring those powers of management, tact, practical method, and domestic instincts which are necessary in a good housekeeper. All these appointments can be well filled by persons of mature years, nor is there danger of a woman, when once established, being removed to make room for younger competitors.

CHAPTER XII

CO-OPERATION

"The multitude which does not reduce itself to unity is confusion; the unity which does not depend upon the multitude is tyranny."—PASCAL.

As the system of co-operation is one which is coming more and more to the front, and as its principles may be applied in many of the spheres of women's work which are discussed in different chapters of this book, it seems advisable to give here some account of its rise and progress in Europe, that Indian women may see how valuable an opportunity it has afforded for the workers here, to rise from the position of mere labourers to that of partners in their special industries.

The theory lying at the base of all co-operative schemes is a democratic one—that those who have helped to produce are entitled to a share in the profits, and to a voice in the direction of the business; also that it is to the interest of the employer that the worker should be admitted to a share in the gains and control of the undertaking. The aim of co-operation is thus the promotion of mutual aid and self-help. Its methods are clearly stated by the Editor of the *Co-operative Magazine*, so early as 1826:—"Mr. Owen (the founder of the movement in England) does not propose that the rich should give up their property to the poor, but that the poor should be placed in such a situation as would enable them to create *new wealth* for themselves."

So co-operation has two tenets as the bed-rock on which it stands: the first, that mutual aid, not individual competition, is the nobler principle to guide the conduct of human life; and the second, that by uniting to sell to others, or to purchase for themselves, a body of people can gain more than by proceeding individually.

Co-operation existed from an early age in many countries, but England was the first to develop it to any great extent. The nucleus of the movement was formed in Lancashire, but had little success until 1844, when an enterprise was started at Rochdale, Lancashire, among the poor flannel-weavers of the north of England, twenty-eight of whom raised a sum of twenty-eight pounds as capital, by means of weekly subscriptions of 2d. each. Now from this very modest beginning, the Toad Lane Store, as it was called, has enlarged until it can count nineteen branches, with as many newsrooms, a great central store, with a huge library and scientific apparatus—such as telescopes and microscopes, for the use of members, science classes, corn and spinning mills, educational funds; and its promoters have become large wholesale as well as retail traders, manufacturers, builders, bankers, etc. The principle on which they conducted their Store was that profits should be divided among all purchasers in proportion to the amount of their purchases; that such profits should not be paid direct to the member, but added to the existing capital, until it amounted to £5, when the owner was made shareholder to that extent, and 5 per cent. interest was paid on the share capital. Anything saved could be drawn out at any time by the shareholder if he desired. So men who had no capital, could, by supporting the Store, gradually become shareholders in the concern, and the more they did to bring new customers to the Store, and the more loyally they purchased from it themselves, the greater their portion of the profits.

Since those early days the system of co-operative stores has spread far and wide. Some are quite humble in area, like the small village shop; others are of huge dimensions, and manufacture clothing, provisions, undertake farming, and provide houses to let or sell to their members, or they advance money to them to help them in building. To start a Store, a meeting must be convened of people interested in such a scheme.

The members will subscribe their own capital, and according to the proposed size of the Store, that capital will be fixed at so many shares, to be held by each (one only, if the concern is a modest one) at £1 each. Then a secretary, treasurer, and collector of subscriptions must be appointed. The profits are usually administered in the following way: part is applied to cover the managing expenses, part to pay the interest due on loans, part to issue the dividends on members' capital (generally at 5 per cent.), part is set aside for educational purposes, and the remainder divided among the members and customers. An account is kept of each customer's purchases, and a proportional share of the whole remaining profit is paid out quarterly to each. Such a scheme is a great incentive to thrift, and also prevents members from running into debt, since no credit should be either given or taken by co-operative stores.

Similar principles rule in what are known as labour co-partnership societies, in which the employees are all shareholders, and receive a portion of the profits. Thus, it will be seen that the actual producer, as well as the consumer, receives his proportion of the profit made by his employers. One of the largest gas companies in London is run on these lines, and contrives to supply the public at cheaper rates than many other companies which do not allow their workers a proportionate share of the gains. Co-partnership would seem to be the ideal condition of labour.

Now, as to the capacity of women in general, and Indian women in particular, for active participation in such projects. It is no new thing for the so-called gentler sex to enter directly upon the high seas of commerce, and where they have done so already it has been found to prove a moral, as well as a material, advantage to them. If anyone doubts the power of work, and commercial work especially, to raise the standard of woman's intelligence, he or she need only look at the lower classes, where the women are frequently cleverer than the men, solely because they are compelled to exercise their faculties. In the Middle Ages in Europe working men and women constituted themselves into "guilds" or industrial corporations, without distinction of sex. In those days women's work was looked upon with favour, and granted a good wage. Women, for various reasons, at present accept a lower rate of pay; but in the co-operative movement there is a chance for them to advance side by side with men, and in India there seem to be opportunities for co-operative organization either between women alone or by women in conjunction with men. By means of such schemes, a fairer distribution of wealth is insured than when the gains of large business concerns are pocketed by one proprietor or raked in by a company.

Besides large co-operative provision and clothing stores, women in India might organize huge furnishing depots on similar lines, such as those described in the chapter on professions connected with the home, where everything connected with the equipment of the household would be sold on co-operative terms. Agriculture, too, affords a vast field for women's co-operative enterprise; and the history of its development in clever little Denmark should prove vastly encouraging to Indian women, because there, in dairy-work especially, women have achieved extraordinary success. Commercially, it has changed the financial position of Denmark as a European Power, for, from being a poor land, it is now transformed into one of the (proportionately) richest countries of Europe. Moreover, it has taken but a few years to effect this improvement, since the first co-operative dairy was not formed till 1882. The system followed there would be one comparatively easy of imitation in India, because the farmers and dairy-keepers do not work in common, but unite in the disposal of their produce. Thus, the scattered villages of India might be organized, and the produce of each co-operative dairy might be utilized to bring prosperity to the whole. In most Danish villages there is a co-operative dairy, which forms a depot for the milk of the cows belonging to all the farmers of the neighbourhood. The owners of the cattle are shareholders, and take a division of the profits, proportioned to the amount of milk, cream, etc., they have supplied. Similar co-operative societies have been formed to produce, collect, and export eggs. Unions also exist to promote bee-keeping and fruit cultivation, and for the disposal of all market produce. There are even co-operative societies for the purchase of farming implements, manures, etc. The funds for carrying out these enterprises are provided by commercial banks.

Since India is pre-eminently an agricultural country, it is thought that large co-operative dairy schemes would very much encourage the poorer classes, and would be a splendid mission for women workers to undertake there. As in Denmark, scientific instruction could be given in India by means of evening continuation classes and technical schools.

Closely connected with agriculture is the system of co-operative credit, by which farmers can obtain sums of money for the purchase and improvement of their farms, stock, and implements. The idea of such banks originated in Germany in 1849-50, the object being that the peasants might be saved from the clutches of the money-lender by borrowing certain sums of money on their united credit, which sums they would lend to their members, for purposes approved by the directors, at a somewhat higher rate of interest. A slight outline of the way in which such a scheme may be carried through in India, and financed by women, will be found in the chapter on "Money-lending." The chief points in the organization of the Raiffeisen banks, as they are called, from their German founder, are:

1. They are local institutions, the shareholders being known to each other. Some affluent members invest their money mainly to promote the welfare of the society, but the majority are poor.

2. The object for which the loan is required must be stated by the borrower and investigated by the authorities. Should any misuse of the loan be discovered, the grant may be recalled.

3. None but members have the privilege of drawing loans.

4. Loans are repayable by regular instalments.

5. A note of hand is given as security.

6. The value of the shares is fixed at a small amount, but no interest is paid on them, all profit being transferred to the reserve fund.

7. The societies act also as savings banks.

8. There are two committees, one active, which transacts the actual business of the bank, and the other managing, to control the operations of the first. Officers give their services free, as the object is to benefit the peasant farmer, not to enrich the directors.

9. The liability is unlimited.

10. The richer members of the committee have the major share of the direction.

The banks in each district are linked in a union, and the total number of unions are joined in a general agency. The scheme is therefore a most practical one to unite the scattered villages of India, and to help the very poorest of her citizens at the lowest possible rate.

Another system of co-operative credit banks, also borrowed from Germany, is the Schulze method, which is employed chiefly to aid by loans the middle-class townspeople. The officers are salaried, interest is paid on the shares, which are of much higher value than those under the Raiffeisen scheme, and the sphere of action is not limited to the immediate neighbourhood. On these two plans, with slight alterations, the whole co-operative credit system is based.

Women in Europe have already taken considerable part in co-operative work. In 1834 they formed their first co-operative society in England, selling tea and coffee in order to establish dwelling-houses for the members. Afterwards they advanced so far that they formed, in 1883, the Women's Co-operative Guild, to teach women the principles of the co-operative movement, to show them how, by dealing at the Store, they may save 10 per cent. upon household expenses, to urge them to take up shares in their own name, and to work with men on the different boards and committees. The Guild has many branches, which meet weekly and are controlled by a central committee of seven members. It holds conferences and annual meetings, and deals with all the questions which concern women, such as Poor Law, Land and Housing, Public Health, etc. It is thus a valuable promoter of the best interests of women. Many authorities consider that such an institution would be a great step towards feminine combination in India, and might become the centre of industrial progress for women. The aim of co-operation is self-help, the development of individuality. Its object is the same throughout all classes, a desire to promote the common good of all, not the particular prosperity of a few. It is the spirit of unity and of friendly feeling to others, and its underlying principle should be universal in every caste and creed.

CHAPTER XIII

MONEY-LENDING

"Since there must be borrowing and lending, and men are so hard of heart that they will not lend freely, usury must be permitted."—BACON.

STATISTICS show that there are about 420,000 money-lenders and bankers in India, of whom 17·4 per cent. are women. For this reason, therefore, we have included money-lending among the professions to be considered by our countrywomen. For a long time in Europe it was looked upon as a moral wrong to require more in repayment of a loan than the amount of the principal lent, and especially between friends such transactions for gain were entirely tabooed.

"For when did friendship take
A breed for barren metal of his friend?"

demands Antonio of Shylock the Jew. In those early days the rich simply hoarded up their wealth, so that to lend money without interest meant no loss to them beyond the risk of its non-recovery. Hence their pecuniary transactions were on quite a different footing. Nowadays, when men borrow to use again for profit, the interest they pay is simply a share of their profits granted to the lender.

Money-lending is one of the oldest callings in the world, and therefore a short history of the trade might not be uninteresting. It was practised in all ancient States both East and West—in China, Egypt, Babylon, India, Greece, and Rome—and a curious point to note in its development is that in each country, though at first confined to a special class, it seems to have extended until it was considered a lawful pursuit for men of all ranks. Thus in ancient India we find that primarily only the Vaishya caste drove this thriving trade, adding it to its other occupations of ordinary commerce, agriculture, and cattle-rearing. But by the Laws of Manu, in times of sore distress a man of higher caste might adopt the calling of the caste beneath him, except that no Brahman nor Kshatriya might lend money on usury. This concession at periods of want with regard to all trades but usury led later on to an extension to the Sudras of permission to lend money on interest in times of necessity. Similarly a Brahman might also accept interest for loans when hard pressed by circumstances. Shortly afterwards the law was stretched a point further, and Vrihaspati about the sixth century A.D. sanctioned money-lending by Brahmans under no other condition except that it must not be done in person, but through an agent. This meant that all classes were now permitted the practice.

Similarly in England we find the trade in the hands of the Jews, from the time when William the Conqueror first granted them admission into England until 1290, when their expulsion took place. During this period Church and State united to restrain the spread of usury among the English themselves, but in spite of the disfavour shown it, it was carried on in covert fashion more or less by men of all ranks. Subsequently, when the Jews were driven out of the country, it was freely practised, though certain checks were put upon the rate of interest to be accepted, and punishments fixed at various times for the violation of these laws. Under Cromwell the Jews were allowed to return to England, and true to their universal character as the world's bankers, resumed their accustomed occupation. So firmly do they adhere to this particular calling that at the present day they still have under their control a great part of the money-lending business of England and, indeed, of the whole world. In 1854, under Queen Victoria, the laws against usury were repealed in England, and money-lending, being now a recognized occupation, may be carried on at a rate of interest to be decided between the contracting parties without direct State control. The law courts, however, are empowered to reduce the rate of interest in a suit by a money-lender when it appears to the judge to be exorbitant.

Money-lending has always been a popular trade in India from the earliest times. It is mentioned in Indian literature, which shows that as early as 600 B.C. it was considered a fit and proper means of earning a livelihood. But Gautama prohibited the taking of interest above 15 per cent. per annum, and also decreed that the total amount of interest could not exceed the amount of the principal.

After Gautama came Manu, the great Hindu law-giver, who in his Code, as we have seen, confined the practice of usury solely to the Vaishyas, or traders. There seems to have been no restriction as to the class from which interest might be demanded; matters were on a perfectly business footing, and a "deal" could be made either with one's own caste or the castes above and below. Like Gautama, Manu also decreed a maximum rate of interest—15 per cent. per annum with security, and without security according to a sliding scale, fixed in proportion to the caste of the borrower, increasing as the recipient of the loan descended in the social scale. Thus a Brahman paid 2 per cent., a Kshatriya 3 per cent., a Vaishya 4 per cent., and a Sudra 5 per cent. per month. So in money-lending, as in law, science, and philosophy, India was ahead of Europe in legalizing the taking of interest and in drawing up a fixed scale of charges. Another rule laid down by Manu to check excessive interest was a clause which stated that no interest can be demanded from persons in distress, since such interest would be exorbitant. An insolvent debtor could be made to repay his loan by personal labour, unless he were of a superior caste to that of the lender. In case of death, the debtor's sons or grandsons had to assume responsibility for the loan, thus proving that there were no bankruptcy laws in those early days.

When India came under the sway of the Mahomedans, who are forbidden by their religion to lend money on interest to those of their own faith, the Hindus were still permitted to carry on the pursuit unhindered, and in practice, though not in theory, some Mahomedans followed their example. There ensued the period of British rule in India, when regulations were passed to fix a maximum legal rate of interest similar to that which then obtained by law in England. When, in 1854, all laws against usury were repealed in England, the same rules were applied in the following year in India, so that to-day only one custom remains, in the Hindu law of *damdupat*, of the old law which forbade a Hindu to exact from a Hindu borrower in a single transaction an amount of interest exceeding the principal.

The trade of money-lending when the borrower requires capital for profit is perfectly legitimate, and one in which women might well take an intelligent share. It is lucrative, for, as Bacon quaintly puts it, "the usurer being at certainties, and others at uncertainties, at the end of the game most of the money will be in the box." In towns money is needed to float business enterprises. In country districts it is required to promote agricultural projects. In India, where the vast majority are engaged in agriculture, one of the chief problems to be contended with is the difficulty the people experience in securing the loan of capital on reasonable terms to carry out their schemes. As is well known, most of the farming class in India are saddled with debt, which only increases as the years go by. The money-lender would find it against his interests to sell up a debtor as long as the latter could continue to pay interest on the sum advanced. Therefore, a farmer's sons and grandsons may find themselves laden with their father's or grandfather's liabilities.

The money-lender's rate of interest is often exorbitant, and in Sir Andrew Fraser's recently published account of his life-work in India* he gives an interesting description of the agricultural community, with suggestions for remedying its financial condition. He estimates the extent of its indebtedness at 500 millions sterling, and he states that the people probably pay 20 per cent. more as interest than they would

* "Among Indian Rajahs and Ryots," by Sir Andrew H. L. Fraser. 1911.

pay if they were solvent. If so, he concludes they are paying in excess every year 100 millions sterling! The cause of the high rate of interest he explains in three ways. Firstly, rates have been retained which were customary in old days when security was not so stable as now, and recovery more difficult. Secondly, in former times the usurer advanced grain at seed-time to the farmer, which was dearer at the time of sowing than at harvest, when the debtor had usually to repay the quantity borrowed with 25 per cent. addition. This was not unreasonable when transactions took place in kind, but the same high rates still continue now when cash and not grain is advanced to the client. Thirdly, interest is often paid in advance, which of course greatly increases the rate.

The idea of co-operative credit is the only one which has been found to relieve the situation of the Indian. It was taken up by the Agricultural Department, under the India Government. In 1904, the Government of India passed "The Co-operative Credit Societies Act," recognizing the Raiffeisen system as suited for country districts, and the Schulze system for towns. Village societies were established with unlimited liability, and a system of repayment of loans from the profits gained through the loan. In many places local investors of capital have deposited money in these banks, and even the money-lenders themselves are beginning to look with more favour upon the enterprise. Several central institutions have been established —a combination of the smaller societies on a joint-stock basis, which have the duties of inspecting and controlling the rest. "In Bengal . . . when I last inquired," says Sir Andrew Fraser, "there were over five hundred societies scattered throughout its Districts, including six central institutions, and the combined capital was about six hundred thousand rupees. . . . The experiment has been most encouraging. . . . The aim is to produce an organization in which isolated societies, in compact areas, in different parts of a District, will be grouped into local unions for the purpose of financial control, and then to link these unions to a Central Bank at District headquarters. Ultimately it may be possible to establish a provincial bank to which the District banks will be affiliated. Some such system is necessary to enable the movement to stand alone, without Government support."

If rich Indian women would grant their patronage to some such scheme, it would give a wonderful impetus to the progress of the people, and to the betterment of their financial condition. The agriculturists are one of the most important sections of the population. It has always been so in India. "Take care, O King," says Bhishma in the Mahabharata, "that the merchants of thy kingdom groan not beneath heavy imposts. Beware also lest the tillers of land throughout thy country forsake it because of thy oppression." "Trade," says Lord Chatham, "increases the wealth and glory of a country; but its real strength and stamina are to be looked for among the cultivators of the land." It is the agriculturists who benefit most by such organizations, and are enabled to carry on their occupations and make improvements in their methods, without paying extortionate rates of interest or hanging round their necks a disheartening and crippling burden of debt. It is a great means of fostering self-reliance, and has been found to have appreciable effect in lowering the rate of interest demanded by the money-lenders. The moral and material condition of the people has ameliorated in those districts where the co-operative system has been brought into play, so that financiers of such a scheme would have the pleasant consciousness that they were furthering a great social movement for the uplifting of their fellow-countrymen.

CHAPTER XIV

CHARITABLE ORGANIZATIONS

"Charity . . . if any duty can be said to be its own reward, or to pay us while we are discharging it, it is this."
—FIELDING.

IT is the duty of the rich to serve the poor. It is especially the rich woman's duty to do something to alleviate the pain of toiling humanity, and the first question she should ask ought to be, "What is the best way to begin?" Method is necessary, whether the help is given in money or in personal service. So a brief survey of England's charitable organizations, may be of benefit in bringing to the notice of Indian women the schemes which have best prospered here. Fortunately there is not much need to preach to our countrywomen the sweet virtues of charity. As well as their religion, their own most ancient and beautiful literature has inculcated the noble principles of compassion for all living creatures. Throughout the Mahabharata this doctrine runs. The old philosophers had a wonderful wisdom in those early days, for even then they saw the difficulty there is in doing good. "There are two things to guard against," they said, in the Santi Parva, "in regard to wealth—one that we give not to him who is undeserving, and the other that we pass not by him who doth deserve it." These are the dangers which can be at least partially avoided by organization.

Before beginning our description of Englishwomen's organizations for the benefit of humanity in their own country, we should like to mention one of their institutions, which has been at work now for many years in our land. No account of women's work for women would be complete without some reference to the justly famous National Association for Supplying Female Medical Aid to the Women of India. The fund raised for the above object is known as the Countess of Dufferin's Fund, and was founded in August, 1885, by Lady Dufferin, for the purpose of providing medical tuition to women in India, to train them as doctors, hospital assistants, nurses, and midwives, and also to provide medical relief in the form of cottage hospitals, dispensaries, and female wards, all under female superintendence, for the benefit of the women of India. Since the inception of the Association it has had as Lady President of its Central Committee such distinguished Englishwomen as Lady Dufferin, Lady Lansdowne, Lady Elgin, Lady Curzon, Lady Ampthill and Lady Minto. The work of its lady doctors, surgeons, and nurses is beyond praise, especially as the exigencies of their profession cause many of them to lead exceedingly isolated lives. The Victoria Memorial Scholarships Fund was initiated by the late Lady Curzon in 1901-1902, as a memento of the keen and thoughtful interest taken by Her Majesty Queen Victoria in the physical well-being of the women and children of India. It was formed with the special object of training midwives of a superior class, and endeavouring to reach the native midwives and persuade them to attend at the Dufferin hospitals, that they might thereby acquire a more practical scientific knowledge of their calling. There is no need to describe at greater length the noble work of the Dufferin Association, which is so well known throughout India; nor for the same reason need we do more than mention Lady Minto's Nursing Association for Europeans in India, with a working staff of forty-two nurses and seven lady superintendents, who carry out their mission over a very wide area, extending from Burma to Baluchistan. But notwithstanding the exertions of the workers in these institutions and in the Countess of Dufferin's numerous hospitals, India cannot yet boast of possessing a high-caste Hindu or Mahomedan Florence Nightingale. What the women of India must learn from the Western woman is action—to imitate not in words, but in deeds, the best of the women of the West.

There would be no end to an account of all the charitable societies of Englishwomen, therefore we can do no more than glance at a few of the most important. The largest general institution which interests itself in every branch of philanthropy, is the Charity Organization Society. It is a society with its headquarters in London, conducted by both men and women, but women take a very large part in its management. The manner in which the association works is as follows:

It acts as a large central union, linking together as far as possible other schemes of charity, and so preventing them from overlapping one another. Its object is to raise permanently the material and moral condition of the poor. It is directed by a council, and locally by district committees. The business of the council is to promote right views as to the distribution of charity, to induce charitable societies to combine to carry on their work, to consider practical schemes for encouraging thrift, to summon special committees to deal with special problems—such as the care of the blind, deaf and dumb, the housing of the poor, etc., to supply the public with information as to how entry to various charitable institutions may be obtained, and as to their working, to inquire into the circumstances of begging-letter writers, and to suppress imposture in appeals to charity. Thus its main object is not the distribution of funds, but to form a central station and information bureau for charitable institutions, and to co-ordinate hitherto unsystematized private charity. The work of the district committees is local, and has the same aims within a limited area as the efforts of the head council. They act as centres in each district for the charitable work of the neighbourhood. Societies connected with them collect subscriptions or donations, which they administer to the best of their ability, investigating each case to insure the genuineness of the appeal. They try to suggest means by which the applicant may be placed on a *permanently* independent footing again, and the old and infirm of deserving character, whose friends are incapable of supporting them, are brought to the notice of societies or individuals, who may aid them by pensions or otherwise. In every case their object is to direct such applicants to the proper channel of relief. Only the deserving poor are aided by this society. None who are known to be of bad character are eligible to receive aid. Begging by letter, or otherwise, is entirely discouraged.

When an applicant for relief comes before the members of committee, if the latter are satisfied that help is required, they first endeavour to find someone on whom the destitute person has a claim. If they can discover no one, relative, friend, or former employer, they endeavour to interest some institution or private individual in the case. If help is still not forthcoming, they advertise in their society's journal, setting forth the wants of the applicant. They also insist as far as possible that *adequate* relief shall be afforded, thinking it preferable to maintain a few decently than to divide their funds among too large a number. Their object is to *cure* distress, not merely to relieve it; to promote thrift, not to encourage dependence by promiscuous almsgiving, which they consider a bad form of charity. This society has its headquarters in London, and its district committees with offices and honorary and stipendiary officials work in all the surrounding neighbourhoods. Similar societies are in operation throughout the United Kingdom.

In India, where calamities—such as famine and sudden visitations of flood or earthquake—are apt to throw whole districts into distress, it is of the highest importance that some system (apart from Government organizations) should be ready in working order to cope with the suffering directly it comes. These misfortunes usually occur as a surprise, and although the money to relieve them may be there, yet if for want of organized effort it is not available at the moment, many valuable lives are lost. Therefore, in every Province and Native State there should be some private league worked on lines similar to the British Charity Organization Society, to point out proper sources of relief in time of unexpected calamity.

Some hints as to the principles on which relief might be granted are to be found in Sir Theodore Morison's "Industrial Organization of an Indian Province." Speaking of Government relief works for the unemployed in the United Provinces in 1896-7, he says:

"The characteristic of this splendid piece of administration was that State aid did not pauperize the people. The relief was so organized that they were anxious, whenever occasion permitted, to return to their normal avocations. This is shown by the extreme sensitiveness of the numbers in receipt of relief to any expansion of the demand for field labour. The spring harvest and the monsoon ploughing and sowing are indicated by the numbers upon the relief works as faithfully as in an agricultural almanack. As soon as the weather permitted it the people resumed their suspended industry with vigour. Agriculture, instead of being, as in the past, crippled for several years after the famine, was resumed upon the same scale as before it was interrupted, and, in fact, the area sown in 1897 was actually 3·3 per cent. above the normal. This simple fact is sufficient proof that State aid did not hamper the resumption of private industry."*

In a footnote emphasizing the fact that relief thus organized did not tend to attract the poor from their usual employment directly affairs

* Edition 1906, pp. 279, 280.

became more prosperous, the same author remarks: "This result was obtained by steadily keeping the pay upon relief works below the 'standard wage' which could be earned in any ordinary labour market. During January, February, and May, the months when agricultural work is always slack, the attractiveness of the relief works for the able-bodied labourer on the look out for a job was minimized by the regulation that no labourer could earn more than the daily wage by doing a larger task; and the daily wage was calculated on a sliding scale, according to the price of grain, as sufficient to purchase a day's rations only. . . . Those who in England demand that in the relief of the unemployed the Government should not pay less than the 'standard wage,' should notice that in the only case in which the State has undertaken to provide work for all the unemployed, success was due to the fact that the Government steadily kept relief pay *below* the 'standard wage' of the country."*

In another comment on the same subject he writes:

"In the relief of the unemployed the practice of the Government of India is in advance of that of any European State. . . . The principle which guided the administration of relief was at an early date declared in the following words: 'The only limitation to the relief to be given

* Pp. 279, 280.

will be the necessities of the people.' But against this principle must be set another, which was not less steadily kept in view—the principle, namely, that State relief must not interfere with the normal organization of industry. . . . . It was a cardinal principle of relief administration in the North-Western Provinces and Oudh [asserts Sir Anthony, now Lord Macdonnell] that some labour should be extracted from everyone seeking relief who was not incapacitated for work by age or infirmity, or in rare cases (chiefly in the case of women) by social status. . . . It was deliberately decided that, in the best interests of the people themselves, industry should be encouraged and idleness or sloth discouraged.' "*

The scheme comprised earthworks, the embankment of roads, and excavation of tanks. The daily wage given was enough to purchase a day's ration. Gratuitous relief was provided at the works for those who from age or infirmity were unable to perform any task. Relief was also given by Government in:

"(*a*) Employment in their homes for women who are debarred by national custom from appearing in public.

"(*b*) Gratuitous relief in poorhouses, chiefly for homeless cripples or casual vagrants, who were drafted on to the relief works when their strength was re-established.

* Pp. 272, 273.

"(c) Gratuitous distribution of relief at their homes to persons who were unable to labour, and were reduced to distress."*

One of the chief methods by which Englishwomen train themselves for charitable enterprises is by "settlement work," which was originally begun in connection with the women's universities and colleges. Settlements are residential training-centres for social, charitable, educational and religious work, and are situated in the districts where the very poor drag out their sordid, monotonous lives. Thus, during her period of training the woman philanthropist is brought directly in touch with those for whom she will afterwards be called upon to organize when she acts as a member of committee or in other capacities connected with charitable institutions and projects. In these squalid neighbourhoods the settlement-workers set on foot schemes for bringing the poor together in bright, social evening amusements. They visit them in their homes; they found clubs with classes in various subjects; they seek out the invalid children and cripples, to whom they try to impart information; they institute lending libraries, and do their utmost to bring about friendliness between all classes of society. Mutual help, mutual kindliness, personal sympathy, are the spirit they strive to foster. They do not actually aim at promoting fresh societies, but rather at

* Pp. 273, 274.

continuing the work of those already existent. For example, they do not, as a rule, supply medical aid, but rely upon the local hospitals for that, and work in co-operation with them. They try to interest the people in questions of sanitation, education, thrift, etc. Sometimes they run savings banks either in connection with the day-schools or by collecting the money from house to house. They encourage the poor in every way to independence, and urge them to take advantage of the provident dispensaries, or to insure in friendly societies, and so place themselves beyond the reach of destitution.

Such training is only attained by residence at the settlement, and the length of time necessary to gain an insight into the work is from one to three years. It is most valuable in accustoming women to act conjointly, so that afterwards, in the management of large charitable enterprises or institutions, they may not fail in co-operation with their colleagues. Women require to be taught this faculty of co-operation. It is not enough for the rich to write a cheque for a substantial amount, and then feel they have rid themselves of their responsibility. Their duty is not ended unless they know that their money will be properly expended. They should see that it is not distributed in directions covered by already existing charities, and to know this they must work hand in hand with others.

Akin to the work done in settlements is that

of the district visitor, who undertakes to visit the poor regularly in their homes, inquire into any distress that may come to her notice, and bring the case before whatever charitable society or institution seems most likely to administer relief. As a rule, she should not distribute money to those she calls upon, but she should put them in the best way to obtain such assistance if necessary. Tact, brightness, friendliness, are essential if she is to succeed in this most difficult and delicate work. Sometimes lady visitors may be able to give valuable advice on many points to the women. They can also persuade them to improve the sanitary conditions of the household, and can insinuate precious hints on health and home management. Occasionally such district visitors can be of practical use in helping the women to save something each week from their small earnings, for if their savings are regularly called for by the district visitor, they have more of an incentive to put by something for a rainy day than if they had themselves to take such small sums to a bank. Information on how to run a collecting savings bank is given in the chapter on "Thrift."

If there be illness in the house, the district visitor sends a district nurse, who comes to the patient's home and sees that she has proper attention. These district nurses are paid from the rates. They do a most valuable work among the poor, who, in time of illness, would often be left quite alone and helpless, with no one to supply their wants. There is usually one or more to each parish, according to its size. Other nurses who give free service among the poor are often supported by the benevolence of private individuals or charitable societies.

The efforts of lady district visitors would be beneficial in India, where matters of sanitation especially are so little understood by the poor. The Maharaja of Baroda, speaking at the annual general meeting of the Bombay Sanitary Association, held last April, emphasized the need for practical, unobtrusive help from educated Indian women in this direction. He said:

"The great value of voluntary workers in this country springs from the fact that the interference of an official in their private lives is usually resented by the people. And the people are so appallingly ignorant. They need to be taught the most elementary principles of hygienic ways of life. For example, one cannot help noticing the utter callousness with which refuse is thrown on to the streets out of house windows. They must be led to understand that a collection of useless rubbish will attract rats and vermin to the houses. All this can be done without arousing any resentment or wounding susceptibilities, for the people are not in reality averse to cleanliness; they are merely ignorant, and unaccustomed to modern sanitary measures. They are, in fact, like children, and must be guided like children by a tactful combination of persuasion and compulsion. Especially are lady workers needed. Womanly sympathy and tact will prove most potent weapons in the war against improper domestic habits, in explaining the dangers of keeping cattle in the houses, in elaborating the precautions to be taken in cases of infectious diseases, in the preaching of the manifold advantages of pure air. Again, the heavy infant mortality, due to parental ignorance, can best be remedied by unceasing efforts on the part of volunteers who will talk to the people in a simple, homely way."*

Women take an active part in England in the temperance movement, and have founded the National British Women's Temperance Association, which aims at promoting temperance by disseminating literature on the subject, by writing in the Press, by meetings and social clubs, by the institution of coffee-houses for the sale of coffee in the streets at the cheapest possible price, by giving scientific demonstrations on temperance in schools, by founding children's temperance leagues, by work among inebriate women and in the police-court cases, by endeavouring to prohibit women from serving in bars, by the institution of temperance societies among working girls. Then, in addition to this, there is the Women's Total Abstinence Union, which holds meetings, provides refreshments on

* *The Times of India,* April 8, 1911.

holidays for working people, shows by lecture the scientific effects of alcohol on the system, and carries on work among nurses, teachers, laundresses, and working girls. It was a woman who started the first Band of Hope, a temperance society for boys and girls, which has spread to an enormous extent. Hundreds of societies exist throughout the country, and in all of them women take a prominent part.

One of the principal problems to which English women have lately given their attention, is the housing of the working poor, especially of the working woman. In this great task Indian women have also abundant scope for their endeavours. It is likely that if adequate provision were made to supply proper lodging-houses for unprotected women, the streets of the large towns would not be crowded at night with women of the lowest classes. A safe, cheap, and healthy lodging-house is an absolute necessity to prevent vice, but it would be better policy to make this provision for the solitary, self-supporting woman *before* she has come to the direst poverty, than to spend large sums in rescue work *after* the process of degradation has been completed.

It may interest Indian women to know the means that have been adopted to supply respectable, cheap accommodation in England. To fight the evil, the National Association for Women's Lodging Homes was formed in 1909, at the offices of the British Institute of Social

Service. The objects of the union are to unite all organizations, and private people interested in the maintenance of lodging-houses or shelters for women and girls; to make known the necessity for such provision by means of literature, meetings, and deputations to public bodies; to further legislative measures for the inspection and legislation of common lodging-houses, for the better protection of the women who use them; and, lastly, to promote the formation of branch committees.

In many towns in the United Kingdom, municipal lodging-houses for women have been built, in which applicants can obtain a bed at lowest possible costs. Poor women in such homes can find a safe refuge, and as they are under municipal control, the immorality, insanitation, and degraded habits so often found in the cheapest lodging-houses are absent. Private individuals have also come bravely forward to help in this great social work, and have established lodging-houses at first on a small scale, afterwards more ambitious in size. This is, of course, a charitable enterprise. It cannot be expected to do more at first than just cover expenses, but the immense benefit it is to poor women and girls makes it one of the worthiest objects to which affluent ladies could devote their attention. Some institutions of this description—such as those run by the Church Army and the Salvation Army—make *no charge* for beds, and remain open all night for the reception of those in want. Others make a very small charge for beds, and they generally provide accommodation for the inmates to cook their own food. A useful plan, which has been adopted in one of these homes, is to reserve one portion of the house for weekly lodgers, and the other for casuals. Some provide board as well as lodging.

These are a few of the efforts made in England on behalf of the very lowest and poorest. But there is scarcely less need for respectable homes for working women of a somewhat higher class. Women's wages are less than men's, and it is more difficult for them to obtain suitable lodgings. They have no capital to start such a scheme as a co-operative plan of living. It would be a work of the greatest benevolence if wealthy Indian ladies were to finance an enterprise by which Indian women, living in common, might be provided with a comfortable, safe and happy home. It would be an investment which would bring them in the usual return for their money in the shape of reasonable interest, and a far greater return than most ordinary investments in the sense of having filled a great social need. The safe housing of unprotected women is a moral obligation of the rich.

This point of proper housing leads us to other efforts that are being made by Englishwomen to supply homes for the needy. Their number is legion, and only a few can be specially mentioned. The many convalescent homes are an inestimable benefit to poor invalids, and subscribers to many of such houses can procure the admission of patients at less than half the usual charges. The Women's Holiday Fund is an institution which helps poor women to take an often much-needed rest in the country or by the sea. An enterprise which must awaken sympathy in the hearts of all women is the homes for the dying: institutions which receive those cases that have advanced beyond all hope of recovery. Some are free. One bears the title, "The Hostel of God": and so it has doubtless proved for many a poor inmate. At others a small charge is made, varying according to the patient's circumstances. In these refuges those who are soon to leave this life on earth may spend their last moments surrounded by every medical care and comfort.

Another enterprise well deserving of notice is the homes for incurables—especially those for women of the working classes. Some are free; others make a small charge. Homes for invalid ladies of reduced means are also in existence, where — at moderate price — board, lodging, nursing, and medical attendance are given.

There is a society whose name—Guild of the Brave Poor Things—well describes those aided by its members. Its object is the helping of crippled men, women, and children, and most of the organization and work is carried on by women. Surgical and nursing treatment are obtained for the suffering, and those who are capable are put in the way of earning a livelihood. A course of training in the Invalid Craft Schools in connection with this society takes three years.

A model for such work among cripples is afforded by the task which has been carried out by the Duchess of Sutherland, who believes that a far greater charitable work can be done and far more happiness brought into the lives of the poor and suffering by teaching them to help themselves than by the most lavish indiscriminate charity. So about nine years ago Her Grace started at Trentham a Cripples' Guild, and now she has 350 cripples working busily under regular supervision. These cripples have been taught a trade, and some work at their occupations in their own homes, others in the workshops of the guild. Many of them were in hopelessly destitute surroundings and badly in need of medical care and suitable diet. These are supplied them by the guild. A band of ladies have arranged to visit them regularly, to see that they have all that is necessary for them, and there are convalescent homes to which the worst cases are sent to recover. The Guild has progressed so amazingly that it is now a limited company, on a sound financial basis. In its workrooms the cripples are taught the skilled arts and crafts, and the beautiful articles they manufacture are the highest possible credit to themselves and to their teachers. The work comprises all kinds of metal-work, jewellery, silver, architectural fittings, repoussé work, enamelling, etc. A London daily paper, in an interesting account of the work, writes as follows:

"Purchasers have the satisfaction of knowing that what they buy is well and truly made by hand, and that they pay no more than for foreign workmanship, and are supporting a very admirable cause.

"The Duchess is very anxious that people should visit the workshops, which are open for inspection every Thursday afternoon from two to four o'clock.

"Among the workers one who has a stiff leg earns a pound a week as silversmith; another has his feet turned in, but this does not prevent him from fashioning exquisite rose-bowls. This hammerman has a short leg; this repoussé worker has his fingers joined; that boy cleaning metals has nearly lost his eyesight, but, as he says, 'He does his best!'"

There are many homes for crippled children, too, which perform a wonderful work of mercy and pity in helping to cure the little invalids and to teach them a trade.

Here it might be well to mention a few more of the English societies mainly organized by Englishwomen for the benefit of children. To start with the babies, the National Society of

Day Nurseries is a centre from which the crèches, or nurseries—where the children of poor women are kept and tended while their mothers are out at work—are organized. These crèches are established all over the country, especially in the large towns, and mothers may leave their babies, with the comfortable assurance that they will be well looked after, fed, and amused. Generally there are two divisions of the crèche: one for rather older children, and another for the newly born. In organizing these institutions it should be remembered that they are intended to be a help to the industrious, not an aid to the careless and idle; therefore the circumstances of the parents should be investigated. A great point to impress upon the mothers is that the children must be sent regularly, otherwise the good work done by the crèche one day may be nullified at home on the next. A crèche is managed by a directress and nurses, and the children's food should be regulated by a doctor in cases that vary from the normal. In some of the crèches girls are admitted as learners, to be taught the care of infants, to qualify them as children's nurses.

A great work is being done by Englishwomen in connection with the boarding-out of destitute children. Under the Local Government Board committees have been formed for the purpose, and suitable homes are found in the houses of the working classes for poor children, orphans, or deserted by their parents, or whose parents are imprisoned, insane, crippled, or otherwise disabled. Ladies acting as guardians under the Poor Law undertake the honorary task of discovering respectable houses, where the woman is willing for a small weekly sum to bring up the child along with her own family, and give it a proper training. So the destitute little one is provided with home life and a mother's care at a comparatively small expense. The woman must sign an agreement before the child is given into her charge that she will treat it well, provide it with all necessaries, admit the inspectors of the Boarding-out Committee at any time to see it, and give the child up when the committee or the guardians require it. Besides the amount paid her for board, a small sum is granted for medical aid, and a certain allowance made for dress. Should the child require extra medical care or any special attention, the expense is defrayed by the Poor Law, which also pays for education. Lady inspectors are appointed to go round periodically and visit these houses where the children are boarded out, to see for themselves that the committees have properly looked to the children's food and treatment. The ladies on the committees are responsible for the welfare of the children they have boarded out, and they undertake to visit them. The system has been found to work well. It has been in existence now for forty-one years; but although an enormous amount of good has been already effected, the supplies of workers and families in which the children may be placed is quite unequal to the demand.

The working of the committees is as follows:

The minimum number of persons on each committee is three, one of whom must be a lady. Ladies may, if necessary, constitute the whole committee. No child may be boarded out more than three miles distant from some member of the committee, and the district within which such boarding out of the children may take place is fixed by the Local Government Board. Committee meetings must be held quarterly, or oftener if necessary, and business must be transacted in the way usual to committee meetings generally. Each member of committee must sign an agreement with the Local Government Board that she will comply with the above conditions.

Rates of payment must be settled before receiving any children from boards of guardians, and such agreement must be sanctioned by the Local Government Board before any steps can be taken.

There are various other societies which also adopt this method to find homes for indigent children. Several make it their object to provide poor children with a holiday. Town-birds, these little ones usually are, who without such help would never be able to catch a glimpse of a green field or smell the sweet breath of the sea.

Some funds are raised simply to let them have a long day in the country. One of the largest of these societies, under the guidance of Mr. Arthur F. Pearson, the magazine and newspaper proprietor, organizes annually a Fresh Air Fund (F.A.F.), and at a small price (9d.) subscribers can make one small child, pent up in narrow city streets, entirely happy for one long day. Out of the Maharaja of Gwalior's Coronation gift of £8,000, King George has devoted £1,000 to this Fund. More ambitious efforts are set on foot by the promoters of the Children's Country Holiday Fund, the Children's Fresh Air Mission, the Ragged School Mission, and many others, which send poor children into the country for a fortnight or more.

Attempts are also made by Englishwomen to interest their children themselves in the lot of their less fortunate little brothers and sisters. The Ministering Children's League, one of the best known of these societies, maintains convalescent homes for destitute children, and supports sixteen foreign and colonial institutions. It is quite a large organization with a central society and many branches. Funds for most of its charitable enterprises are raised by the personal efforts of children, who are thus practically taught the duty of sympathy with the poor and suffering.

A similar society is called the Sunbeam Mission, to elicit the compassion of children in better circumstances for their poor little brethren dwelling in the crowded cities. A separate branch is instituted for the benefit of blind children. The League of Pity is the children's branch of the Society for Prevention of Cruelty to Children; it endeavours to interest children in the welfare of those little ones who are cruelly treated by parents or employers.

Yet another charitable enterprise, undertaken to bring a little light and gladness into the existence of poor children, is the Play Centre or Playground, established in poor districts, where for a few hours daily the little ones are amused with games, music, physical drill, etc. This is a work which requires support both in time and money, for an organized band of helpers has to be brought together, who will undertake to give their services in turn regularly for a certain number of hours each week. It is a wonderful break in the dull grey monotony of the youngsters' lives. The "Schools for Mothers," to train mothers in the management of their children, are also an attempt to influence for good the surroundings of the little ones.

We must now pass on to consider what is being done to protect young girls from poverty, and the ever-present temptations of the crowded cities. There are numbers of orphanages and industrial Homes, where destitute girls of good character are received, some free, others at a moderate charge, and taught a trade or trained in domestic work. The funds for their support are obtained either by voluntary subscriptions, or in part by the earnings of the girls themselves. There are several societies interested in these homes, notably the National Union of Women Workers of Great Britain and Ireland, which has a special committee dealing with preventive and rescue cases, and also the Ladies' Association for the Care of Friendless Girls. These societies give particulars to inquirers concerning the nature of each institution, and if they are informed of the candidate's circumstances, they are able to say in which she might most suitably be placed. Without some such authority to consult, a girl might be sent where she would not benefit by her surroundings. Some homes are for "naughty, tiresome, unmanageable" girls; others are for those who at home would be under the influence of undesirable parents; others again are simply for orphans or destitute girls. The two above-named societies with their branches act as bureaux to disseminate information concerning them. Rescue homes and reformatories are dealt with in another chapter.

There are also numbers of boarding-houses for young women earning their livelihood, maintained in part by the payments of those who take advantage of them. There is a home of this kind in almost every large town of the United Kingdom, as well as in most of the big cities on the Continent. Many have two sections, in one of which the better-class girls—students, teachers, governesses—may live, and in the other, servants and young women of the poorer classes are taken in at a very low charge. In the large towns on the Continent such places are an inestimable boon, for it is almost incredible how often girls find themselves stranded, without friends or money, and would have nowhere to turn were it not for these homes. They will admit such applicants, and maintain them without payment until they have had time to communicate with their friends. If apprised of the arrival of a young woman in a strange town, the authorities will also meet her at the station, conduct her safely to the home, and endeavour to find her employment. They are managed by one or more directresses, who keep an employment registry for the purpose. The moderate charges of these institutes make them a great boon both to the poorer boarders and to those of better family who are, nevertheless, not earning a large income. A similar function is filled by the homes in connection with the Young Women's Christian Association.

The Association for Befriending Young Servants also does good work in connection with destitute girls from fourteen to twenty years of age. These girls must be recommended to it by the guardians of the Unions, or by the principals of industrial or orphan schools. After the girls have left school and are ready to prepare for domestic service, the Association finds room for them in one of its certified training-homes, where they receive instruction in laundry and other household matters. A small charge is made, except in certain cases recommended by the guardians, which are admitted free. There are free registry offices, and suitable situations are found for the girls on completion of their course.

A class of institution which is particularly useful is that which provides homes for gentlewomen in reduced circumstances. It is pitiful to think how many women of gentle birth there are who are eking out a miserable existence on a pittance which is insufficient to keep body and soul together. Many people here, as in India, hold that to relieve such poor gentlewomen, who are often too proud to confess their poverty, is a greater act of benevolence than helping to support the lower classes, whose want often springs from idleness and improvidence. Such homes for gentlewomen are usually for those possessed of very small income. Some are for officers' or merchants' widows, some for poor governesses, some are for poor women over a certain age (fifty to fifty-five years) who are unable to earn a living. Some are for invalid ladies, in which case no limit is fixed to the age at which they may be received.

There are numerous charitable societies which supply pensions to women in need. They are chiefly financed by bequests, and are usually for gentlewomen and others living within a certain area, or who belong to a special class—such as widows or unmarried daughters of officers and clergy. One is for the support of trained nurses who have reached the age of fifty, and are in necessitous circumstances. There are numbers of homes and almshouses for such cases. Candidates for admission must usually have a small income, not below a certain low amount; and in many cases they are provided with an annuity, unfurnished rooms, gas, coal, attendance, which, in addition to their own little property, enables them to live in comparative comfort amid respectable surroundings. The fact that these people have seen better days makes it doubly hard for them to bear poverty, with all its lowering circumstances; therefore the founders of such institutions meet with special gratitude from the recipients of their generous bounty.

An insurance scheme on the lines of the Hindu Widows' Annuity Fund, which was started in Calcutta some years ago, by which a woman on being left a widow might, if she or her relatives had been prudent enough to insure her against such an event, receive a monthly sum for her maintenance, could be worked out with advantage. A few leading women in England and America are devising a pension scheme of this nature to benefit single women of their respective nationalities.

The blind are a class of sufferer for whom

much well-organized work is done by Englishwomen. Several papers and pamphlets give definite information regarding societies, classes, homes. One society—Gardner's Trust for the Blind, which has a pension fund, and grants money for teaching the blind whatever trades or professions are thought most suitable to them—also issues leaflets showing that in many cases blindness might be prevented, and setting forth the precautions that should be taken against it. There are numerous homes and pensions for men and women thus afflicted, and schools where they are taught a craft; also funds to assist them in commencing their trade, and funds to teach them music as a profession—an art which is such a solace to them in their lonely, darkened lives. Basket-weaving is found to be a trade in which they achieve great skill, and, in connection with it, many shops are established, where articles made by the blind find a ready sale. Then there are lending libraries, supported by voluntary contributions, where volumes in raised Braille and Moon type can be obtained; and there are societies for teaching the blind to read this type. Newspapers and magazines are printed for their benefit. Many organizations exist for visiting them in their homes, for reading, talking to them, and arranging meetings. One, the Ladies' Mission to Outdoor Blind (Glasgow), visits blind women in their own houses, teaches them knitting, and supplies them with work and a market for their goods. Regular grants of money are made to the older protegées.

Similar institutions and training colleges exist on behalf of the deaf and dumb, and a great work is also being carried out for the benefit of the feeble-minded—a class which, especially among children, has been a source of much difficulty. In dealing with the problem, the National Association for Promoting the Welfare of the Feeble-minded—with a lady as its president and another as its secretary—has done much to bring the various societies and workers into touch with each other, and acts as a centre where all interested in such work can gain information and interchange ideas. Its aims are to organize homes for the feeble-minded, to provide after-care and supervision for those who have left the London County Council's Special Schools, and to promote legislation with regard to the feeble-minded. One of its latest projects is the establishment of a farm, on which the mentally weak of both sexes are taught agriculture, etc. Farm-work has been found to have a very favourable influence upon such cases. In the care of the feeble-minded, women's influence is of course almost an indispensable adjunct, and the study of the subject is one well worth their attention. Many pamphlets are issued by the National Association for the Feeble-Minded, which give information concerning the best ways of helping this unfortunate class, the cost of founding and maintaining homes for them, the means to prevent such social degeneracy. The association also arranges lectures on the subject of the treatment of these unfortunate weaklings.

Any account of Englishwomen's work of charitable organization would be incomplete without a description of their efforts as Poor Law Guardians. Their share in the boarding-out of destitute children has already been indicated, and in their general work as guardians they are performing a great philanthropic duty. The first woman guardian was appointed in 1875, and since then their numbers have increased, until women sit on almost two-thirds of the boards of guardians for England and Wales. Their work consists in helping with the internal management of the workhouses, asylums, hospitals, and homes under the control of the Poor Law. They are sometimes elected by public contest, sometimes appointed by the already existing members of the board. They have proved themselves indefatigable in suggesting improvements, and the care of the sick in the infirmaries is an especially successful sphere for them. They have lately been appointed relieving officers in connection with Poor Law work, their duties being to receive applicants for relief, and those women who require admission to the maternity wards of the hospitals, to visit the sick and poor who are recipients of aid from the Poor Law, and to find suitable situations in domestic service, or as apprentices, for girls who have been brought up and trained in the workhouses, or boarded out under the system previously described. In the granting of outdoor relief (that is, money doles to applicants not living in the workhouse), they have great opportunities for the exercise of their intuition, and for the investigation of cases to see that the money thus given is not put to wrong uses. In the administration of the Prevention of Cruelty to Children Act, of which further details are given in another chapter, they have a wide field for humanitarian effort, since it devolves on them to investigate cases in which complaints have been made of cruelty from parents or employers, and to prosecute the offenders under the Act. If ill-used children are found by the police and brought to the workhouse, the guardians have to maintain them there until inquiry has been made and the prosecution set on foot. Women guardians have also had much success in dealing with the pauper feeble-minded. It is universally acknowledged that women are exceedingly suited to such labours as these, and it has been found that boards which consist of both men and women have done the best work. There is much of course that can most effectively be done by women, especially with regard to women, boys, girls, and infants, while at the same time there is much which man can better perform. The combination of masculine and feminine effort would seem to produce the best results.

Woman's sympathy, keen intuition, enthusiasm, and perseverance are her great assets in this department of public service; but she cannot be an efficient helper without constant study of social problems, and also of the business side of charitable management. To work for a society like the Charity Organization Society gives valuable experience in method. It is, however, useless for a woman to go in for charitable work of this description unless she has ample leisure and abundant energy at her command. Perfunctory effort may here be worse than useless.

Societies to promote the employment of women are achieving great things in England, mainly under the direction of women. A central union to which applicants can come for information on all employment questions, is provided in the Central Bureau for the Employment of Women. In connection with several of these free agencies, there are funds to supply special training for women who have not the means to prepare themselves for a particular calling. No interest is charged on these loans, and when the borrower has obtained employment, she repays the money in instalments. Such funds are usually derived from charitable bequests. Strict inquiry is made into all cases, and the loans are as a rule for fees, not maintenance.

In addition to these projects in which Englishwomen are mainly concerned to alleviate the sufferings of their own race and sex, there are other humane societies in which they take an immense interest. Englishwomen have always been noted for their sympathy with and fondness for dumb animals, and in the many leagues that exist for the protection of these faithful friends of men, none are more enthusiastic workers than their female supporters. To prevent God's harmless creatures from being tortured and misused is the aim of the Royal Society for the Prevention of Cruelty to Animals, the Canine Defence League, the Royal Society for the Protection of Birds. Ladies who belong to the latter pledge themselves to wear no feathers which shall have been obtained by cruelty from any bird. The osprey thus finds itself banned. The Society for the Prevention of Cruelty to Animals prosecutes offenders who are found culpable of cruel conduct towards animals. Most of the work in organizing these leagues is done by honorary effort, and the various pamphlets and literature on the subject, as well as the general funds of the societies, are obtained by voluntary subscription. There are also homes of rest for horses, a huge home at Battersea (London) for lost and starving dogs and cats, and in "Our Dumb Friends' League" British children have an opportunity of doing something to aid the humane work. It supplies, by private subscription, an animals' hospital and cats' shelters, and part of the funds are applied to maintaining trace-horses at certain steep hills, to assist horses struggling under too heavy a load. The task of raising subscriptions for these societies is almost entirely carried on by ladies, and a great part of the practical organization is in their hands. Such charitable enterprise is entitled to much sympathy from Hindu women, whose religion expressly enjoins kindness to every living creature, teaching us—

> "Never to blend our pleasure or our pride
> With sorrow of the meanest thing that feels."

CHAPTER XV

THRIFT

"If you know how to spend less than you get you have the philosopher's stone."—FRANKLIN.

IT is a difficult task to teach all classes of the poor of India to be thrifty. The labourer or mechanic, although he can live on so much less than his brother worker in England, finds it very hard to practise economy in the way of storing up a hoard for a rainy day. Yet the principle of saving something, even from scanty wages, is such a valuable one, that it should be universally inculcated. By the independence that accrues from it the standard of the poor will rise. Gradually they will see the necessity of greater comfort and greater decency of living, and the result will be an endeavour, by dint of greater efficiency, to obtain higher wages. So from the point of view of economics the encouragement of thrift is most important.

The improvident nature of the Indian factory worker is made evident in the Report of the

Indian Factory Labour Commission (1908) where it is stated that "what the Indian labourer needs is to be trained to a system. . . . Lessons should be introduced describing the advantages of thrift. The regular showing of magic-lantern plates such as those prepared by the local Temperance Association, may tend to do material good. . . . The Indian factory labourer lives a longer and leads a happier life than any other Indian who has to depend on manual labour for his living. He is the best paid coolie [labourer], and but for the ruin brought by drinking and reckless expenditure on pay-days, he would be richer, healthier, and happier by far, than the middle-class man of India."*

The improvidence of the Indian agricultural community, from which the factory hands chiefly spring, has been commented on both by British and Indian observers. In 1874 Mr. R. C. Dutt, C.I.E., who was for some time Prime Minister of Baroda, wrote thus in his book, "The Peasantry of Bengal," from personal experience of the peasant:

"The peasantry of Bengal, therefore, it may be asserted as a fact, have never deprived themselves of a single comfort in order to save, and have always lived from hand to mouth.†

* East India (Factory Labour Commission, 1908) (Cd. 4519), vol. ii., p. 17.

† "The Peasantry of Bengal," by R. C. Dutt, p. 20.

"The peasantry of Bengal have always been remarkable for their improvidence.*

"Under such circumstances it was not a matter of surprise to find the peasantry devoid of all energy.†

"Alas! poor Bengal ryot! When will education enable thee to hold thine own against all others and make thee a prudent, provident, and independent creature?"‡

This evidence of a distinguished Hindu officer of the Indian Civil Service has recently been corroborated by the Factory Commission, as we have already noted. It goes to prove that thirty-four years of Government action failed to achieve their object in making the people thrifty. Evidently the promoters of the thrift movement must be able to appeal personally and sympathetically to the workers, and hence private schemes set on foot by ladies' enterprise—schemes to reach the people in their own homes—seem more hopeful than those officially adopted in the past.

It may be urged that there are cases where it is false economy to lay money aside for emergencies, that a poor man or woman with a young family to support is not justified in stinting the children's appetites and stunting their bodies by such saving. The argument is that if the head

* "The Peasantry of Bengal," by R. C. Dutt, p. 181.

† *Ibid.*, p. 78.

‡ *Ibid.*, p. 127.

of such a household tries by expending the total wage in domestic comforts to bring up himself and family in the healthiest possible condition, the children will in a few years' time be able to help their parents, and the parents themselves, through having thus maintained themselves in strength and vigour, will have increased their own wage-earning period considerably. Doubtless this is true of the extremely poor sections, but for the classes above them in somewhat better circumstances the practice of thrift cannot be too strongly urged. We therefore propose to discuss what is being done in England to further this end.

To begin with the poorest classes, the Penny Banks have proved most successful as a means of helping the improvident to save even the smallest sums. These Penny Banks are often worked by collectors, and the money thus saved is returnable to the depositor at a week's notice if desired. Many of the poor are quite willing to reserve a small sum if it is called for by the collector, whereas they would not take the trouble to go to a savings bank and put it in themselves. This is work which may be well undertaken by respectable women, and, as is mentioned in the chapter on charitable organizations, it is a great aid in district visiting among the poor, the collector often gaining admittance where an unauthorized person would meet with an uncordial reception. Now, suppose an Indian lady wishes to start a Collecting Bank in a poor neighbourhood, the best method of floating the enterprise is to broach the project to some person of credit in the district with whom the people are acquainted—at least by name. This person should then, either by a visit or by written intimation, inform the people of the proposed scheme, and tell them the day and hour at which the collector will call to receive their savings. She should not only take great care to select honest collectors, but should do everything in her power to convince the public that the collector is thoroughly honest, and that reliable security has been taken to insure against loss. The best time for collecting is as soon after pay-day as possible, and it is of the greatest importance that the collections should be made regularly, otherwise the housewife may have yielded to the temptation to squander the savings before the collector arrives on the scene.

The Charity Organization Society has drawn up a plan for the conduct of these banks. Each depositor is given a card with spaces ruled for payments made in every week of the year. The collector enters the money received upon the card and also in the bank's own book. When the money has been collected each week, it is given over into the hands of whoever undertakes that part of the management of the bank, and in England the plan usually adopted is for the manager to pay the total weekly amount received into the Post Office Savings Bank, where a special account is opened for the purpose. From the Post Office Savings Bank $2\frac{1}{2}$ per cent. interest is obtained, which can be applied to cover the cost of printing and other expenses connected with the enterprise. No interest is granted to the depositors, because it is thought desirable to train them to apply their savings to insure themselves in friendly societies or provident dispensaries, or to start a proper banking account of their own. The collecting savings bank is only a means to an end. It is not considered right that they should be dependent on the collector's call to remind them of the necessity of economy. Any sum of one penny upwards may be entered, but no depositor may have more than £5 in the bank.

Another plan of saving advocated by the Charity Organization Society is the issue by the collector of forms supplied by the Post Office and which have to be filled up with twelve stamps. The visitor on her weekly calls sells stamps to the would-be depositor, who affixes them, one or more at a time, to the form. When twelve have been collected and the form is full, a Post Office account may be opened by the depositor, who still continues to buy the stamps from the visitor and fill up the forms. In this case no entry of the amount is necessary, as the stamps themselves answer that purpose. From beginnings such as these great strides have been made in the direction of economy, and the effort required for such management has in itself the best possible bracing effect upon the poor. There is an immense feeling of satisfaction in the thought that one has even a small banking account between one's self and poverty. If once the poor can be induced to give themselves that pleasant sense of security, they usually appreciate it so highly that saving becomes a habit with them. Besides, when want drives people to the money-lender the latter is more likely to accommodate those who are in the habit of saving than those who have never made such an attempt.

These are two of the methods adopted in dealing with women of the poorer classes. But Englishwomen in better circumstances have also been looked to, and at present there is in London a bank which has a department entirely for women, with a woman manager and a staff consisting of women. This enterprise was started in response to the demand occasioned by woman's great and increasing activity in spheres outside her own home. Now, when most of the professions are thrown open to women in England, it is felt preferable by many of them to apply to members of their own sex for information on business questions. Moreover, it is frequently considered advisable even in small households that a woman should have her own banking account and cheque-book. Women of ample means have for a long time been in possession of this privilege; but the institution of this bank makes it possible to open an account for quite a moderate amount. The check to lavish expenditure which the bank supplies has been found of great benefit to women who were formerly accustomed to spend without taking much heed of the consequences. Now, when the extent of their outlay is plainly visible to them on the counterfoils of their cheque book, they feel it a deterrent to extravagance. The returned paid cheques are also useful as receipts for money paid out. In this women's department all the usual business carried on by Joint-Stock Banks is executed: also the business which is undertaken by the People's Banks of the Continent. Current accounts can be opened with £5 and upwards; deposit accounts with any sum from one shilling upwards. Banking business is also transacted through the post, so that an account may be opened by customers at any distance. To encourage thrift among the less well-to-do clients, home savings banks (small steel safes and wooden money-boxes) can be obtained from the bank, also automatic thrift machines, which are issued chiefly to tradeswomen, schools, or public institutions, and in which quite small sums can be inserted and registered. Many other exceptional lines are taken up by the bank for the benefit of its women clients. Tradeswomen can have their books kept and accounts and balance-sheets made out; businesses can also be converted into limited liability companies. Besides these services, women can also obtain the bank's advice on legal matters connected with financial affairs. The bank acts, if desired, as sole or joint trustee or executor under wills, marriage, and other settlements. It even undertakes surveys of land and house-property. In many cases women find themselves badly in need of some disinterested adviser, and the bank under such circumstances supplies a long-felt want.

On the model of this bank a similar scheme for Indian women would probably be found a great boon. It would afford women of good financial standing an opportunity of starting an enterprise which might save many of their poorer sisters from the grip of the Marwari. The women's department of the London bank we have been describing is not independently financed by women, but is capitalized by the head office of the bank. In days to come we may perhaps have the pleasure of seeing in India a women's bank entirely financed and controlled by members of their own sex, as now in Germany, where the only bank in the world financed and conducted entirely by women for women has just completed its first year of existence. This "Mutual Bank for Self-Supporting Women" (*Genossenschaftsbank selbständiger Frauen*) was founded last year in Berlin to enable girls and women who have entered into, or are about to embark in, trade, or any self-supporting women to obtain such financial advantages as men have long possessed. The scheme has been started on a small scale, the present capital being only £5,000. Any German woman can become a member of the co-operative body which controls the bank by payment of a membership fee of 5s. and by taking up at least one £5 share in the concern. Not more than £500 of capital may be held by one woman. Women may open an account even without their husband's knowledge, and many cases in which financial help has thus been granted to enable them to start in trade afford remarkable instances of the bank proving a veritable stepping-stone to success.

There is another sphere in which it has also met with much acceptance—through granting small temporary loans which enable tradeswomen in difficulties to tide over a crisis. By this means many an honest woman has been saved from bankruptcy or from the clutches of the usurer. In such cases, men would probably find no difficulty in raising the sum necessary; but women's credit has been, so far in Germany, a non-existent article, and the foundation of this bank supplies a great want.

The bank proceeds cautiously, and will not lend more than £25 to a borrower, while security is required for any amount over 50s. Loans must be repaid within three months. All the usual business undertaken in ordinary banks is transacted, the board of control consisting of four women, and the staff, comprising two directresses, with seven women-clerks under them. The lady-authorities in charge state that their past year's work has been most gratifying, and they hope to publish shortly a balance-sheet, which will prove reassuring to any who may perhaps have hesitated to entrust their business affairs to feminine hands. Doubtless it will take a little time before women themselves—to say nothing of men—have confidence in the gentler sex where the sterner realities of life are concerned, and the general ignorance of business evinced by the average woman will make progress somewhat difficult; but this Berlin Bank for Self-Supporting Women can, at any rate, boast that, so far, it has incurred no loss whatever in any of its transactions. Its premises are situated in one of the best quarters of the German metropolis, and it may be remarked that the feminine element in the management is apparent in the fresh green plants decking the windows, the cut flowers that shed their fragrance in the abode of commerce, and the spotless white draperies which adorn the casements. This is a new venture for women, and novelties are often looked at askance, but surely

> "Who rights a land's finances is excused
> For touching copper, though her hands be white."

It is more and more felt in England that some organized effort is necessary to inculcate thrift in the young. To this end, School Banks, and Girls' and Boys' Clubs have been started, and meet with quite an enthusiastic reception from their juvenile supporters.

There are many societies which confer benefits on their members in case of sickness or unemployment, and defray funeral expenses in case of death. Some of the trade unions, founded to promote organized action for the raising of wages and conditions of employment, carry with them such privileges, and act as provident societies. On the whole, comparatively few of the female workers of England belong to unions consisting entirely of women. In Birmingham, several societies have been organized, and may serve as a model for similar unions.* "The Birmingham and District Lady Clerks' Society" has been formed for women employed in clerical work. The number on the rolls in 1908 was 190, which has probably increased since then. The advantages afforded to members are: employment registry, free medical attendance and money grants in case of illness, weekly payments to those out of work, annuities to the aged or disabled, and funeral expenses in case of death. A sliding scale of subscription regulates the amount of the payments. This society is managed by a

* "Women's Work and Wages," by Cadbury, Matheson, and Shann, p. 254.

committee of lady-clerks, and has proved of great assistance to members when ill or out of employment.

Most unions require a small weekly subscription. They give legal advice free to members, and in case of excessive hours, bad pay, and extravagant deductions from pay in the shape of fines, they are able to interfere to prevent injustice with far greater weight than the isolated woman-worker could possibly hope to do. Some return 50 per cent. of a woman's contributions as a wedding portion if she gets married after a two years' membership without having taken advantage of the sick or unemployed fund. Women shop-assistants are strongly urged to join such trade unions. The Women's Trade Union League, founded in 1874 by Mrs. Paterson, a working printer, does all it can to encourage workers to become trade unionists, and the number of members in the various unions throughout the United Kingdom is now about 200,000, the majority of whom are engaged in the textile industries.

Other provident societies which confer benefits on members are sick clubs, friendly societies, clothing clubs, slate clubs, boot clubs, etc. The sick clubs grant a certain weekly sum during illness, and the balance is usually divided equally between members as a bonus at Christmas-time. These clubs are, as a rule, re-started annually. Their disadvantage is that no provision against prolonged illness or want during old age can be made by them.

Friendly societies exist in England chiefly among men of the working classes, though women may also belong to, and enjoy the privileges of, the most important of them. It is a movement which is spreading extensively among the female working population of the United Kingdom. In Australia, Tasmania, Canada, the West Indies (Barbadoes and St. Lucia), and New Zealand, the Reports of the friendly societies show that women there avail themselves largely of their advantages. In the 1908 report of membership in Victoria (Australia), it is stated that the "number of registered friendly societies composed solely of females was 11, and the number of branches 154." In connection with the sick and funeral funds the amount of £2,812 was expended in sick pay, and £200 in funeral assurances, proving that many women had profited by the benefits of the societies. The excess of receipts over expenditure in these funds was £3,109. A sum of £6,446 was laid out in benefits by the medical fund, leaving a balance of capital to the medical and management funds at the end of the year of £2,209. These official figures clearly show that friendly societies run entirely for the benefit of women can be made to pay well.

Women in England who belong to the men's branches have their own "lodges" and hold their own meetings. Many of the societies are on quite an ambitious scale and are organized for a great variety of purposes: to provide relief for "the members, their husbands, wives, children, fathers, mothers, brothers or sisters, nephews or nieces, or wards being orphans, during sickness or other infirmity, whether bodily or mental, in old age or in widowhood, or for the relief or maintenance of the orphan children of members during minority"; they also pay insurance money on the death of a member, and funeral expenses of husband, wife or child of member, or of widow of deceased member; they make grants to members out of work or looking for employment, and loans for special purposes; they insure against shipwreck, or loss of or damage to boats and nets, against the destruction of a worker's tools by fire, and against disease or death in cattle; they grant annuities, and also insure for a lump sum (endowment) payable at a certain age.

The work of the registered friendly societies of the United Kingdom was highly approved of by King Edward, who did all he could to encourage the people in habits of thrift and mutual aid in time of trouble. He and Queen Alexandra were present in person and opened the new office buildings of the Hearts of Oak Benefit Society in 1906. His present Majesty, King George, also takes a great interest in these provident societies, and about the time of the late

King Edward's most sudden and lamented death he had promised to preside at a banquet at Southampton in connection with the centenary of the Independent Order of Oddfellows, one of the largest societies in the Kingdom, but the Royal bereavement prevented him from carrying out this intention.

Some of these clubs are known as deposit friendly societies, and act as savings banks with the additional benefits which a friendly society affords during illness. Each member has his own deposit account, of which a certain amount is applied to afford him relief in case of illness. Should he not require to draw upon the society's funds, his own money remains intact. Should, however, his illness prove lengthy, it may easily in time swallow up the whole of his savings, after which no further benefit can be derived by him from the society.

Other friendly societies for life, sickness, and funeral insurance, are carried on by means of house to house collections, and the collectors usually work among the very poor, gathering small sums regularly from them for the purpose. The advantage of these societies is that they reach a class of people who would not insure in the ordinary way; their disadvantage is that, because of the poverty of the people they work among, the insurance money is very apt to be discontinued, whereupon the whole policy lapses and the members get no advantage whatever from their little savings. Rules have been drawn up for the protection of the members, the chief of which are:

1. Every member is to receive on payment of a trifling charge a copy of the rules and a signed policy.

2. Fourteen days' written notice must be given before the lapse of an insurance can become legal.

3. No collector may act as manager, or vote, or take part in any of the society's meetings.

4. One general meeting must be held annually, formal notice of which is to be sent to each member.

5. The society's balance-sheet is to be open for inspection seven days before the meeting, and to be attested by a public accountant, not an official of the society.

6. Disputes to be referred to justices or county courts.

The officials of these collecting societies have, unfortunately, been too apt to regard them simply as a means of money-making on their own account, not as benefit societies for the poor, and the expenses of management have therefore often been extravagant. If Indian ladies could finance such a scheme to be run, not for personal gain, but on straightforward lines as a real means of encouraging thrift and foresight among the very poor, they would be doing a truly philanthropic work. There is no reason whatever why such an enterprise should not be conducted by Indian women for the advantage of their sex.

These collecting societies allow a member to insure the funeral expenses of his child, parent, or other specified relative. They are not permitted, as a rule, to grant insurances on the life of any person other than a member. At the death of the member the insurance of the third party's funeral expenses lapses, unless the society specially grants the right to the person whose funeral expenses are insured, or to some other person, to take up the insurance, and become a member instead of the deceased.

Under the Housing, Town-Planning, etc., Act, 1909, societies may be formed in England on a co-operative basis, with the object of erecting or improving the dwellings of the working classes. The County Council is empowered by Section 72 of this Act to assist such societies by grants or advances, or may guarantee advances made to the society, upon such terms and on such security as the Council think fit. The housing question is one in which the co-operative movement has been taken up with great success. Some co-operative societies advance money to members for building; others build houses, and let or sell them to members.

The need for some system to improve the housing of the people of India is very great. Perhaps the co-operative scheme might help them, as it has aided some of the English popular tion. Speaking last April on the subject of town-planning at the annual general meeting of the Bombay Sanitary Association, the Maharaja of Baroda thus stated the problem which faces us: "We have to deal in both towns and villages with masses of human habitations irregularly huddled up together, intersected by narrow winding lanes through which no air can penetrate into the dwelling, from which also, owing to faulty construction, the light of day is excluded. Such areas are plainly most suitable for the development of disease, and we must remedy the existing insanitary conditions by a gradual process of pulling down some houses, and the cutting of wide rectangular roads. We must have building by-laws for both towns and villages, providing for future expansion by a regular system of town-planning. . . . You have in Bombay city a striking example of what an Improvement Trust, backed by an efficient Health Department, can do in gradually improving the sanitation and appearance of the town. The poor appreciate the chawls provided for them, and learn the advantages of sanitary dwellings. I have recently started in Baroda an Improvement Trust for my capital, and I trust much good will be done to the city and its people; that chawls of a sanitary design will be provided for the housing of the poor; that in the midst of the agglomerations of houses provision will be made for better ventilation and light. Something has already been done in Baroda. The streets have been widened, and the pols opened to some extent to the admission of light and better ventilation. Much, indeed, remains to be done; but I look for steady improvement, and, above all else, for the intelligent co-operation of the people and the Municipality."*

All ordinary co-operative societies, as well as agricultural credit societies, are registered under the Friendly Societies Act. There are also various temperance societies which confer benefits upon their members, and juvenile societies composed of young persons, who take the precaution to insure against future sickness or misfortune.

As a proof of the extent to which the industrial classes of England can provide against times of bad luck and old age, the Report of the Chief Registrar of Friendly Societies for the year ending December 31, 1909, draws special attention to the annual return of the Dunmow Friendly Society for that year: "Of the 1,015 members on December 31, 1909, 622 were agricultural labourers whose average wages amounted to 13s. per week; 222 servants and artisans, with wages averaging from about 15s. to 25s. per week; and the remainder, tradesmen and small farmers.

* *The Times of India*, April 8, 1911.

"The present pensioners are principally agricultural labourers; and it is interesting to note that many of them, in the first instance, contributed to the society when their wages were between 7s. and 8s. per week. . . .

"On December 31, 1909, 155 pensioners were in receipt of pensions varying in amount from 4s. to 8s. per week, according to the scale of contributions under which the members contribute.

"The benefits provided under the rules are as follows: during sickness, fifty-two weeks' full pay, and half-pay so long as sickness lasts; and, at age of sixty-five, contributions cease, and a pension is provided for the remainder of life, equal in amount to half sickness pay."

This society started in 1832 with a capital of £174. Its capital in 1909 totalled £39,554, showing that, even when members are drawn from the humblest ranks of the working classes, the result, under efficient directors, can be most gratifying. The managers in this case are honorary, and discharge their duties in the most capable manner. We have deemed these returns worthy of quotation, because from them it may be argued that the poorer agricultural population of India may be induced with great advantage to save even from scanty earnings. The above wage-figures represent an exceedingly low rate of pay in England. There are many other societies conducted on a similar basis whose books can show a good surplus on the right side.

If men with such slender resources as the labourers above described can manage to secure to themselves benefits in sickness and old age, it is evidently a matter into which Indian women will find it worth while to look.

Provident dispensaries are another institution in England by which the poor can guard against lack of medical care in sickness. In return for a very small weekly sum they may, in case of illness, obtain medicine and a physician's advice free of cost. The hospital almoners, whose work in connection with the public hospitals is described elsewhere in this book, do all they can to induce the out-patients to exercise this forethought, as do also district visitors and health visitors, sanitary inspectors, and any women whose work brings them into contact with the poorer classes. In the famous 1909 Report of the English Poor Law Commission these provident dispensaries are specially commented on, and it is recommended that local medical assistant committees should aid in their organization, that working people whose wages come below a certain standard should be persuaded to subscribe, and also that the assistance committee should supply the aged, and widows with young children, with the money requisite for subscription.

Pensions for women is a subject which has awakened attention for some time past. The State in England now provides a pension of not more than five shillings a week to members of both sexes of seventy years and upwards, whose yearly income does not exceed £31 10s., but there is, as yet, but little provision for women who are incapacitated through sickness at a much earlier age than seventy. For nurses something has been done by the Royal National Pension Fund for Nurses, whose capital exceeds £1,250,000, and whose aim is to enable nurses to insure for themselves, at lowest cost, an old age free from want, and money-grants during sickness; it also constitutes a savings bank in which they can safely invest their property.

Of course there are the ordinary forms of assurance in companies, by which women through payment of a certain annual amount, will receive in, say, fifteen or twenty years time a considerably larger sum than if they had invested their savings in the ordinary way; or upon reaching a certain age they can draw an annuity. The drawback that women feel in investing in such companies is the heavy payments that are required. Only women of some property can possibly afford the yearly sums necessary to effect the insurance, and for others some different plan is needed. In this connection it might be interesting for Indian women to consider what is being done by Germany to provide against ill-health in early or middle age among both men and women. In Germany eleven infirmity pensions are granted to one old-age pension, showing the great demand there is for such provision among the working classes. The present German system is, that workers in regular employment with an income of less than £100 a year are compelled to pay a small weekly subscription to a national insurance fund, the amount of which subscription varies from seven-eighths of a penny to twopence-farthing a week, according to the income earned. Employers are also obliged to contribute a like sum, and the State supplies a similar amount, with the result that an average pension of £8 12s. a year is given in case of permanent disablement or sickness. This scheme has some glaring drawbacks. According to Mr. Pember Reeves, Director of the London School of Economics and Political Science, the pensions are too small, and widows and orphans are not allowed to benefit by them. A married woman cannot subscribe to the fund, and a single woman has to forfeit her benefit when she marries, her money being returned to her. He advised that the standard of income below which pensions should be granted should be raised, so as to include everybody earning less than the average income of £160 a year, and also urged that the pension be made larger. It is thought that if some scheme as this were set on foot, which would admit the widow and orphan to a share of its benefits, it would do much to alleviate the hardships so often suffered by women when overtaken by premature sickness and forced inactivity. The Workmen's

Compensation Act indemnifies those who meet with accidents during the actual service of their employer, but it obviously cannot cover the majority of cases when women workers succumb to the ravages of untimely disease. In Denmark, the extent to which old-age pensions are taken up, is conveyed by the facts contained in the consular report on the year 1906–7, which states that about a quarter of the population there over sixty years of age draw their weekly pensions, and particularly the women are eager to take advantage of help thus afforded.

British friendly societies, as has been seen, have long recognized the need for insurance, and have done great service in the cause both to men and women, but it is felt in England that voluntary insurance is not sufficient, that it fails to reach more than half of the working population, who unless forced to be prudent, will never make an attempt to provide for times of misfortune. Therefore the Chancellor of the Exchequer would like to carry through a scheme for compulsory insurance, insisting that every man and woman not earning more than a certain weekly income (amounting to £160 per annum) should contribute to insure against sickness, invalidity, provision for widows and orphans, and for medical treatment. It is his belief that no project could meet with success *in any country*, which is not to some degree compulsory. He also feels that, both on financial and on moral grounds, the classes directly concerned must themselves contribute to the fund. A purely charitable scheme is destructive of independence. But there are many whose means would be quite inadequate to contribute the whole of the sum required for the insurance, therefore the State and the employer must aid by contribution to the scheme. So high is his opinion of the good work done by the friendly societies, that he declares "it must be the aim of every well-considered plan to encourage and work through these organizations." There are, however, many in England, who consider any State-aided scheme of compulsory insurance to be subversive of independence, and actually a discouragement of thrift. The whole problem of poverty is an exceedingly difficult one to tackle, and great diversity of opinion exists on the subject.

The above is but an imperfect sketch of public institutions for the furthering of thrift among the poorer classes in England. It may serve to give the women of India some small idea of the intense importance attached to the subject, and to awaken them to a sense of the need for that economy which is "the beauteous sister of temperance, of cheerfulness, and health." "When we have reached the end of our property,' says Seneca, "it is too late then to become economical."

CHAPTER XVI

ANTI-SWEATING

> "Still from one labour to another thrown;
> Nor ever fold our wings, nor cease from wanderings."
>
> TENNYSON.

It has been considered by many thinkers that throughout the period of human existence upon this planet, the labour of women has always been more or less exploited for the benefit of the public. This result is not necessarily a consequence of man's disregard for the interests of the other sex, for man exploits the labour of men as much as he can with impunity, and in many instances in the present day we find it is women themselves who are demanding from their poorer sisters an amount of work at such inadequate rates of pay, that it is quite impossible for the producers to live in the commonest decency upon the proceeds of their toil. Nor is this state of affairs peculiar to any one country. England, Germany, France, America, India—each and every nation has its particular sweating problem, and its special conditions depressing to woman.

Woman is only now beginning to learn the lesson of defending herself from such exploitation! Many causes have contributed to silence her. Her training has not been calculated to foster independence of speech or action. Until comparatively recent years her lack of education has helped to keep her in the background and to narrow her horizon, so that she has been content to muddle on with a poor salary rather than make a fuss about it. To all women in India matrimony is the final goal. Marriage is an important factor, which militates even in Europe against women entering on a thorough course of training which would render them efficient enough to demand a really good wage. After marriage they work merely to supplement the family income, and so are satisfied with a lower rate of pay than the woman who has to depend entirely on her own exertions could possibly manage with. All this tends to depress the general level of women's salaries. Lower scale of payment is as rife among the better class of wage-earning women as among the poor. Except in a few of the higher professions—such as medicine, music, and the stage—they generally receive from one-third to one-half a man's rate of pay; not necessarily because they are entering into undue competition with men, nor because their work is always inferior to men's, but perhaps for the same reason for which the uncovenanted officer in British India draws less pay than a member of the Indian Civil Service, though the former may do as good work as the latter.

But the point to be considered by every employer should not be a comparison of women's earnings with those of men. The quality of the work should be compared, and women should be paid accordingly. If the quantity and quality are good, she should receive a wage which will enable her to live in decency and comfort. The issue at stake has been put so well by Messrs. Cadbury, Matheson, and Shann in their interesting account of "Women's Work and Wages," that it may be quoted here:

"When the salary of almost any worker is discussed one hears almost invariably the easy reply, 'Oh, she *can* live on it.' She generally can live on it, but that is not the question. The vital point is, Can she improve on it? Can she live as her education and class of work demand? Can she keep pace with the times and the rising standards required in her particular work? Can she have the necessary minimum of recreation? (a point rarely noticed as a necessity), and can she, whoever she be, save against sickness, loss of work, or old age? . . .

"In dealing with women common custom permits us to calculate not the worth of their work, not even what they can live on, but, if we consider the question at all, what they will consent to live on."*

* Pp. 185, 186.

Underpayment of women is censurable for various reasons. It condemns her, if very poor, to a life of incessant, soulless toil, as the only means by which she can keep the wolf from the door. "No foreman in the world," says Miss Clementina Black in her book on "Sweated Industry," "can drive so hard as her own low wage drives the piece-worker, who has to support herself, and, often enough, to help to support relatives. The most worn-out girl whom I remember ever to have seen, was engaged upon no harder task than the packing of cocoa. My attention was called to her, in a room full of girls, by her ghastly appearance. She may have been eighteen or nineteen; she was absolutely colourless, and although there was no sign about her of any specific illness, seemed exhausted literally almost to death. She sat day after day pouring powdered cocoa into ready-made square paper packets, of which she then folded down the tops and pasted on the wrappers. She received a halfpenny for every gross. In the week previous to that in which I saw her she had earned seven shillings. Each shilling represented 24 gross of packets; she had therefore filled, folded, and pasted in the week, 168 gross, or 24,192 packets. . . . The firm has now, I believe, disappeared. Would that its methods had disappeared with it."* Numberless other painful instances could be quoted of similar exploitation of women workers, and it is to the

* Pp. 25, 26.

women factory inspectors that the exposure of such abuses in England is, in a great measure, due.

Besides rendering women physically inefficient, underpayment also brings in its train mental inefficiency. Under the conditions in which many of them are forced to labour, the brain cannot possibly develop, and mental deterioration is an inevitable consequence. Even in the higher callings, if a woman is not paid a sufficient salary and given hours short enough to allow of a little rest and recreation, or time for mental improvement, stagnation is the result. This may very likely be one of the reasons which have hindered women's mental progress during recent times. The salary earned has seldom been ample enough to afford the recipient room for progress. Doubtless the same is true of many men also, but it applies even more closely to women's labour.

Women's willingness to accept low wages causes them to be chiefly employed in inferior kinds of work which lead to nothing, lines that men will not undertake. If women were better paid, it has been suggested that the help of machinery could be called in to perform the mechanical tasks over which so many sweated workers are wasting body and soul. The women could then be left free to exercise brain and hand on more skilled labour, for which they would receive higher pay. It might be argued that higher pay for the women would bring down men's wages, but it is put forward in "Women's Work and Wages" that "in many cheap articles there must be a considerable consumer's surplus, and thus the consumer would pay more rather than go without. Excessive cheapness leads to waste, and if the price of many things—*e.g.* hairpins, pins, matches, etc.—were doubled, it would not decrease the demand."*

It is notorious that the poverty of the women workers is one of the chief factors in Europe and America in leading many to adopt the life of the streets. So by the underpayment of its women a community is actively encouraging immorality.

If it were the rule and not the exception with regard to men and women alike to pay according to the quantity and quality of work done, we should not find it authoritatively stated that about 12,000,000 people in England are on or under the poverty line. Remember, as we said before, this condition of affairs does not exist in England alone. Germany has a huge mass of sweated workers; the United States of America are also confronted with a most formidable labour problem; India's teeming population abounds in examples of the oppressed toiler of both sexes. Civilization has had as one of its effects the breaking down of barriers between different countries. Communications

* P. 143.

are possible now within a space of time that our forefathers would have thought incredible, with the result that the sociological conditions of the various nations have been, and are, gradually approximating. Hence the similarity of the sweating problem in all civilized lands. Great riches are acquired by the few, a rather larger number are moderately well off, but the mighty mass of the remainder are left to flounder in the abyss of poverty. Hence the antagonism of class that is sweeping over the world to-day; hence the deep chasm which yawns between rich and poor. The underpayment and oppression of the worker has a great deal to answer for. Ruskin put his finger on one method of healing when, nearly fifty years ago, he thus addressed the women of England in words the spirit of which is applicable still to women of all civilized lands:

"The real, final reason for all the poverty, misery, and rage of battle throughout Europe is simply that you women, however good, however religious, however self-sacrificing for those whom you love, are too selfish and too thoughtless to take pains for any creature out of your own immediate circles. . . . I tell you more: that at whatever moment you chose to put a period to war, you could do it with less trouble than you take any day to go out to dinner. . . . Let but every lady who has conscience toward God vow that she will mourn—at least outwardly—

for His killed creatures. . . . Let every lady in the upper classes of civilized Europe simply vow that, while any cruel war proceeds, she will wear *black*—a mute's black—with no jewel, no ornament, no excuse for, or evasion into, prettiness, I tell you again, no war would last a week."

If such be woman's wonderful influence to stem the red tide of blood and bid the clash of arms to cease, surely in this matter of the grinding war that is waged against the helpless poor, and especially the poor of her own sex, she could work useful reforms. Now, when education and enlightenment have done so much to bring the question before the public, is it not time that educated women of all lands, East and West alike, combined to put down this great social scandal, and so help mankind to journey onward towards that "gleaming goal" of peace which should be the aim of all endeavour? If women of every nation would steadfastly set their faces against the purchase of any article which they knew or could discover to be the product of sweated labour, there would be a certain end of the worst of this injustice.

If such be the state of affairs in England, where women workers, following the example of the men, are waking up and learning to protect their own interests, how great is the need of measures to prevent the undue exploitation of women and children in India where most of the workers are illiterate, without education or example to guide them! Among factory-workers of both sexes, we are told, there is little or no combination. "If the mill-owners desire to increase the hours, the operatives have no real power to prevent them. Their power of combination is, as yet, exceedingly limited; a large proportion will always continue to prefer to get as high wages as they can, regardless of their own welfare in the long run; and, finally, the system of withholding pay and of inflicting fines renders the great mass of the workmen helpless to resist the far more intelligent class which exercises authority over them."* This statement holds good of the working population of India generally. As regards the benefits obtained by shorter hours, it is stated by the Commissioners in their Report of the Indian Factory Labour Commission (1908) that "the physique of the female workers is uniformly excellent," and that they "are not in any way injuriously affected by their employment in factories."† But it is pointed out by Dr. Nair, of Madras, in his Minute of Dissent to some of the points considered by the Labour Commission, that "the excellent health of women factory operatives in India at the present time is *the result of the short hours they are now worked* [eleven hours maximum]. . . . They come when they like, go when

* East India (Factory Labour Commission, 1908) (Cd. 4292) vol. i., p. 101.

† *Ibid.*, p. 28.

they like. The reeling-room containing no dangerous machinery, they, in some cases, bring their infants along with them to their working-room. All these arrangements are very suitable to women's work in this country, and so they are the one class of factory operatives who have managed to earn their living without ruining their health. . . .* At present, whatever the hours of starting and stopping of a mill may be, women seldom turn up before seven, and seldom stay at their work after six. This gives them time, both in the morning and evening, to attend to their household duties. . . . Long hours and good work are rather antagonistic than concomitant.† . . . Women workers all over the mills in India loiter less than men, for the simple reason that they work shorter hours."‡

So it is stated here that Indian women factory hands do better work in their shorter hours, and can show a better bill of health than those who are forced to toil for longer periods. Thus, on physical, economical, and ethical grounds, as Dr. Nair says, it is a calamity when the hours which women work are excessive. We have taken factory work as an example, because authentic statistics are readily obtainable concerning it; but the rule holds good with regard

* East India (Factory Labour Commission, 1908), vol. i., p. 105.

† *Ibid.*, p. 106.

‡ *Ibid.*, p. 84.

to all labour. Good pay and reasonable hours mean superior quality of work.

In the vast mass of unregulated labour there are far more abuses going on than in the regulated employments, and naturally it is much more difficult to reach and remedy these injustices. It is very hard to teach home-workers, especially, the habit of combination. The poorest classes of all who labour in their own homes are almost impossible to reach. The manufacturers of little toys, sweets, and fancy articles to be sold in the streets—these are the toilers who drag out the most wretched existences in India in the slums and back alleys of the crowded towns. Such women as these cannot possibly maintain themselves in a fit state of health, with the consequence that hunger and misery produce their inevitable effect upon the quality of the work performed. Surely, from the economic point of view, a country should look to it that its women may not deteriorate into ineffective, faulty machines, which, in the end, break down and become useless under the excessive strain! The result is national pauperism instead of a happy, healthy, busy life.

Conditions of labour are quite different in England and India, therefore no exact comparison can be made between the two countries. Nevertheless, in regard to factories it is generally granted that the protection which Indian factory women and children at present enjoy under the law, they owe, to a large extent, to British factory legislation which is adapted to Indian requirements. If, then, some of the English regulations have proved of such benefit to Indian workers, it may also be advantageous to them to consider one or two of the means which are already adopted, or merely put forward for consideration, to ameliorate the lot of the sweated labourer there. Sweating has been defined in the Report of the Committee of the House of Lords (1889) as—(1) underpayment of the worker, (2) excessive hours of labour, and (3) insanitary condition of workplaces. The first cause, the underpayment, can be shown to lead, in the case of home-workers, inevitably to the other two. This sad state of affairs has materially improved in some respects. The work of the woman sanitary inspector and that of the public health committees have done something to better the dwellings of the very poor. Education has also contributed to raise the ideas of decency among the workers; and the keen interest taken by public bodies has helped greatly in ameliorating the housing of the lower classes. The Factory Acts have been of inestimable service in setting a standard of sanitation, cleanliness, hours of work, below which the employer is forbidden by law to go. But the great mass of sweated workers are beyond the reach of Factory Acts. Their ranks are chiefly recruited from the wives of men out of employment, of men unfit or too lazy for work, widows with young children, deserted wives, girls with relations dependent on them. For such as these there has been established in England the National Anti-Sweating League, which works to secure a minimum fixed wage in all underpaid industries both for in- and out-workers. This league from the outset thought that nothing could be done to raise the wages of the worst-paid trades except by definite legal regulation of salaries. In the year 1908 the Sweated Industries Bill was brought before Parliament, its aim being, as the Memorandum preceding it well puts it, "to provide for the establishment of wages boards, with power to fix the minimum rate of wages to be paid to workers in particular trades. The Bill will apply, in the first instance, only to the trades specified in the schedule. Power is given to the Home Secretary to say to what other trades the Bill is to be extended, and no doubt at first the extension will be made only to what are known as the 'sweated industries'—that is, industries in which out-workers are largely employed, and in which the rate of remuneration is low. A wages board will have power to fix a minimum rate for any single kind of work, and will have the widest discretion as to fixing time rates or piece-work rates, and as to varying the minimum according to the locality, the kind of work, and the persons employed. The Bill provides that a wages board shall be composed of representatives of employers and representatives of employed in equal numbers, with a chairman chosen by the members or nominated by the Home Secretary. It is proposed to entrust the enforcement of payment of the minimum rate to factory inspectors." This Bill was to apply, in the first instance, only to tailoring, dressmaking, and the making, altering, trimming, finishing, and repairing of shirts. It was proposed that separate boards should be appointed for different trades, and also for different districts, as local circumstances would vary, and naturally require separate consideration. The Trade Boards Act, which came into operation on January 1, 1910, established trade boards composed of equal proportions of representatives of employers and employed, and of three members appointed by the Board of Trade, one of whom must be a woman, if women are engaged in any numbers in the trade affected by the Act. These representatives fix the minimum wage, and publish the legal rates of pay by time or by piece. Any employer paying less than the fixed sum is liable to a fine. Factory inspectors are appointed to visit workshops and see that this rule is enforced. The Act can be extended by special order of the Board of Trade to other trades than those originally determined, if the wages in such trades are excessively low.

Such regulation by the State of wages affects, of course, only a certain number of sweated industries in England. In Australia and New Zealand the system has been universally adopted, and has been working since 1896. The result there has been reported as favourable. It is said (1) to have raised the standard of goods produced, because when an employer is forced to pay well, he makes it his business, it is argued, to purchase new machinery and seek out other better processes of manufacture, thus improving the quality of the goods turned out; (2) to have abolished, or greatly modified, the evils of sweating; (3) to have increased wages, but, it is stated, not increased the cost of the goods nor their selling price; (4) to have equalized the conditions under which the honest employer and the "sweater" work. These facts are found in Mr. Ernest Aves' Report on the Wages Boards and Industrial Conciliation and Arbitration Acts of Australia and New Zealand, quoted by Miss Constance Smith in her able little pamphlet, "The Case for Wages Boards," published by the National Anti-Sweating League, London. She also points out that the principle of a minimum wage is not a new one in Britain, since it is adopted in the large Government factories and workshops, arsenals, dockyards, clothing manufactories. Coal-miners, engineers, cotton-workers, doctors, lawyers, officers in the Army and Navy, Government servants, all work according to this system. There seems no reason why, in many Indian trades which are more or less "sweated industries," a similar rule should not succeed. If found to work well, the principle could then be more widely extended.

Trade unions have done much to keep up the standard of wages and shorten hours of labour in Great Britain. These are associations of workers, formed to protect themselves from the oppression of bad pay and excessive hours. The benefits—such as insurance, pay during unemployment, etc.—which members obtain by joining them, are described in the chapter on Thrift. By the payment of members when out of work, they enable them to resist any attempt on the part of employers to reduce their wage, as through the unemployed benefit granted by the union they can afford to refuse any terms of employment lower than those recognized by their union.

A brief history of Trade Unionism will show the change of attitude and the recognition it has wrung from the law in England. It should also help the women of India to understand a little of the method by which labour-protection organizations are worked here. At first such organizations were punishable by law, since they were considered as conspiracies restricting trade. Any individual workman might refuse work if the terms were unfavourable to him, but if even as few as two agreed together to resist the terms of employment, their combination was a legal offence and punishable by law. At the end of the eighteenth century, when machinery brought about so vast a revolution in the methods of manufacture, the numbers of operatives increased to an extraordinary extent in England, and with this increase a number of secret societies, or trade unions, sprang up among factory workers. The Act of 1800 was aimed against these secret combinations, decreeing that any persons uniting to control the wages or hours in any trade or manufacture should be liable to three calendar months' imprisonment, or two months' hard labour in the house of correction. So great was the discontent of workers with existing conditions that in 1824 a law was passed, rescinding the restrictions upon meetings of masters and workmen, but this Act was only in force a short time, being repealed in 1825, and another Act passed rendering it lawful to hold meetings to discuss wages, hours, etc., except if the matter under discussion involved anything prejudicial to freedom of contract. The Act of 1859 permitted such combinations to be made if the persons making them acted "peaceably and in a reasonable manner, and without threat or intimidation, direct or indirect . . . in order to obtain the rate of wages or the altered hours of labour." Matters were in this indefinite and unsettled state when in 1867-1869 a Royal Commission on Trade Unions examined the whole question, their deliberations culminating in the Trade Union Acts 1871 and 1876. By these Acts trade unions are not illegal merely because they are in restraint of trade. But the malicious breaking of a "contract of service or hiring, knowing . . . that the probable consequence of . . . so doing, either alone or in combination with others, will be to endanger human life or cause serious bodily injury, or to expose valuable property, whether real or personal, to destruction or serious injury," is punishable by fine or imprisonment. These Acts also define other violations of contract and malicious actions, which are legal misdemeanours. In 1906 a further Act was passed more carefully defining the law of conspiracy, all tending to justify the peaceable combination of persons to settle a trade dispute.

The constitution of English trade unions varies, beginning with the simple local club, in which a small number of people engaged in the same trade unite together, paying a small weekly subscription, which confers various benefits upon them in case of sickness, death, or unemployment. From this primitive society there are unions ascending in scale, until we come to such vast organizations as the Amalgamated Association of Operative Cotton Spinners, which is a great federation of all the branches of workers in the cotton-spinning trade. This association deserves special mention in any book on women's industrial questions, because it contains the majority of the women trade unionists of England, most of whom are employed in the textile trades. It can be readily seen how mighty an influence can be wielded by such a huge body of operatives (in 1905 there were 239,539 members in the textile trades alone), uniting against any attempt to decrease wages or increase hours.

Women in England are beginning to see the advantage of trade unions, and in the cotton trade the women trade unionists outnumber the men. It is stated in the latest (eleventh) edition of the "Encyclopædia Britannica," that of all the women employed in factories and workshops in England, about one in twelve belongs to a Trade Union.* The Women's Trade Union League, with its headquarters in London, forms the centre for the women's trade unions of England. Its founder was Mrs. Paterson, a working printer, its chairman and secretary are also women, and its secretary and committee organize meetings all over the country for the formation of new unions and for the help of those that already exist. Among the bodies which hold meetings at the headquarters in London are women book-binders, tea-packers, telephonists, etc. If complaints as to oppressive conditions of labour are received, the league investigates such claims. It endeavours to promote legislation for the benefit of women, and obtains legal advice for them on trade matters. Its quarterly journal is known as the *Women's Trade Union Review.*

There are of course opponents to the system

* Vol. xxvii. 146.

of trade unionism and that regulation of hours and wages which forms the object usually aimed at by its policy; but the trade union champions, in answer, proudly point to the cotton-workers of Lancashire, the majority of whom, as has been seen, are women and all trade unionists. In this industry shorter hours and better pay have produced a state of prosperity unequalled in any other country. The English cotton-hand is better paid and works far shorter hours than any of her foreign rivals, yet the numbers employed in the trade have multiplied, exports have increased, the skill and intelligence of the worker have gone on developing in proportion. The efficient state of sanitation and ventilation, which the mill-owner is obliged by law to observe in his establishments, has caused an improvement in the physique of his workers, until as a body of skilled cotton operatives the Lancashire people have no equals throughout the world.

Trade unions, the Factory Acts, and wages boards are the chief means that have been adopted so far to put down sweating in England. Now let us consider some of the other very important methods that Englishwomen are taking to accomplish this end. One of the largest societies which interest themselves in questions affecting the woman worker is the Women's Industrial Council, formed for the organization and social education of women workers, and for the improvement of their conditions of employment. The council is non-political and non-religious. It gives free legal advice on industrial questions to women, and has done much in this way to remedy abuses and expose infringements of the Factory Act. It issues a quarterly journal, *The Women's Industrial News*, in which it reviews various trades and discusses industrial problems. It also publishes in pamphlet form at very reasonable rates a number of papers, the titles of a few of which will give the best ideas of the scope of the society's efforts: "Separate Courts of Justice for Children," "Labour Laws for Women and Children," "Boy and Girl Labour," "Women Workers and the Factory Act," "Women Laundry Workers and Legislation," "Summary of the Factory Act," "Women's Wages in England in the Nineteenth Century," "How to Clean a House," "How to Cook a Simple Meal," etc. It has an Executive Committee, an Education Committee, an Investigation Committee, a Legal Committee, a Clubs Citizen Committee, a Publications Committee, a Training School Committee, and an Advisory Committee to the Association for Trained Charwomen. In each case the chairman is a lady. If any instances are known to the general public of infringements of the Factory or Public Health Acts which are detrimental to the health of women or girl workers, the Women's Industrial Council will, if informed, investigate the matter thoroughly and see that it is set right. From time to time the Investigation Committee makes special inquiry, within a certain radius, into the conditions of some particular trade in which women are engaged, and by means of personal visits to employers, employees, workrooms, and any officials from whom information can be gained, it discovers and rectifies abuses, should such exist. In this way it examined into and reported on the condition of shop assistants in London, by which report a reform in the rules and accommodation for shop assistants has been set on foot in the metropolis. The investigation of home industries, which are carried on by the poorest class of women toilers, has been one of the special duties undertaken by this committee, which has also inquired into the conditions under which women printers labour, and has given reports on twenty-eight separate trades for women. The Education Committee has concerned itself particularly with the wages earned by school children, and the influence of its inquiry was seen in the Children's Act of 1909. Technical training and trade schools for girls have also engaged much of the attention of this committee, with the result that numbers of such schools have sprung up in London. The Legal Committee, besides being the "poor woman's lawyer," voices its opinions through questions put by members of Parliament in the House of

Commons. It draws up petitions, organizes deputations, and makes known abuses through the medium of the Press. The matters to which it proposes to devote its attention at present include street trading by children, and the management of unemployed women's workrooms. A volume might be written on the work of the Women's Industrial Council, but we must content ourselves now with describing the latest of its projects—a nursery training-school to teach girls of the industrial classes to be good wives and mothers, and to train them as children's nurses. To start this scheme a well-built house has been taken in Hackney (North-East London) and has been adapted as a training-school for fourteen girls. The intention is that these girls shall be taught the practical management of twelve babies, aged from one month to five years. The laundering of these children's clothes will be done by the students. Each student has her own curtained cubicle to sleep in. She will be instructed how to wash, dress, and feed the babies; to amuse the children sensibly; to keep house economically; to cook, wash, and sew. A knowledge of infant hygiene will also be imparted, as well as the principles of first aid, of home nursing, and invalid cookery. The matron in charge is a trained nurse, and the entire work of the house is to be done by the students under the direction of a domestic economy teacher. After a year's residence each girl will be expected to enter for an examination, upon the results of which, if she prove successful, a certificate will be granted and a position found for the candidate. Each student will be on probation for the first month, and may be refused further training if she be considered unsuitable. The inclusive sum charged for a year's residence and training is fixed at £26, payable in weekly instalments if desired. It has been suggested that a loan fund might be started for the benefit of those unable to pay the fees, which would allow them to refund the money gradually after they had begun to earn. The need for reliable, capable children's nurses is very great, and the initiation of this project will no doubt do much to raise the status of children's nursing as a calling for respectable girls. This is a fresh effort which is being made in England to train girls to be good mothers and careful housekeepers, and as such we feel sure that its principles will commend themselves to our countrywomen in India, who might consider the advisability of practically organizing a similar scheme to promote the welfare of their children.

Some of the other organizations started under the auspices of the Women's Industrial Council are the Clubs' Industrial Association, the Girls' Club Library, the Association of Trained Charwomen and Domestic Workers. The Clubs' Industrial Association, founded in 1898, and now incorporated in the National Organization of Girls' Clubs, consists of delegates from a number of working girls' clubs, and its object is to extend a knowledge of industrial law among the girls in their separate clubs. For this purpose lectures on factory law are given by experts, to which representatives from neighbouring clubs, whether members of the association or not, are invited. It is often the case that girl workers are in absolute ignorance of the laws affecting their trades, and so they suffer silently under grievances which could be redressed. The aim of this and similar associations is to remove such ignorance and to interest the girl workers in their own social and moral welfare. In the poorest parts of London, where dwell the hardest pressed of all the toilers in that great hive of industry, "citizen classes" have been held to teach the girls something of their duties as citizens of a mighty empire and to discuss matters of industrial and social importance. These have already met with success. A course of lectures on industrial questions has also been drawn up for lecturers to study and deliver in the different girls' clubs.

The National Union of Women Workers of Great Britain and Ireland, affiliated to the International Council of Women, is another society which exists to promote the welfare of women. It encourages the formation of women's unions, circulates information to help women workers, and acts as a central council, to which all societies of national importance may send delegates. Each local society is quite independent, and membership of the union is open to all women interested or occupied in women's work on payment of a small subscription. A conference of women workers is held annually at a different centre each year, and the published reports serve to make known the conditions of women's employment throughout the kingdom. The titles of the sectional committees show the extent of its influence. There are Committees of Publications, Finance, Legislation, International, Industrial Committees, Girls' Club Committee, Preventive and Rescue Committee, Education Committee, Women's Indian Study Association, Committee for promoting Rest-Rooms for Women Employees in Exhibitions, and a Public Health Committee. There are branches of this huge organization all over the United Kingdom. In connection with the National Union of Women Workers, there have also been formed the Central Bureau for the Employment of Women, Moral Education Committee, Rural Housing and Sanitation Association, Association of Teachers of Domestic Service, School of Sociology and Social Economics. The work of the Industrial Sectional Committee is more particularly concerned with the industrial questions affecting women workers.

Another scheme to insure better wages to the woman worker is one to render her more efficient, and so able to command a higher wage. It is argued by some that higher pay is the *cause*, and not the *result*, of efficiency, and therefore that any measure which does not begin at once by aiming at good wages and good hours for workers must be ineffective. Nevertheless, it is generally acknowledged that girls' lack of ambition leads them to remain in the lower branches of a trade instead of trying by greater skill to rise into the better-paid sections of work. Something should be done, it is felt, to spur on these laggards, and so the Apprenticeship and Skilled Employment Association was formed in London to promote an efficient industrial training for both boys and girls. The National Institution of Apprenticeship has the same aim—*i.e.*, to apprentice boys and girls to skilled trades. The great importance attached to the technical training of the young is shown by the number of scholarships which the London County Council offers to train boys and girls in special trades and callings. Trade schools have been established, and are attended every day by boys and girls who have been through the elementary schools, and who, in addition, wish to spend about two years in the acquirement of a skilled trade. Their general education is also continued, but the greater part of the time is devoted to specialized technical work. Teachers of practical experience in the different trades are engaged as instructors, and the organization of the whole is directed by a committee of experts in each branch. It is stated that after such instruction the pupils are able to obtain good employment in the particular branch they have taken up. These trade schools at present exist only in London, except a few elsewhere due to private enterprise; but it is a movement which is certain to become very general, since skilled training is regarded as a national question, one which closely affects the great problems of poverty.

The scheme of free apprenticeships leads us to a further discussion of the same problem—the question of boy and girl labour, which may take its place here in the chapter on anti-sweating. This is a point in which Englishwomen have greatly interested themselves, and it was a woman, Mrs. Hogg, who was the first to force a legal regulation of children's employment out of school hours. At present, in the big English towns especially, children are employed, in addition to their school work, in casual labour—odd jobs, such as the delivery of milk, running errands, the selling and distribution of newspapers, the hawking of flowers, fruit, vegetables, and toy trifles. Most English authorities are agreed that this premature employment of children has the very worst results on their after careers, the chief reason being that it is so often practised in occupations which need no preparatory training whatever, and therefore lead to nothing. In England, where education is compulsory, it is considered by many most desirable that children should not be engaged in any kind of labour during school years. Throughout India, except in the Baroda State, education is not compulsory, and therefore the child labour question assumes a totally different aspect from that which it bears in England. If there are not sufficient schools for Indian children to attend, one can hardly object to their parents employing them in some useful and healthy work, such as agriculture, which, as discussed in some chapters of this book, exercises so beneficial an influence upon those engaged in it, and may save them from becoming loafers, if not criminals. The question of compulsory education for India is now before the Government, but it is not likely to be settled soon, since there is the difficulty of finances to be surmounted. The Government of India has recently lost a large portion of its income in opium revenue. The reduction in the salt-tax has also curtailed its financial resources, and we all know that there is no hoarded wealth under the control of the Viceroy which he could immediately transfer to aid the cause of compulsory education. Doubtless there is a difference of opinion as to compulsory education in India, but there can be no two opinions as to the advisability of the spread of primary education. In Baroda, where compulsory education has been introduced, it might be worth while to attempt the prevention of street-trading by children, which western sociologists think is detrimental to the interests of the nation. One of the dangers they fear is that where the cheap services of children can be obtained, an employer may not bestir himself to find new and quicker methods of production; therefore, a trade in which children and cheap labour generally are employed wants careful looking after.

This is a subject which demands attention in other countries beside England; indeed, it calls for close scrutiny in every civilized land, and India may be no exception to the rule. It is impossible to obtain accurate statistics as to the ages at which Indian children are employed in the many casual trades which occupy them, nor whether it be true that they are overworked; but the evidence of the Government Factory Inspectors in India may be examined, and the conclusion will probably be that if children be overworked there, among a class which is under official supervision, then the evil may be even worse in places which are subject to no regulation or control.

In the first place, it is evident that children are often employed in factories under the legal age of nine years. The Report of the Textile Factories Labour Committee (1906-07) states: "In the opinion of the Committee, the present law relating to certificates of age calls for drastic and immediate reform. The intention of the Factory Act is to protect children from overwork, and, further, that children should not be classed and worked as adults before they have attained the prescribed age of fourteen years laid down by law. . . .* An equally important question—namely, whether certificates of physical fitness for employment should be required—has engaged their serious attention. It will, of course, be remembered that from the very earliest days of factory legislation affecting the United Kingdom, this certificate has been required, and, presumably, if valueless, the united influence and intelligence of the manufacturers of Great Britain would have been sufficiently powerful to secure the repeal of a useless and unnecessary requirement. In England the exact age of candidates for employment can without difficulty be ascertained. In India this is impossible—a fact pointing to the necessity for physical condition being considered and stated, in addition to a merely speculative statement in regard to age. . . . In their [the Committee's] opinion, serious abuses exist, and have for long existed, in regard to employment on full time of so-called adults professing to be fourteen years of age, but, in reality, one or two or even three years below that age. It is common to find children certified as being over nine, in one year, employed within a period of, say, twelve months on full time. The proof other than the evidence of one's observation is difficult to obtain, conviction in court almost impossible."† The Report of the Indian Fac-

* P. 11.

† *Ibid.*, p. 13.

tory Labour Commission (1908) gives a similar account. It says: "The most serious abuses which have arisen in connection with the neglect to observe the provisions of the existing law relate to the employment of children in textile factories. In the United Provinces generally, except Agra, in the Punjab, in Southern Madras, and in the cotton-mills of Bengal, children have, as a rule, been habitually worked during the whole running hours of the factories, not on the excuse that they were over fourteen years of age, but in pure disregard of the law. The importance of this will be more readily appreciated when it is mentioned that the factories which have been illegally employing children in this manner work from ten to fourteen hours a day."*

"The next abuse which we find to be prevalent in connection with the employment of children is the working of children under nine years of age as half-timers, and of children under fourteen years as full-timers, on the excuse that they are over fourteen. . . . In *cotton factories* a large number of children under nine years of age are undoubtedly employed as half-timers."†

"The children, where they are employed for half-time only, are frequently required to work for seven hours continuously without any interval of rest."‡

"The children examined during the course of the tour were in general of poor physique, thin

* Vol. i., p. 14. † *Ibid.*, p. 15. ‡ *Ibid.*, p. 18.

and weakly looking, especially in cotton textile factories. . . . In Cawnpore and Northern India generally, where the adult mill-hands are as a rule of fine physique, we were specially struck with the poor appearance of the children. There can be no doubt that doffing, even though intermittent, is hard work for a child of nine years of age; and some relief from present conditions seems to us to be called for in the case of children."*

Delicate children are often employed in the mills, though mill labour is not a suitable occupation for them. The evidence given before the Commission in 1908 by various inspectors and mill managers supports this statement. For instance, speaking of the condition of child labour in the mills at Ahmedabad, Mr. W. B. Chambers said that he had seen some cases of puny children who could hardly do the work to which they were put. He knew of no suitable outside employment which these children could undertake if they were not employed in the mills, but work in the open air was preferable to mill labour for such weaklings.† Again, Mr. Dadabhai Nasarvanji Nanavati, City Magistrate of Ahmedabad, gave evidence that he had seen children at work who were incapable of carrying out their duties; some were very small children

* East India (Factory Labour Commission, 1908), vol. i., p. 29.

† *Ibid.*, vol. ii., p. 9.

quite unfit to do the work required. The rules regarding half-timers were not generally observed.*

A similar report came from the officiating Civil Surgeon at Broach, who said he would have rejected about one out of every eight boys for physical unfitness, had there been a test for that.†

Mr. Haigh, I.C.S., Chief Inspector of Factories, Bombay, also gave it as his opinion that many children were passed as over fourteen when an ordinary observer would place them about twelve years of age. He said he had also seen children who did not appear to be nine years of age, but the discrepancy in this respect was not so marked as in the case of children passed as fourteen.‡ Likewise Mr. Hatch, I.C.S., Collector, Bombay, reported that he found occasionally "young children of from six to nine years entered the mill with their parents, and were put to work."§

At Aligarh, Lieutenant-Colonel Woodwright, I.M.S., asserted that he had seen children in gins, who in his opinion were under fourteen years of age, working as adults.||

In Calcutta, Mr. D. R. Wallace estimated "that from five to eight per cent. of children

* East India (Factory Labour Commission, 1908), vol. ii., p. 13.

† *Ibid.*, p. 31.

‡ *Ibid.*, p. 49.

§ *Ibid.*, p. 155.

|| *Ibid.*, p. 180.

were under nine years, and probably about ten per cent. of the spinners were under fourteen years of age."*

Such evidence coming from both prominent Englishmen and responsible Indians, can leave no possible doubt as to the existence of a certain abuse of boy and girl labour in the Indian factories. It can readily be imagined how much greater the evil may be in the employment of children in other trades, which are known to be sweated industries.

Moreover, Indian parents of the lower working classes, like those of most other countries, are naturally anxious for their little ones to begin to earn money. They cannot afford to wait for them to gain first some education, and so fit themselves to acquire a skilled trade, but owing to poverty, they usually have to put them to the first employment that offers, not reflecting that an occupation which can be entered upon without training cannot afford a lucrative livelihood. The result is a body of unskilled workers, unable to rise above the rank of the lower labourers. What a waste of good material, and what a loss to the nation is this squandering of the early years of its children!

England now fully recognizes the gravity of the problem, and a Committee appointed by the Home Secretary to inquire into the legislation

* East India (Factory Labour Commission, 1908), vol. ii., p. 253.

required with regard to street-trading and other occupations in which children are engaged, has recommended that street-trading by boys be wholly prohibited by statute up to the age of seventeen, and street-trading by girls be also prohibited up to the age of eighteen years. Street-trading is, of course, defined, so as to exclude the delivery of newspapers and other goods by young persons to regular customers of trades-people. It is naturally a difficult question to settle satisfactorily, since there is no doubt that considerable hardship would be felt by many parents who cannot afford to let their children remain idle up to the age of seventeen or eighteen, but the Committee is fully alive to the necessity of providing some means for these children to enter other occupations more suitable for them, and have recommended that the functions of the local education authorities should be extended, so as to include the giving of advice and assistance to children at or leaving school, to help them to find proper employment. This Bill to prevent street-trading by boys under seventeen and girls under eighteen has been discussed in Parliament without awakening much opposition. It was moved by Lord Shaftesbury, a nobleman who bears a name famous in the history of philanthropy, and especially philanthropy towards children. It was insisted, however, that something should be done for the young people thus deprived of the means of getting their livelihood. In moving the Bill, Lord Shaftesbury urged the dangers—moral, mental, and physical—which encompass the young who are exposed to the life of the streets. He said that trading of this description is the worst possible occupation for the minds of children, exposing them to the worst evils, and forming an unquestionable danger to girls. Among the 25,000 boys and the 10,000 girls who had registered at the Labour Exchange for employment after leaving school, the street-trader figured only to a very small extent. "In time," said Lord Shaftesbury, "they go to swell the ranks of the unemployed—and, what is worse, the unemployable. The opportunities of employment for boys and girls leaving school are improving, but some parents are too lazy to work, and get part of their living from the street-trading of the children." Other ardent supporters of the Bill spoke in its favour, the Bishop of Southwark maintaining that "the life of the nation is really bleeding away through the conditions of boy life." Dr. Talbot also gave an account of gambling among boys who work in the streets, and the harmful influence which these excitements exert at a time which is the most important period of a youth's life.

The question of how to provide for those children whose means of subsistence are thus removed from them by this Bill is taken into consideration by the establishment of children's labour exchanges. These work in connection with trade schools and apprenticeship committees, with the object of helping boys and girls to choose a suitable career, to find places for them, and, after they are thus launched, to supervise them, both as to their material and moral welfare. Parents are frequently quite ignorant as to the comparative advantages or disadvantages of the various trades, but many could well afford to let their children spend a year or two longer in acquiring proficiency in a superior occupation, if they were acquainted with the facts of the case. The labour exchanges, therefore, act as registries to bring children, on leaving school, into touch with suitable employers and employments. Local apprenticeship committees exist for this purpose, working under a central association in London, and while the children are apprenticed or learning their trade, their progress is watched over by "visitors," or "guardians," who report to the committee on the well-being of the young beginner, and give him or her advice as to attendance at technical classes or evening continuation schools. Books have been published by these apprenticeship committees, containing particulars of various trades and the means of embarking in them. The titles of such little pamphlets indicate their nature: "Trades for London Boys," "Trades for London

Girls," "A Handbook of Employments," "Occupations for Girls." The children's bureaux are a most valuable attempt to organize the employment of the young. With the work of the bureaux, the help of voluntary workers, men and women, is associated and much sought after, and although the bureaux themselves are managed by paid officials, the voluntary workers' aid in the after-supervision is considered essential to the success of the project. The organization of such a scheme in India is one in which the combination of masculine and feminine effort would achieve the happiest results. Men's co-operation is necessary, because these labour bureaux have to keep in touch with the whole of the labour market, and it requires a man to maintain a connection with the employers of male labour: but women could do much in the placing of girls; and in the task of supervision of the young of both sexes their aid is absolutely indispensable.

At Munich, in Germany, this system of children's labour exchanges is generally worked in connection with the schools. When children are about to leave school, the teacher explains to them the important nature of the choice of calling which they are going to make. With the teacher's advice and that of their parents, they fill up a form with various particulars as to their age, acquirements, and any calling which they may feel a special inclination to enter. When these have been sent in to the exchange, they receive from it another form, which they fill up and take to the exchange in person, to apply for a post as apprentice or otherwise. These proceedings are carried out some little while before the children are ready to leave school, so that there may be an opening waiting for them directly they have completed their studies. In Strassburg the same co-operation between the school and the labour exchange is observed, and, in addition to the form filled up by the child, the latter may also, if willing, undergo a medical examination in presence of the teacher, parents, and the superintendent of the exchange. Representatives of the English Poor Law Commission visited Strassburg, and reported most favourably on this voluntary medical examination of apprentices, as a deterrent to those who might wish to enter callings unsuited to their physical strength.

A useful little book entitled "The Labour Exchange in Relation to Boy and Girl Labour,"* by Mr. Frederic Keeling, gives much information on the subject, and urges that all branches of the work of organization of the labour market should be carried on in the same building, in order that, if a candidate be found unfit for one section of work, he or she may be passed on at once to something more suitable. Similarly, a single prominent building in the capital of

* P. 54.

every Indian Province and every Native State should be made a labour exchange, where workers could apply at any period during their industrial careers, and obtain the best help and advice as to employment. The apprenticeship committees deal only with skilled trades, but "the object of the labour exchange is to organize the *whole* of the labour market. Its ideal is an organization which arranges—or, at least, is cognizant of—every contract for the employment of labour in the whole country. As long as the industrial system is so arranged that there is a demand for a large number of boys and girls for purely unskilled work, it is better that these boys and girls should obtain their work through an exchange rather than in the unregulated market."* Speaking of the work of the apprenticeship committees, Mr. Keeling says: "There is no doubt that their efforts tend to raise the *standard of skilled work*—(1) owing to the selection of more suitable children than would otherwise obtain places as apprentices; (2) owing to the encouragement and assistance given to apprentices already placed, to make the most of their opportunities of attaining a high degree of skill. There is some reason to believe that efforts of this kind may indirectly tend to raise the *proportion of skilled workers* in the whole community."†

* "The Labour Exchange in Relation to Boy and Girl Labour," by Frederic Keeling, pp. 57, 58 (1910).

† *Ibid.*, p. 17.

Thus, England is speaking with no uncertain voice as to the wrong done to the youth of the nation in withholding from it the entry to more skilled callings. The Wage-earning Children's Committee is an organization which has done much to restrict child labour out of school hours. Through its initiative the Government passed the Employment of Children Act in 1903, which chiefly concerns the employment of children within the school age. This Act has done much to prevent the overworking of children out of school hours, and many towns in England have passed by-laws which regulate the hours during which children may be thus employed. This is, therefore, a considerable advance in checking the evils of sweating among the young. The same Act also dealt with the street-trading problem, and the Act of 1908 brought about the establishment of the special courts of justice for children which are now an English institution. That children convicted of crime should be tried in the same court as adult offenders has been considered to have a most deleterious effect upon their morals and character. They are, therefore, since 1908, brought up for trial in separate courts of justice, their imprisonment under the age of fourteen is forbidden, and they are not permitted to be present in ordinary police-courts except at the moment of giving evidence.

To sum up the chief agencies adopted in

England to check sweating among both women and children: These are: (1) Factory and Workshops Acts; (2) Public Health Act; (3) appointment of women sanitary inspectors and women factory inspectors; (4) trade unions; (5) National Anti-Sweating League; (6) Women's Trade Union League; (7) Women's Industrial Council; (8) trade boards for the establishing of a minimum wage.

The chief means projected by English men and women for the better development of boy and girl labour are: (1) prohibition of street-traders under the age of seventeen (boys) and eighteen (girls), according to the Bill recently before the House of Lords; (2) regulation of child labour outside school hours, under the Children's Employment Act; (3) Factory Acts limiting the age and hours in which children may be employed; (4) trade schools, continuation classes, and technical schools; (5) apprenticeship committees and skilled employment associations; (6) labour exchanges.

It is clearly impossible to give anything more than the briefest outline of all these schemes, each of which could easily be expanded to fill a chapter equal to, or much longer than, the present one. But enough, we hope, has been said to prove the growing interest which is felt now in Europe, and which it is the duty of the women of India also to take, in the intelligent education of the youthful element of the population. An aimless *laisser faire* policy will but result in a purposeless, formless muddle. Here, as in so many other questions, it is absolutely necessary to have a definite plan. The watchword in India should be "Educate, organize: organize, educate," and then the country can look forward to the time when this terrible waste of youthful power and talent shall be checked, and the reproach of the oppression which now lies heavy upon the working women and children of wellnigh every land shall be removed. Surely this is a sphere in which Indian women may labour as ardently as the men, that their "sons may grow up as the young plant, and their daughters be as the polished corners of the temple."

CHAPTER XVII

RESCUE WORK

"There is a future left to all men who have the virtue to repent and the energy to atone."—Bulwer Lytton.

"Criminals collected together corrupt each other," said the great Napoleon; "they are worse than ever when, at the termination of their punishment, they re-enter society." Here is one of the burning questions of the day: What can be done to help those who, having been once convicted, and having passed through the ordeal of punishment, are thrown back again upon the world which pronounced them unfit for freedom? Their stay in prison does not exercise a reforming influence upon them, as is proved by the figures quoted by Mr. Churchill, the Home Secretary, who states that three out of every four convicts released from jail in Great Britain from 1900 to 1903 returned under long sentences. British criminal statistics for 1908 also show that out of 11,628 prisoners, 8,222 had previous convictions against them, a proportion of 70·71 per cent! Nothing further is required to prove the need for societies and projects to turn these released prisoners to some profitable employment, and make them into useful citizens instead of criminal outcasts. If they relapse repeatedly into crime, then it must be admitted that the whole system of imprisonment is a failure, since its object—to deter from vice—has not been attained.

Women especially, on leaving prison, where they may have been sent for what is really a trifling offence, find most avenues of employment closed to them. This is one of the causes that go to swell the ranks of women of ill-fame in most countries—the lack of suitable occupation for women on the expiry of their sentences. In England practically the only organized trade for them is laundry-work; and although the efforts made in this direction are most praiseworthy, it seems regrettable that some fresh lines of labour could not be devised. It was a woman (Mrs. Meredith) who did so much to improve prison life, and who first (in 1867) started a laundry to employ discharged female prisoners. From that beginning the system has extended in all directions in connection with British prisons, and has partly filled a want which was felt by women on leaving jail. There are also various homes in which female ex-convicts can be received and trained for domestic service; but the project which seems to afford the brightest gleam of hope for them—that of a farm colony—has only been tried in isolated instances, or for younger criminals—boys and girls.

The Salvation Army, whose work is known to dwellers in most of the large towns of India, has been so singularly successful in connection with ex-convicts that it is very hard to pass it over here without a word, and as India is pre-eminently an agricultural country, we feel that it may not be out of place to give a short history of the enterprise through which men released from prison have been started on a fresh life of purpose and hope by setting them to work upon the land. A similar scheme has been tried on a comparatively small scale in Baroda at the Model Farm, where, under the Thana system, selected male prisoners are sent and allowed to work at agricultural pursuits practically as free men. The result of the project has there been found satisfactory. Doubtless the same system might be turned to the benefit of women also. The regenerating effect of labour on the soil is so strongly evident among the ex-prisoners at Hadleigh Farm in Essex, on the east coast of England, that perhaps our countrywomen might think the example worthy of imitation as a means of redeeming the woman convict in India. Those who wish to read an inspiring history of this undertaking will find it described at greater length in chapter ix. of "Waste Humanity," by F. A. McKenzie.

The estate at Hadleigh consists of about 3,000 acres, bought by the Salvation Army ten years ago. This, when first taken over, was waste land, unproductive and apparently undesirable. At present it is a thriving farm colony, with orchards, vegetable gardens, poultry farms, strawberry and other fruit gardens. Cattle and horses are reared on the estate. All the usual farm produce is grown. Greenhouses furnish a huge supply of tomatoes and early salad. Brick-works occupy a large number of men. Experts are engaged in the various departments to teach the men their trades. The workers come from all classes of society. As well as ex-convicts there are professional men, who, through drink, gambling, or other misfortunes, have sunk, until the farm has proved their one means of salvation. There are tramps and wastrels gathered in from all parts of England. Here on the fresh Essex land they are given work to do, the only conditions being that they submit to the regulations of the colony, and indulge in neither alcohol nor drugs during their stay. On entry, most of them have to be taught to perform the simplest farming operations, and it can readily be comprehended that for some time their labour is not very productive to the colony. As the months go on, however, if they be industrious, they can improve so as to earn a small weekly wage as well as board and lodging. This wage they are encouraged to save to provide capital for themselves when they leave the farm. If they continue to show progress and prove steady, efficient workers, they are gradually raised from grade to grade, their food and accommodation are bettered, and their wages slowly increased. There is a reading-room and library for their use, social intercourse is promoted between the men, and when they have been trained into useful, capable workers the Salvation Army finds places for them either in England or the colonies. Naturally this system of taking in wastrels, boarding them, and paying them a small weekly sum as pocket-money, does not pay, in spite of the fact that tons of market produce are dispatched to the neighbouring towns. But what it does do is to make men out of what are often mere wrecks of humanity—the flotsam and jetsam that seems as if it can find no room for itself among the capable workers of the world. Then another point to be noted is that the labour done by them is all toil performed with a definite object—that of fitting them to become once more useful members of the State. It is not work merely extended to them as charity, which would be of no real use to them or to their employers. An objection sometimes urged by the opponents of the scheme is that the produce of the farm competes in the market with the labour of other men who are paid a higher rate of wages. Hence, such objectors assert, the tendency of employing this cheaper labour is to lower the rate of wages generally, and to substitute poor labour for good and well-paid work. But no employer could possibly afford to take such incapable workmen as these usually are at the beginning, pay them the full rate of wages, teach them their business, and sell at a profit. The whole enterprise, as we have seen, does not pay, in spite of its fine organization—that is to say, from the material and immediate point of view it does not pay; but in the end it achieves a far higher result than present percentage in pounds, shillings, and pence—*i.e.*, the transformation of the outcast and hopeless into honest, capable, and healthy men. Many of them emigrate to the colonies, and are helping there to extend Britain's great Empire beyond the seas. Certain it is that they carry with them over the water the best wishes of all true philanthropists in England.

In other ways, too, the Salvation Army does a wonderful work for good among ex-criminals. The officers are permitted by the Home Office to visit the English prisons, where those prisoners who wish to interview them are requested to give in their names to the authorities. When the officer visits the jail, he interviews each man privately in his cell, and converses with him either about religion, or his relations, or his prospects on leaving jail. Particulars concerning each individual are kept on record, and if the man's sentence for any reason be shortened or remitted, he is often given over to the care of the Salvation Army officers, with a photograph and a statement of his record, as a help to them in subsequent dealing with him. The Salvation Army then supports him until some employment opens for him. Women officers also work in the prisons, spending their whole time in visiting the women detained in the jails, talking and praying with them, and assisting them when their sentences have elapsed.

The success of the work thus undertaken is marvellous, considering the hardened criminal natures with which it has to cope. Mr. H. Rider Haggard ascribes its good progress to the fact that the promises made by the Salvation Army to convicts are always fulfilled, and also that, by its loving sympathy even with the most degraded, it reawakens in them a fresh hope and a new self-respect. Moreover, the social worker is often one who has himself been rescued from a life of sin, and so appeals directly to the prisoner as a living proof of what can be done for the fallen.

The work of the Salvation Army has already proved almost as successful in dealing with Oriental as with Occidental nations, and especially the criminal tribes of India have benefited greatly by its efforts on their behalf. These are stated to number about three millions, are of a roving, wild, gipsy nature, and are supposed by some to be the descendants of the primitive races of India. The greater number subsist by means of pillage and theft, frequently committing dangerous crimes of violence, and the British Government has found it practically impossible so far, in spite of constant imprisonment, to restrain them from crime. A few years ago, gangs of these marauders were expelled from the United Provinces, to which they nevertheless returned; and about three years ago, Sir John Hewett, Lieutenant-Governor of the United Provinces, invited the Salvation Army to attempt some schemes of regeneration among them. Soon the people saw the advantages of earning an honest living, and came of their own accord to beg for admission to the carpet-weaving factory and other places where the Army had devised modes of employment for them. Now, as set forth in one of the latest pamphlets issued by the Salvation Army, they are taught weaving, *durrie*-making, the manufacture of money-bags and boxes for the Treasury, rope-making, towel and duster hemming, etc. The work among them has progressed rapidly—probably because of the method adopted by their reformers of treating them, not as outcasts, but as fellow-beings. They are reported to be quick to learn the processes of weaving, but, as might be expected, are difficult to induce to work steadily. The success which has attended the Salvation Army's labours among this dangerous class of hereditary criminals, whom the police have hitherto been powerless to restrain, is a great testimony to the efficacy of the methods of British organization applied to Indian life.

A new system has just come into force in England, from last April, for the treatment of ex-convicts, which may prove advantageous to the fallen. On leaving prison, the convicts are handed over to the care of a Central Association. The money they have earned by their labour during incarceration is given over to this association to use for their benefit and to find them employment. Hitherto it has been difficult to secure posts for these men and women, as employers have naturally been reluctant to engage them except in very menial occupations. There are about one hundred societies that deal with the task of befriending the ex-convict, and also with those who have served short sentences. The above Central Committee of Discharged Prisoners' Aid Societies only takes up cases of long sentences, but a scheme is being mooted at present to set up a similar association to benefit those undergoing short sentences.

It is increasingly evident in England that imprisonment has on many natures a hardening, evil influence, and hence every effort is being made to save the young from familiarity with the jail. Those who are acquainted with female criminals assert that it is far more hopeless to redeem a hardened woman offender than a man. There is, therefore, the greater need to consider what can be done to help Indian women and girls to trample vice under foot at its outset instead of attempting to smother it when it has passed beyond control. We shall, accordingly, consider a few of the correctional schemes adopted in England, America, France, and Germany, for the youth of either sex.

The depressing and demoralizing effect of prison life upon the young had been so clearly shown by the statistics of English convictions, which proved that a very considerable percentage of young persons committed to prison returned there again and again, that the Reformatory School Act was passed in 1854. Since that date all youthful offenders over twelve and under sixteen, guilty of deeds rendering them liable to a period of imprisonment, are sent to a reformatory instead of to jail. The procedure is the same in India. The industrial schools, on the other hand, are intended for the education of children who are not guilty of any actual offence against the law, but who are either outcasts or found living in degrading circumstances. By taking the children thus early from their vicious surroundings, it is believed that their downward career is checked, and that those who would otherwise go to swell the number of criminals in the jails are transformed into happy and useful members of society. The classes of children admitted into these industrial schools under a magistrate's order are those found begging in the streets; those found destitute, either orphans, or whose parent is a convicted criminal undergoing sentence; those who are found wandering without any visible means of subsistence and without a home; those whose parents or guardians are morally unfit, through crime or intemperance, to take charge of them; those who are known to associate with thieves or women of ill-fame, or to be living in a house of ill-fame. In these industrial schools, which are for children of both sexes, the girls are educated, kept for at least a year, or often considerably longer, and when they leave they are found situations to enable them to make a good start in life. There are also many voluntary industrial schools, not under State control, which receive friendless girls, either free or at a small cost, and give them a training. The certified reformatories and industrial schools, as well as many of these voluntary institutions, are all affiliated with the Reformatory and Refuge Union, whose secretary keeps an account of each, and gives valuable advice to any who require information regarding particular cases. Where there are such numbers of similar institutions, the advantage of applying to an authority who is familiar with the special character of each is very apparent, and the effect of such organization under a special head is to insure the effective placing of children in the institutions best suited to them.

As well as resident industrial schools, there

are truant schools in England, to which children who have committed offences against the law are sent for short periods, and receive food, instruction, and some industrial training. There are also day industrial schools, intended for young persons who are found in an uncared-for, dirty, ill-fed, ill-clothed condition, where they are fed, given an elementary education, and taught some means of getting their livelihood.

The scheme of institution-life for the inmates of industrial schools is approved in England, as giving a better discipline and more regular mode of living than would be afforded by boarding out the young persons in private families, as is so often done on the Continent. The statistics of the after-employment obtained by the inmates go to prove the success of the English plan. Of the girls the majority become general servants, cooks, housemaids, laundry - workers, nurses, dressmakers, mill-workers, factory hands; many marry, and only a *very* small proportion accept casual employment. It is only fair, however, to give some opposite views held as to the evil effect on the individual of such large institutions. In the report of the Second International Congress of Women held at Paris,* Mlle. Lucienne Marin made a pronounced attack upon large correctional establishments, and gave an outline of what she considered would be a much more beneficial organization for boys and girls. Detention in

* Vol. ii., p. 505.

reformatories, she said, had had a very insufficient result. The inflexible disciplinary régime only awakens in the child a longing to escape. The practical instruction is useless or inadequate to produce skilful, honest workers. The life in common is fatal to the good, who deteriorate by contact with the bad; among the worst specimens a slight improvement usually manifests itself, the result being a general levelling, and the creation of a low standard of morality. Most of the children, she asserted, only require to be placed under conditions which are morally and materially healthy to transform them into useful members of society. They are not criminals, they are only unfortunates, who must be elevated by education and placed in a well-organized school, where they may become good citizens, good fathers and mothers, and excellent workers. Instead of gathering together 300 or 400 children, she recommended the division of these numbers into sections of about fifteen children, over whom it would be possible to exercise an effective moral control. At entry into the school the children, up to the age of ten for girls and twelve for boys, would be educated together. At first primary instruction would be given, including sewing for girls and wood and iron work for boys. After the ages of ten and twelve for girls and boys respectively, an apprenticeship of at least three years would be given to each child in carpentry, house-painting, building, locksmith's and glazier's work, for boys; and for the girls domestic duties, gardening, poultry, dairying, the preserving of fruit and vegetables, confectionery-making, etc. These duties would occupy about six hours a day: the ideal aimed at being to create workers with a good, all-round knowledge and capable of fulfilling any functions connected with their trade. The school should be the prototype of the family. The girls would be taught the entire management of the house; no servants would be kept, as the whole work would be performed by the pupils. The cookery would be carried out on strictly economical and hygienic lines. It was proposed to have a "trial group" of children just admitted to the school, who for three months would be kept under surveillance, to see if there were any evil so deep-rooted in their character as to make it inexpedient for them to associate with the rest. These incorrigibles, who are, however, rarely met with, would then be sent to a reformatory proper, where more repressive measures could be used. The aim of the school would be to turn out intelligent artisans, capable workers, honest women, who would later on become the parents of families not likely to yield to drunkenness or vice. They would also be able to earn their living in whatever surroundings they might be thrown, either town or country, since they would have studied agricultural pursuits as well as other trades and callings carried on in cities. The objection urged against a new organization of this kind is the initial expense, and also the cost of providing the technical education; but Mlle. Marin maintained that such expense would only be initial, and that the debt could be wiped out gradually by the proceeds of the labour performed on the farm. Half the money earned by the children would belong to them, the other half would go to the maintenance of the school. After leaving the school, a friendly society of former pupils would serve still to link the young people with their early associations, and they could return to the school, either to find employment if they should be out of a situation, or even to be nursed in case of illness. Thus the school would continue to act as counsellor and guide on their path through life.

In all reformatories the rôle played by women has been most important. It was a woman, Mary Carpenter, who was one of the original promoters of English ragged schools (first devised by John Pounds, a Portsmouth shoemaker), reformatory schools, and girls' industrial schools. Hers is a name well known also in India, as the promoter of the female normal schools established in each Presidency. Now, when reformatories form an essential part of philanthropy in England, whether they be for boys or girls, a woman is always either in entire charge or at least associated with the management. In many cases the inmates of both sexes are children of degenerate parents rather than actual criminals, the offspring of intemperance or of vice, who require to be taken care of rather than punished. Some are simply weaklings in body and mind, who need a woman's influence, and it is in this sphere that she can do so much in the noble task of developing honest, industrious women and capable workers out of the apparently unpromising material committed to her charge.

It has long been felt in England that some sort of correctional education is required for young delinquents between the ages of sixteen and twenty-one, who are too old for admission to State reformatory schools. Therefore the Borstal system for dealing with young criminals was adopted in October, 1902, and a penal establishment, under State control, was set on foot, which is neither a reformatory nor a prison, but an institution where youths sentenced to six months' imprisonment or longer receive an education both mental and manual. The inmates are divided into classes—penal, ordinary, and special. By their good conduct they can be promoted from one division to the other. They are taught agricultural work, market-gardening, and various useful trades. In addition to this, their mental equipment is cared for by the provision of a sound elementary education. The measures adopted are therefore not repressive, but developing, and include gymnastics, exercise, libraries, and pleasant evening amusements. The effect upon the youths has been very gratifying, as after they leave the prison the majority of the inmates do well. The authorities in charge recognize fully the grave necessity of finding employment for these young men upon their release; and the Central Borstal Association, which numbers among its patrons the most prominent men belonging to the English Church, law, and politics, is a central society to direct those liberated to suitable occupations. The practical, sensible nature of the trades taught during the stay in the institution makes the provision of openings for them not so difficult a task as might be imagined. This scheme has been generally adopted throughout England; and the Prevention of Crime Act 1908 still further extended its sphere of action by empowering the court to send to a Borstal institution, for a term varying from one year to three years, such young offenders between the ages of sixteen and twenty-one as appear to be acquiring criminal habits, and who have been sentenced over and over again for minor offences. There is also provision made for releasing some of the inmates of these institutions on licence if they seem likely to lead steady, decent lives. During the time that the offender is liberated on licence he is superintended by some society or individual interested in his welfare, who reports on his progress. Should any inmate of a Borstal institution be found unamenable to the discipline there, he is removed to prison, lest his evil influence should affect his companions. The Borstal system has been introduced in Baroda since April, 1908, for the benefit of young male criminals, who are taught weaving, sewing, warping, cane-work, tape-making, gardening, and carpentry. The main outlines of this attempt to check crime and to preserve the young from the often fatal familiarity with prison life might be adapted for wayward girls, or those young women who are convicted of a first offence, but whose natures are not actually criminal. Concerning this class it may be urged that their faults are generally due to evil surroundings or mental and physical defects, for which they personally are not responsible; therefore it would appear advisable to adopt some different method than mere imprisonment for their regeneration.

In America there is a remarkable institution for women at Sherborne, Massachusetts, where most of the inmates are confined on charges of insobriety, and are undergoing sentences of more than a year. It partakes more of the nature of a hospital than a prison or reformatory, and there are various divisions to mark the good conduct of the women. For example, in the worst class the crockery used at meals is inferior and imperfect, in the one above it is rather better, in the next better still; while in the first division the prisoners enjoy the privilege of using quite good china and neat table equipment. The care of animals and birds is also granted as a special favour for good conduct, and the influence of this occupation is said to have a most beneficial and humanizing effect upon the women.

In France there are many societies for visiting women prisoners during the time of their detention, and helping them to prepare for a useful and industrious life when they leave prison. There is usually no hard-and-fast rule laid down; the ladies who visit the women each proceeding in her own fashion, according to the character of the person with whom she has to deal. At Montpellier they interview each one separately in a special room set apart for the purpose; and in the report laid before the Second International Congress of Women, held at Paris, Mme. Max Bonnet asserted that much had been done to bring the prisoners into communication with their families; but she also maintained that an institution, to serve as an intermediate abode between leaving prison and re-entering the world, would be of great benefit to those who were unable or unwilling to return to their relatives. Such an establishment could do much to prevent women who are set at liberty from relapsing into their evil ways.

Various societies throughout France are occupied in this work, and have opened refuges, where women and girls are temporarily admitted pending suitable employment or their return to their families. It is universally granted by all those who work among ex-prisoners that the real moral struggle only begins on leaving the jail. During their forced confinement they are no longer exposed to temptation, but once freed from this restraint the old evils assail them again. Recognizing the dangers that beset these women, the Maison de Famille Saint Augustin at Sainte-Foy, in France, was founded some years ago to receive young girls from the age of thirteen to twenty-one, who had just left prison. Only a few were admitted at a time, the superintendence was careful and firm, but there was not the same gloomy restriction as in prison life. These girls were allowed to engage in gardening and agricultural work, and it was often found here, as in so many other countries, that an open-air life worked wonders both for their moral and physical regeneration. More active and less sedentary labour is what is required for ex-prisoners. Part of the day the girls spent in ironing and sewing, the proceeds of which went to defray some of the expenses of the institution; the rest of their time was occupied with work in the kitchen-garden, the poultry-yard, in housework, and cookery. On Sundays some educational instruction was given them, and walks were taken. From the earnings of each girl a certain percentage was saved for her; and when she reached her majority this sum formed a little fund for her, to help her to set up in life.

An establishment on these lines does much to solve the problem of the after-career of the ex-prisoner, who without it has often nowhere to turn. Some have no families to go back to, others have relatives who are worse than useless to them, others, again, have friends or families who are ashamed to receive them. For such as these, life in an institution like the one described is the best intermediary stage through which they can pass before returning to the battlefield of the world. The success of the Maison de Famille Saint Augustin was ascribed by the Bulletin de la Société Générale des Prisons to three causes: (1) the small number of girls received, (2) the great care taken in their selection, and (3) the unremitting, motherly supervision exercised over them. A committee of ladies undertook the direction of the house.

The idea of an agricultural colony is one that has always been felt to be full of hope for the youthful offender. It has been tried in France: first at the colony of Mettray, near Tours, where, under the guidance of M. Demetz—a judge whose experience of the law courts had impressed him with the injustice of exposing young criminals to the dangers of prison life—an agricultural community was founded. Young criminals were sent there instead of to prison, and the wholesome effect of rural occupations and outdoor life showed excellent results. Farming, gardening, vine-culture, cattle-rearing, and silkworm breeding are their chief employments. The toil is severe, but healthy; and many colonies have been formed on the same model, including several for girls.

The project of agricultural employment for street urchins and unmanageable children—both boys and girls—has also been in vogue at the celebrated Rauhe Haus, near Hamburg in Germany, where the inmates receive instruction in agriculture, gardening, and certain trades. On leaving this establishment, posts are found for them in whatever capacity they seem most likely to succeed. The children here are not necessarily criminal, but unruly and wayward. Two important points distinguish this school: first, the housing of children in separate dwellings, each containing about twelve to sixteen occupants; and second, the teaching and constant supervision of the boys by young men of good education and character who are training for posts as prison officials, heads of industrial homes, or schoolmasters.

Lastly, among the many charitable institutions connected with reformatory and prison life, there is one which should not be forgotten, though it does not deal directly with the convicts themselves. It is the Duchess of Marlborough's Homes for Prisoners' Wives and Children, situated in London. These homes were started about three years ago, with the idea of helping the wives of prisoners—particularly those under short sentences. It was thought that if the wife could be enabled to keep her home and family going while her husband was removed from her, it would be a great encouragement to the man to make a new beginning when he left jail. The chaplains of the various prisons report the cases to the Duchess and her lady secretary, who have an office for the reception of the women, where the secretary interviews them, explains the character of the employment offered, and then introduces them to the home if they are pleased with the prospect. The home is a daily institution: the women arriving with their young children about 8 a.m., and leaving at 6 p.m. There is a crèche for babies, and children not old enough for school, aged from one to five years. Each morning they are left by the mother at the crèche, which is close to the workrooms. Here they are given a warm bath, dressed in clothes provided by the crèche, and are then kept in a nursery, fed, amused, and the older ones taught a little. When the mothers leave in the afternoon, they call for their babies and take them home with them. The women work in a pleasant room at sewing, and the results of their labours are sold to defray the costs of the Home. Each woman receives two shillings a day, as well as her food, and if she comes from a distance, part of her travelling expenses are paid for her. As well as the sewing-room there is also a laundry, where sixteen women are occupied under the tuition of a skilled laundress, and after three months' training they are able to take up laundry work as a means of livelihood. The Duchess of Marlborough herself frequently visits these houses, and is familiar with every detail of their management, which is entirely financed by her. There is ample scope for rich Indian ladies to follow the excellent example of the Duchess.

The next subject presents an even sadder and more difficult problem than the reclaiming of the female convict. Rescue work is essentially a woman's business, and it is one of the hardest tasks with which she is confronted. For in all large cities like London, Paris, Bombay, and Calcutta, there are numbers of women and girls who gain their livelihood by immoral means. In London, as in most large towns, the streets at night are the places where those work who devote themselves to the duty of redeeming women and girls from evil associations. There are, roughly speaking, two sections into which English rescue work may be divided: (1) that in direct connection with some religious body, such as the efforts made by various sisterhoods, by the Church Army, the Salvation Army, the West London Mission; and (2) work undertaken in connection with different societies, non-religious in so far as they are not directly affiliated with a particular Church or creed. To this latter division belong the Ladies' Association for the Care of Friendless Girls, the preventive and rescue work carried on under a branch committee of the National Union of Women Workers, and many miscellaneous independent enterprises which exist to remedy the social evil.

The Sisterhood of the West London Mission is one of the best known rescue societies. Its work is performed by educated women who have devoted their lives to the mission of aiding the poor and sinful. Two of these philanthropic women go every night from 11 p.m. to 1 a.m. through the streets of the West End of London, where vice displays itself most openly, and try to persuade the girls to accompany them to one of the numerous refuges or homes which charitable enterprise has provided. There they are housed, fed, and sheltered for a certain length of time, varying from a few days to three months, according to the exigencies of the case. During this period they are carefully supervised, and attempts are made to influence them for good and to procure them work. In this particular refuge in West London numbers of new inmates are received each year, and it is estimated that out of the number fully 85 per cent. *never* relapse into their old way of life, but become useful and helpful members of society. Nay, more—those who have been thus rescued often themselves take up the good work, and help others who have fallen to escape from the snares of evil which are spread around them.

Numbers of such sisterhoods exist in Great Britain, doing their work in quiet, unobtrusive fashion, and mostly acting under the guidance of some religious body. They manage homes, refuges, houses of mercy for fallen women, some for those who have committed their first fault, and whom it is held inexpedient to mix with more hardened wrong-doers, others for outcast women of every class. In connection with the English Church, a number of educated women, called deaconesses, receive a thorough training in social work and religious knowledge. At the end of this course of instruction, which lasts two years, they are appointed by the heads of the Church to work in particular parishes, either town or country. One special object of their endeavour is the reclaiming of girls, who are taught to follow some useful calling. A point to be noted in regard to these workers is that they are all women of education and culture, and they have met with much success in their unselfish and noble toil. Many other religious bodies train women to aid in this field of labour. The Roman Catholic religious orders do much for the raising of outcast women, while men and women of the Salvation Army carry on this work amid the very worst of the flotsam and jetsam of humanity.

The head of the Salvation Army, General Booth, whose name is well known in India, aided by his capable and sympathetic wife, founded about forty-five years ago the religious organization which is now established in fifty-six countries and colonies. The extent to which a woman can help her husband in social labour is proved by the life-work of this noble woman, to whom General Booth dedicated his memorable book "Darkest England," speaking of her as "the Companion, Counsellor, and Comrade of nearly forty years, the sharer of my every ambition for the welfare of mankind."

At present, under the auspices of the Army, its work is carried on in thirty-three languages; every night over twenty-eight thousand poor are housed in its institutions; it has two hundred and twenty-nine food depots and shelters for men, women and children; one hundred and fifty-seven labour factories, where destitute and outcast people are employed; seventeen homes for ex-criminals, thirty-seven homes for children, one hundred and sixteen industrial homes for the rescue of women, sixteen land colonies, five hundred and twenty-one day-schools for children, one hundred and forty-nine slum stations for the assistance of the poor, sixty labour bureaux for the unemployed, criminal and general investigation departments, inebriate homes for men and women, maternity hospitals, prison visitation staffs, etc., etc.*

* "Regeneration: An Account of the Social Work of the Salvation Army in Great Britain," by H. Rider Haggard, p. 9.

Apart from its religious aspect the Salvation Army especially merits attention, since women hold such an important place in its ranks. Its workers are drawn from the poorer classes; they speak at meetings and hold public religious services, generally in the open air. It is universally admitted that they reach a stratum which would otherwise be totally neglected, and the love and zeal which the women show for their work among the most degraded of their sex, is a wonderful proof of the feminine power for good amid the vilest surroundings. Women as workers for God are fully recognized in the Salvation Army. They may hold any position from the lowest to the highest in its ranks, and they have frequently managed the affairs of large organizations with the greatest skill. They have numbers of rescue homes, nursing institutes, maternity hospitals, lodging homes and shelters for the distressed. They deal with women thieves, ill-used children, inebriate, aged, and destitute women, victims of the white slave traffic, women leading immoral lives, illegitimate children, and unmanageable girls.

A description of one or two of these projects must suffice to show the lines on which the rest are run. In the homes for fallen women the sisters of the Salvation Army have scored what is perhaps their most signal success, although much of their work in this direction is done so unostentatiously that its far-reaching results do not always come before the public. The Army recognizes the fearful temptations that have often assailed those women who have gone astray. Therefore, their most important principle of action is to proceed without the slightest hint of superiority. There is no preaching to them about their past: nothing but an atmosphere of sisterly kindness and helpful love. Many of the Army officers are women of good birth and education. These do not disdain to associate with the very lowest of their poor sisters, but frequently take their meals with them, talk with them as friends, pray with them if they seem desirous of it, and bring them such bright messages of hope and courage for the future that miracles are wrought among the women to whom they devote their lives. When a woman in straits appeals for help to the Salvation Army, the first thing the Army does before the babe is born is to urge the prospective mother to reveal the name of the father of her child. This is generally, though reluctantly, done, and after the infant's birth a detective is set to find out the other parent, who ought to be equally responsible for the little one whom he has helped to bring into the world. When the discovery is made—and this is always done by means of a personal interview, not by correspondence, no matter where the man lives—the officer persuades him to acknowledge his child and to give so much a week, according to his means, towards its support until it has reached a certain age. A form of agreement making this undertaking is given to him for signature.

For the mothers there are maternity receiving-homes, where the young women are taken in and sheltered pending the birth of their children, and there are hospitals where they are sent for lying-in. The charges made by these establishments are entirely in proportion to what the patient can afford. Sometimes no contribution whatever is required. During their stay in these homes the Salvation Army does all it can to give them moral instruction, that this slip they have made may prove the last. When they are well enough to leave, the greater number are provided with posts as domestic servants, and generally they do well afterwards. A foster-mother has to be found for the child, for whose maintenance the mother agrees to pay so much weekly. There are working-homes organized to train the mothers as servants, where all their surroundings are made as bright and hopeful as possible. It is said that three pounds will save a woman from an immoral life,* and though this cannot be inclusive of the after-training and after-supervision that is an integral part of the Army's work with "fallen" women, yet to help forward even the first stage of the process for three pounds seems a good investment for money.

The labours of these ministering sisters are

* "The Great Idea," by Arnold White.

not entered upon lightly and without preparation. To fit women for the great task of raising their submerged countrywomen there is a training home for the workers where they receive a year's practical instruction in religion, plain sewing, cookery, laundry, nursing and household duties generally. The discipline is no sinecure, for the candidates have to learn their work thoroughly, that they may be able to teach the women something by which they can earn a livelihood. It is evident that none need embark upon this career unless they are filled with sound, sensible enthusiasm for their cause, and feel themselves to possess plenty of pluck, resource, and tact. The remuneration paid to the women officers is so trifling as barely to suffice for the purchase of their simple uniform. It is solely the love of poor, suffering, toiling humanity which draws them into the work. Some notes given at a lecture on "Success," at the Training Institute in London, are so indicative of the spirit which animates the Army that we cannot refrain from transcribing part of them here. The remainder will be found quoted on page 134 of "The Great Idea," Mr. Arnold White's book on the social work of the Army.

"Success consists of:—

(*a*) Godliness—both spiritual and practical.

(*b*) Cleanliness—clean yourselves, and make others clean.

(*c*) Industry.

(*d*) Cheerfulness—be cheerful when you do not feel like it.

(*e*) Tact—be tactful with comrades and tactful with your girls."

As well as training in a home, the probationer is sent to live for a time in a slum settlement, where families of the sick and poor are visited, maternity cases aided, mothers taught the care of their children, the homes of the poor cleaned and attended to, and words of comfort spoken to those who require them. The public-houses in these poverty-stricken neighbourhoods are a recognized source of evil, and the brave sisters of the Army are not afraid to enter the "palaces" where strong drink is sold, and to speak a word of warning to those tempted to over-indulgence. To the credit of the proprietors of such houses, it must be said that they usually place no obstacle in the way of the officers entering, but even encourage them to do so, and to persuade the pitiful wrecks of humanity to leave the place whose allurement is so strong to them.

This would seem to be a favourable opportunity to make brief mention of the Army's efforts among women inebriates. A hopeless task indeed it has often proved to redeem women from the fatal habit of drug or dram drinking, and yet in it the Army has met with a measure of success which makes it amply worth its while to persevere. For the better classes who can afford to pay, good residences in pleasant neighbourhoods are taken, generally with bright gardens attached. Here, as in the rest of the Army's organizations to combat the drink evil, the method relied on is vegetarian diet, physical exercise, the training of the patient's will-power, the cultivation of her memory, and the imparting of religious hope. Hot milk has been found to have a wonderfully stimulating effect, and grapes are also in vogue, with apples and oranges next in order of merit.* When the patients have left the homes, their after-career is watched over for a period of three years, after which they are left to pursue their lives independent of supervision. The homes run for the poorer clientèle are on similar lines, but simpler accommodation is provided for the inmates. The restoration to happiness and usefulness of some of the most degraded, dirty, apparently impossible specimens of female humanity forms one of the brightest chapters in the annals of women's social work in England.

Among the many countries abroad to which the Salvation Army has extended a helping hand, India is one of the most important. A little band of Army officers began their mission in India in 1882, and since then, apart from numerous village day-schools, industrial homes, farm colonies, weaving schools, hospitals, dispensaries, and village banks, they have also instituted three rescue homes for friendless and fallen girls

* "The Great Idea," by Arnold White, chap. xiv.

in Calcutta, Bombay, and Madras. The methods by which the social uplifting of this class of girl is effected in India would, if studied, probably afford useful hints to Indian ladies who feel it their duty to do what they can to improve the position of those of their unfortunate countrywomen who need such care. The Salvation Army, as well as most other English agencies that labour in this direction, make it their aim not only to increase the material comfort of their protégées, but above all to strengthen and confirm their moral character. They are great optimists, and believe thoroughly in the principle set forth by Bulwer Lytton: "Every man has in him good and evil. His good is his valiant army, his evil is his corrupt commissariat; reform the commissariat, and the army will do its duty."

Apart from the Salvation Army, the Ladies' Association for the Care of Friendless Girls should also be mentioned as playing a most important part in connection with preventive and rescue work in England. This society believes in warding off the evil before it has occurred, even more than helping to repair the fault already committed; and therefore it aims at helping young girls who, from poverty or evil surroundings, are in danger of falling into wrongdoing. A ladies' association can be formed in any neighbourhood, and an annual conference of workers is convened by the preventive and rescue committee of the National Union of Women Workers. Representatives of each association are invited to the conference. The extent of the work done may be gathered from the fact that there are no less than forty-five associations in London, and sixty-six others throughout England and Scotland. The aims of the organization are to further in systematic fashion preventive work among rough girls of the poorer classes who are leaving school and entering upon some occupation. These are provided with free registry offices, where they are found suitable employment; clothing clubs, where by small payments they can obtain clothing at lowest cost; and a training home, where a number receive training in various occupations. The girls are also visited by ladies who take an interest in them and try to influence them for good. The removal of children from unsuitable or dangerous surroundings, the enabling of young women to emigrate, and the establishment of aid committees to help girls after their first fall, are likewise among the aims of the Ladies' Association. The visiting of outcast girls, and special efforts to rescue the very young, addresses to poor women on the best ways of bringing up boys and girls, the issue of various books, pamphlets, etc., on these subjects to teachers, parents, and social workers, together with the raising of the level of public opinion on matters of morality, and the inculcation of an equal standard of morality for both men and women, form an important part of their programme.

Rescue work in England is both paid and honorary, and its brave missionaries venture in pursuit of their task into the common lodging-houses, police courts, and, as we have seen, into the streets of the large cities at night. Not everyone can visit in person the districts of ill-fame where these unhappy girls and women dwell, but all can take an interest in the movement and help it by their money and their influence. The chief preventive and rescue homes which are of benefit and for which subscribers' funds are sought in England are medical homes, convalescent homes, refuges for those who are morally deficient, homes for epileptic, deaf, dumb, or blind girls who have been led astray, also homes for doubtful cases and for preventive cases of girls over sixteen.

When women and girls have been set once again on the right path, and when some useful occupation has been found for them, there frequently comes the pressing question of where they are to live. Charles Dickens again and again by his tongue and pen expressed his conviction that "the reform of their (the mass of the people's) habitations must precede all other reforms, and that *without it all other reforms must fail.*" This applies with peculiar force, both in India and elsewhere, to the class which is now under discussion. Those who are merely provided with work, and not with a home as well, have to find for themselves a cheap, respectable dwelling, to which they can return in safety after their day's toil is over. Such a place is often difficult to discover, and the financing of an institution on these lines, where women who are trying to lead a better life could be furnished with reasonable accommodation and decent surroundings, would be an enterprise well worthy a rich woman's charity. Without some provision of the kind many a girl whose feet have been placed on the upward rung of the ladder will be drawn down again into the abyss from which she has just been rescued. A woman, more than a man, appreciates the comforts and refinements of a home. She is more influenced by her environment. Without such comforts her susceptible nature is prone to relapse quickly into its former state of mental and moral deterioration. The crying need of the Indian working woman is for a decent home.

No account of the work done for the suppression of vice in England would be complete without mentioning the National Vigilance Association, which issues a "Warning to Young Women," printed in ten languages and placed in the cabins of steamers sailing between England and Continental or other ports. The booklet published by the society contains addresses of ladies and gentlemen in all parts of the world, and the addresses of the National Committees in Europe, Egypt, and South America, who will be of service to any women or girls requiring help in difficult or dangerous circumstances. Ladies who are good linguists meet arriving trains in London, to help those young girls who may need their aid or advice. The Travellers' Aid Society carries on a work of similar nature, meeting young women and girls by appointment at stations or ports, directing them to respectable lodgings, and making inquiries into the character of the posts they are proceeding to. Young women are frequently placed in positions of grave peril through arriving in strange cities where they have no one to look after them. Workers in connection with this society are found all over the world, and notices of warning to young women travellers are placed in railway stations, trains, and steamers. Where the girls can afford to pay, a trifling fee is charged to cover expenses, but in many cases no money is required. Railway officials and porters at the large London stations are acquainted with the office or other address of those ladies who meet the trains, and can apply to them at all times in cases of difficulty.

The task of preservation and rescue should not be left entirely to missionaries and special bodies. It is a work which contributes in the highest degree to the development of a higher morality: therefore it should be the concern of every woman to do something for the cause. It requires a special temperament to succeed in the practical part of this arduous and often repellent undertaking, but it is essentially work for women. for those resolute enough to say:

> "I would be bold, and bear
> To look into the swarthiest face of things
> For God's sake, Who has made them."

Many a woman's fault partakes of the nature of those sins which Massillon has classified as "surprises" rather than "infidelities." To such as this the gloomy treatment of prison or penitential life would be the worst possible remedy to apply. It is with her as Molière, the great French philosopher-dramatist, has said of feminine natures in general: "They are not easily kept in the path of duty by harshness; distrust, bolts, and iron grating do not produce virtue in women and girls. It is honour which must keep them to their duty, and not severity." To rouse in them that sense of honour the all important thing is to find them some useful occupation which may re-awaken the sense of self-respect so necessary to the leading of a decent life. With the employment there must be found for them a home. These two things so dear to the heart of every true woman will often be of saving grace to those who have been tempted from the beaten track of good behaviour. Even if there be some few who appear ungrateful, let the benefactress remember the words of the quaint old author Quarles: "In giving of thy alms, inquire not so much into the person as his necessity. . . . If the man deserve not, thou hast given it to humanity."

CHAPTER XVIII

WOMEN'S INTERESTS

"Philanthropy, like charity, must begin at home. From this centre our sympathies may extend in an ever-widening circle."—LAMB.

THE subject of this chapter is the way in which the well-to-do women of India may combine to protect their own interests, and more especially the interests of the less wealthy members of their sex. There is a quaint saying of Shakespeare, that "a fish hangs in the net, like a poor man's right in the law, it will hardly come out." If this be true of poor men in general, it is doubly true of poor women, for working industrial women have usually neither leisure nor ability to defend themselves from oppression. The case becomes more complicated if they happen to be *purda* women. It should therefore be the aim of the more influential Indian women to watch that all laws passed by the Imperial and Provincial legislatures, as well as by the Native States in India, should keep women's welfare in view. We have seen how women in other countries have been at the head of most of the great movements for social reform. In America, Mrs. H. Beecher Stowe was one of the pioneers in the abolition of the American slave trade. In England, Miss Elizabeth Fry and Mrs. Meredith, besides others, have done much for the improvement of prison life ; Miss Louisa Twining brought about a marvellous change for the better in the administration of the Poor Law ; Miss Florence Nightingale by her wonderful enterprise and noble example revolutionized the system of training for hospital nurses, and made her name a household word ; Miss Mary Carpenter was the great promoter of ragged, industrial, and reformatory schools ; Miss Tod, Lady Henry Somerset, Miss Frances Willard (the latter an American), together with many other valiant women workers, have led the van in the crusade against intemperance ; Miss Agnes Weston's brave, practical spirit has found its life-work among the sailors of the British Navy, and those who wish to read the record of one of the happiest, simplest, most heroic careers will find it in her book, "My Life among the Blue-Jackets." Many women authors have used their literary talents for the benefit of humanity, witness Mrs. E. B. Browning, whose pathetic poem, "The Cry of the Children," did so much to awaken public sympathy with the little ones condemned to toil amid the deadening, unceasing whirr of factory machinery

> "Do ye hear the children weeping, O my brothers,
> Ere the sorrow comes with years? . . .
> They are weeping in the play-time of the others,
> In the country of the free."

Many a heart in England was touched by the sad music of her verses, as it could never have been by the cold figures of a factory commissioner's report, and so we find the great movement urged forward for the improvement of children's position as workers. In various other ways women of Europe and America have used their influence, both publicly and privately, to stem social abuses. Indian women who desire that they, too, may not be behindhand in the record of unselfish work performed for the benefit of their fellow-beings, and especially for their poorer sisters, might well consider what feminine societies already exist, to serve them as groundwork on which to base some of their schemes of public service. All may not be suitable for transplantation to Eastern soil, but the leading ideas of a few might be transformed to suit Indian requirements.

One of the broadest associations for social amelioration and progress is the International Council of Women, which has as its great object the extension of a feeling of common humanity throughout the world. This council is a federation of National Councils of Women in most of the civilized countries of the globe, including the United States of America (whose women were the first to unite, in 1888, at Washington, in a National Council), Great Britain and Ireland, Canada, Australia (comprising the federations of New South Wales, Tasmania, Queensland, Victoria, South Australia), Germany, Sweden, Denmark, the Netherlands, Switzerland, Italy, France, Austria, Norway, Hungary, Belgium, and Argentina. Greece and Bulgaria are the latest recruits to the ranks. This huge organization, comprising about a million women, is non-political and non-religious, its aim being simply to act as a link between the women of various nationalities, and to afford them sympathy and suggestions in their work. No council which joins the association is in any way pledged to adopt different modes of work or organization, nor is it committed to any views held by the International Council or any of the affiliated national councils. Meetings are convened at intervals, which are attended by women representatives from all parts of the world, who are thus afforded an opportunity to confer upon matters of common interest to their sex in all its relations. In this way a valuable interchange of views is made possible, and the sentiment of good-fellowship maintained between people of widely different nationalities. "Everywhere, in every land," as Mrs. May Wright-Sewall so well expressed it, at the International Congress of Women, held in Paris, 1900, "there are unfortunate women, women utterly deserted, children who are poor, ill, and unhappy. And everywhere there exist societies to aid these unfortunates. . . . If I were asked: Is it possible that women belonging to different countries should meet in a universal and general cause? I should answer: It is not only possible, it is the final and eternal cause for which women exist. It is only because men, absorbed in their public and private business, cannot alone bear the burden of the sick, the poor, the destitute, the unfortunate, that women, who have to-day as yet no share in political life, find it easier to meet and cultivate the spirit of universal brotherhood."

One of the chief causes which the International Council of Women has at heart is the maintenance of peace, and to that end it formed a committee, composed of one member from each National Council. Each national council has a president, vice-president, treasurer, and executive committee—all ladies. Sectional committees, mainly of experts, are also appointed to collect information on various subjects affecting women's interests. In connection with the National Council of Women of Great Britain and Ireland these sectional committees meet quarterly, and report the results of their efforts to the executive officials. In Great Britain and Ireland the National Council of Women is the governing body of the National Union of Women Workers, whose efforts are described in other pages of this book, and which has done so much for the cause of the working women in England.

Mrs. May Sewall, in pointing out the influence that could be exercised by this International Council, emphasized one point out of many as an example. She said:

"Your discussion this afternoon, to which I have listened with the keenest interest, touched upon a situation which exists everywhere; the same question confronts us in all countries. In all countries there are deserted women and illegitimate children; well, perhaps it would be possible for this committee, formed of representatives of each nationality, to find some means of improving this sad state of affairs by studying it under all its aspects, and by appealing to the intelligence and goodwill of women of different lands."

The symbol of the Conference that year was two clasped hands, which were meant, she said, to signify two things: first, that men and women must walk hand-in-hand, since it is necessary that those who wish to advance upon the path of social progress should be agreed together, both men and women; and second, it signified that the hand of one nation must be clasped in that of another, so that in the twentieth century no civilized country should make war upon another.

Some other questions taken up by the Councils in England and America are the appointment of women on all state commissions in which women's interests are concerned, the promotion of hygienic reform in household cookery, the securing of equal educational advantages and a similar industrial training for men and women, the advocacy of an equal standard of morality for men and women.

These, then, are a few of the aims of this great feminine federation. But it cannot truly be called an "International" Union unless women of every nation belong to it. Therefore the women of India might interest themselves in its work, which concerns matters to which no woman of intelligence can afford to be indifferent. A National Council of Women of India affiliated to the great International Council would probably do much to link the nations in the bond of a universal friendliness, and to span the gulf that still yawns between the East and West. Advancing civilization is doing much to lessen the breach. The bounds of space that formerly severed distant lands are being contracted each day by the marvellous inventions of mankind. With the fresh knowledge of each other that the peoples of the earth can thus easily gain, surely a mutual understanding should not now be so difficult of attainment as it was in days of yore! By their association in such an International Council, the women of every land may do their share in furthering that great day when the nations shall recognize the futility of war, the "Great Illusion," and feel that their truest interests are served, not by storms of internecine strife, but by the civilizing hand of peace, a new order, whose advent shall usher in

> "A time when brotherhood shows stronger
> Than the narrow bounds which now distract the world;
> When the cannons roar and trumpets blare no longer,
> And the ironclad rusts, and battle flags are furled;
> When the bars of creed and speech and race which sever
> Shall be fused in one humanity for ever."

The principles of such co-operation are especially capable of extension in India, where there should be co-operation in economic, as well as sociological organizations between British Provinces and the Native States. The influence of women might do much to break down the barriers of misunderstanding that often exist within their own country as well as outside it.

There are numerous societies whose special object it is to safeguard the interests of the English working woman. Several have been described in other chapters of this book. One of these, and perhaps the most important, is the Women's Industrial Council, described at length in Chapter XVI., which was founded in 1894, and has a separate department to watch over all legal matters affecting women's interests, and also to prepare official reports, Parliamentary bills, etc. The Council is constantly publishing information about women's work, and among its latest subjects of inquiry may be mentioned the industrial employment of married women and widows, regarded from an economic and sociological point of view.

The Industrial Sectional Committee of the National Union of Women Workers is another society which has been already dealt with elsewhere, also the National Anti-Sweating League to secure a minimum wage, and the Women's Trade Union League. In Scotland there is an important body, known as the Scottish Council for Women's Trades, with its headquarters in Glasgow, and having as its President the Countess of Aberdeen. Its object, like that of the Women's Industrial Council in London, is to watch over the interests of women and children in every trade in which they are employed. There are four departments of the Council's work: (1) An Inquiry Department, which examines into and reports particulars of women and children's employment; (2) an Organization Department, to further trade unions and combination among women, also insurance societies, to provide them with support during illness or unemployment; (3) a Parliamentary Bills Department, to further legislation in favour of women and children; (4) Women's Employments Committee, which supplies workers and those interested with particulars concerning openings available for women, and the conditions of labour in the different trades. Each of these departments is governed by a separate committee.

Breaches of the Factory Act and other

measures for the protection of women and children are reported to the Council, which undertakes to submit such cases to the authorities. In this manner many measures of a sanitary and industrial nature have been furthered by the Council. The result of inquiries into various trades is published from time to time. For example, pamphlets have been issued on "The Employment of Children," "The Housing Problem in Glasgow," "Summary of Factory and Workshop Act," "The Problem of Home Work," "Women Shop Assistants: how they Live and Work," "Guide to Occupations for Girls" (containing information on thirty-six trades), etc. Lectures on social and industrial problems are given by members of the Council.

Another English society which has as its object the promotion of legislation in favour of women and children is the Christian Social Union, which has made a study of labour conditions, and sends in reports to the Home Secretary upon the results. It has thus supplied details for and furthered Parliamentary legislation, and has given valuable information regarding work in such industries as laundering, fish-curing, brush-making, artificial flower manufacture and fruit preserving. The committee have also conducted an investigation into the employment of home or casual workers after childbirth, and into the hours and wages prevalent in the drapery, dressmaking, and millinery trades, where women are engaged.

The Industrial Law Committee was formed in 1898, and is an association of women created with the object of enforcing the observance of the law regarding industrial work. Lectures by inspectors of factories and sanitary inspectors are held throughout England before meetings of ladies, for the purpose of teaching social workers the provisions of factory and sanitary law. Offences against the law may be reported to the committee, and any other particulars regarding the employment of workers. These reports are sent in to the proper authorities for redress, and where an improvement in legislation is deemed desirable, it is brought before the public notice.

The British Association for Labour Legislation, with its headquarters in London, is the British section of the International Association for Labour Legislation (central office at Basle, Switzerland). This International Association has as its purpose the union of persons of every nationality who recognize the need for industrial legislation. It issues a periodical bulletin published in English, French, and German, giving an account of all that has been recently done in every country to promote labour legislation, a list of the laws passed, and the full text of such measures. Reports of labour congresses and the resolutions passed are also printed, and a list of the most recent literature dealing with labour.

The society aims at promoting uniformity of conditions of labour in different countries, and every two years it convenes international congresses to discuss industrial problems in various lands. Individuals may belong to the association on payment of 5s. yearly subscription, while 10s. 6d. includes the receipt of the periodical bulletin, or labour magazine; societies may also become members on payment of one guinea. The association is non-party, and through its organized efforts labour treaties have been adopted, scientific work has been carried on by the international labour office, and statesmen and social workers have been enabled to study and follow the laws of other lands. Thus each country is able to benefit by the experience of others, and laws beneficial both to employers and employees can be passed without endangering national interests. Four new sections have been added to the association in the year 1910-11, Norway, Sweden, Finland, and South America, and a special British magazine entitled the *World's Labour Laws* has been started, as a companion to the bulletin. The international aspect of this new labour journal is well emphasized in its first number (May, 1911), which contains an article on recent legislation in the East, with reference to (1) the Japanese Factory Act, and (2) the new Indian Factory Act. The motto of this latest labour publication is Goethe's famous dictum: "Das Gesetz nur kann uns

Freiheit geben" (The Law alone can give us Freedom). Some idea of the scope of the association may be formed from this year's report of the work of its five commissions, which dealt with (1) Finances and Business Affairs of the Association, (2) Industrial Poisons, (3) Home Work and Sweating, (4) Night Work of Young Persons, (5) Maximum Working Day. Other subjects were Equal Treatment of Foreign Workmen and Child Labour. Three English-women contributed reports on several of these themes. Women's industries in most other countries were also well represented, though more frequently by male delegates, for although many distinguished ladies have given able support to the British and American sections, it does not appear that European women in general have as yet taken a very prominent part in the work. The last International Meeting took place at Lugano in September, 1910, but few of the sections sent women representatives to the conference, showing that even in Europe women's practical interest in labour matters still requires considerable stimulus. The Association has dealt at length with the question of women's employment in industrial occupations, and has promoted an international treaty by which the contracting States agreed to forbid the employment of women on night work. The advantage of joining such an important international association will doubtless appeal to Indian women when they begin to take a more active part in promoting the welfare of their working sisters than they do at present.

These are the chief societies in Great Britain which deal with labour legislation as it especially affects women. But it would hardly be fair to pass over such associations without a brief mention of another which would seem to have as its object the antithesis of those we have been discussing—*i.e.*, the Freedom of Labour Defence, which exists to protect workers, and particularly women, from restrictive enactments which might militate against their salaries and restrain their liberty in their private lives. According to this party, the protective laws, by prohibiting woman from free employment on a completely equal footing with men, place her in an inferior position and make her employment so irksome that employers consider the difference in men and women's salaries does not counterbalance the inconvenience caused by the restrictions placed on female labour. Now, in England this view is not generally held, chiefly because the idea that restrictive legislation would prove a bar to women's advancement has been found untrue, and especially so in the case of an industry which employs a vast number of female operatives—the Lancashire cotton trade. Formerly in this calling the women and children suffered under terrible hardships. Children toiled all day long in the mills; they were over-worked, ill-paid, corrupt in morals, physically degenerate. Women, also, were fearfully over-worked. All were condemned to labour in factories dirty, ill-ventilated, insanitary. The hours of work were excessive. But now with the improved legislation, under the Factory and Sanitary Acts the hours during which women and children may be employed are limited, a definite standard of sanitary accommodation, temperature, ventilation, etc., is fixed, and various rules are laid down to guard women and children from employment in dangerous trades. With what result? Not that women and children have been driven from the Lancashire factories, but that, proportionately to men, they are employed now in larger numbers, that in the textile trade unions women outnumber the men, that wages have gradually increased. Legislation has helped the women as well as the men to acquire more money, better health, greater skill, additional leisure. It has not militated against their relative position in the labour market. Protective legislation has not diminished the number of callings open to them. On the contrary, the number of trades in which women are employed has increased, and the result of better laws in England has been that the reduction of the working day has led to the employment of more women, to complete the tasks which the others, without regulation, would have been compelled to finish over-time.

On the other hand, in the two English occupations which are more unregulated than any others—domestic service and agriculture—women are growing scarcer every year. The conditions of labour in these two spheres in England are worth looking into, and the difficulties experienced here in the organization of domestic service should afford a valuable hint to India, for that is a branch which should not be neglected there.

The party who oppose legislation specially protective of women maintain that the right to work should be considered as one of the most precious interests of women. The present legislation is regarded by them as hurtful to women, from several points of view. It prohibits, they say, or strictly limits, their overtime work, it restricts the home-worker, who requires all the money she can obtain to keep body and soul together, and it regulates the labour of females in dangerous trades. Instead of imposing restrictions, they assert that the proper method of procedure would be to substitute better processes in the dangerous trades, to instruct the employee so that the risk to her would be practically removed, and to insist on proper precautions being observed by the employer. As far as liberty to work at dangerous trades is concerned, they declare that the health of the men employed in the manufacture of white lead, matches, etc., probably suffers quite as much as that of the women would. If no better processes can be invented, say the upholders of the women's equal right to work, then the hours of labour in those callings should be shortened, so as to minimize the risk, and at the same time, employees in those industries should be paid as much for their few hours' labour as others gain by a whole day's work in less dangerous pursuits. Those industrial occupations which are really unsuited to the feminine organism will naturally, they assert, be avoided by them. For the rest, hard work is preferable to hunger or pauperism. The right to work means with women the right to live. Work in its various shapes and forms is their stock-in-trade. They ought to be encouraged to enter other branches, instead of being cramped in those departments to which they are admitted. The printing trade, they declare, is an example of the exclusion of women from a calling, which, as far as compositor's work is concerned, seems eminently suited for them, and yet there are only a few women in England engaged in it, and every effort has been made in the past to shut them out.

In answer to these objections, we would remark that the enactments against the employment of women on night work, have naturally an effect in excluding them from labour in connection with the daily papers. True, there is no great fatigue or very prolonged effort necessary, but the legal prohibition based on moral considerations rightly puts them out of the running. Women's health suffers more no doubt in other callings—such as laundry-work and street-hawking—than it would in the ordinary printing trade, but *night-work* with men printers must be viewed in a different light. In many other industries, too, where from the nature of the business there is inevitably a slack season followed by a rush, the restrictions placed on women's overtime work are frequently misunderstood.

The intention of the laws to protect women are good, but in practice they are considered by some to defeat their object. The limitations of hours of work for married women are also objected to by the "Freedom of Labour" party, who assert that there are women without children who require employment, and, moreover, that it is not guarding the interests of the coming generation to deprive the future mother of the good living which her extra earnings could procure for her. Every woman who has attained her majority, whether she be single or married, should have the right, they say, to decide herself on the hours and conditions of her labour. These are the chief arguments in favour of freedom of labour for women, whose advocates see in it an escape from want and suffering for the poor woman, and the promotion of the dignity of the so-called weaker sex. But the opposite party, who hold that woman's interests ought to be protected, are in the majority in England, and

Mr. John Burns has in view a measure by which women shall be restrained by Act of Parliament from working in factories, workshops, etc., within ten or twelve weeks after child-birth. The present Factory Act imposes an interval of only four weeks as necessary.

There is another association, called the Stansfeld Trust, which makes it its object to further the position of woman under the law. Its principle is the legal equality of men and women, and it distributes to subscribers (societies and private individuals) reports on Bills before Parliament which affect the status of women or children, also on all educational methods laid before Parliament. Its secretary and treasurer are both ladies, also its scrutineer of Parliamentary Bills. The work of the latter is to study all bills immediately upon publication, and to report on those parts which concern the position of women and children. These reports are printed at once and sent out to subscribers, thus serving to keep those interested in questions affecting women *au courant* with what is going on, and enabling them to take direct measures if anything injurious to their interests should be attempted. The observance of an equal law of morality by both sexes is another aim of the trust, which owes its existence to a fund raised in memory of Sir James Stansfeld's great work in promoting the cause of women.

One of the best examples of an English

association—the work of which is carried on by means of cordial co-operation between both men and women—is the National Society for the Prevention of Cruelty to Children, which exists for the purpose of safeguarding the welfare of the children of English parents at home and abroad. "The sole object of the Society," says the latest report (May 30, 1911), "is that every child in the land shall live an endurable life." Surely there can be no more noble sphere of effort, especially for a woman, than to see that the young children of her country shall be enabled to exist without suffering oppression or wrong. In India, fortunately, the child born in wedlock is seldom treated cruelly by its parents; but to insure the safety of illegitimate offspring there is room for such a society there. "No organization in England," it is stated in the annual report, "owes more to the splendid work of women than does the Society." They act as patrons, vice-presidents, as secretaries and members of committees, as collectors of funds by subscription or otherwise, as distributors of leaflets, as lecturers, and those who have taken up the cause have spared neither time, money, nor ability to make their endeavour a success. The result has been that, mainly through their efforts, the proportion of misery and cruelty in Great Britain has been sensibly diminished. In this year of the Coronation the Society makes a special appeal to all British subjects who love their country and who love children to assist in advancing the principles, methods, and claims of the National Society for the Prevention of Cruelty to Children. On the score of humanity the furtherance of such an endeavour should appeal to women of every land, since the future of every country depends on the health, safety, and happiness of the younger generation. The National Society for the Prevention of Cruelty to Children was founded in 1884, and has as its official organ a journal, *The Child's Guardian*, in which a regular account is given of the work of the association. The organization of the Society is remarkably good. It has now a total of 201 branches and 1,231 district committees, and the Society does not intend to slacken its effort until it has representatives in every city, town, and village throughout the kingdom. Public meetings are held to bring the cause before the people and so stimulate fresh interest. A new feature has lately been started in the shape of meetings organized and addressed by ladies for the purpose of speaking to mothers on the educational principles of the Society, warning them against the use of highly inflammable clothing for their children, teaching them the way to rear healthy babies, and numerous ways by which to promote the welfare and comfort of their little ones. Numbers of working women attended these meetings, which, it is hoped, will be of great benefit in fostering an intelligent comprehension of the Society's aims and the duty that even the poor owe to their children. The women at Holloway Prison and the young men at two Borstal institutions have also been addressed by the director on the subject of the care and regard that should be observed towards the young. The National Society for the Prevention of Cruelty to Children does not, however, confine its scope to England, for in these days, when the other side of the world has been brought within a few weeks' journey, a movement that only included England would be but a limited scheme. Therefore, the question of international federation has been successfully initiated to look after the interests of British children abroad, and to provide a central bureau in London, where persons from other countries who are interested in the cause of children may meet and discuss methods, legislation, and any other matters of common interest. Those who seek for instruction on the subject can readily find there an answer to their inquiries. The method of federation adopted might be usefully employed to link up the scattered parts of India, since without such a central bureau no thorough plan of organization could be carried through.

The Society is primarily one to enforce the Acts of Parliament for Prevention of Cruelty to Children. Its object is not so much the *punishment* of cruelty as its *prevention*. It is incorporated under a Royal Charter, and is non-political and non-sectarian. It is governed by branches formed of the subscribers of the districts. The branches appoint representatives to the council, the council elects an executive committee, and the executive committee appoints officers and transacts the whole administrative business of the society. Its mode of procedure is the same in all cases, and is as follows: anyone who knows of a case of ill-treatment of a child should communicate either with the director of the head office in London or with the nearest local inspector of the Society. An inspector is then sent to inquire into the circumstances, and in many instances a warning stops the cruelty without recourse to prosecution. When the ill-treatment is so aggravated and continued that legal measures become necessary, the Society undertakes the action, paying expenses and assuming the care of the children, who are afterwards boarded out in suitable homes at the Society's expense. Cases of cruelty may be reported by the general public, the police, other officials, and by the Society's inspectors. Numerous leaflets distributed from door to door, chiefly by women, explain what constitutes infringement of the Acts for Prevention of Cruelty to Children, and supply information as to whom cases of ill-treatment may be reported, assuring the public that the informant's name will be kept private unless the complaint be proved a malicious one. The majority of the cases are not discovered by the inspectors, whose time is chiefly occupied in investigating cases reported by the public. The Society carries on its work without encroaching on the province of the police, and its inspectors are able to do by warning and supervision what no ordinary policeman could possibly undertake. The inspectors are often granted admission to houses where a policeman's visit would not be tolerated, to homes where parents are merely careless or ignorant in the upbringing of their little ones. Another important factor in the procedure is that prosecutions are only undertaken on advice from the legal staff of the central office. No personal or vindictive spirit can therefore enter into the case. In each instance a solicitor is instructed, and the decision remains with the magistrates. The Society also undertakes the investigation of cases where a parent refuses to support his children, and insists, by legal means if necessary, that a fixed amount be contributed out of the man's wages. The Society is not extravagantly managed, and numbers of voluntary workers greatly aid the financial as well as the moral side of its organization. It has no endowment, no State grant. There are no less than 11,000 lady collectors, and the report of the director for this year states that "the whole Society is a triumphant exposition of the glory and beauty of woman's work. No restrictions surround its workers; they are found in all classes, they excel in noble deeds. The government of the Society is shared by women; on local committees, on the central executive, on the general administrative council—a democratic body, consisting of two representatives from each branch—they have rights of speech and of voting. This is as it should be in an organization that seeks to improve home life, to establish the right of the child to proper treatment at the hands of its parents."

Such a eulogy of women's work should be a wonderful incentive to Indian women to follow their Western sisters' good example. The effect of their intervention would no doubt be a tangible gain to their country in the shape of a perceptible increase in the sum-total of its happiness.

CHAPTER XIX

WOMEN IN JAPAN

"The woman question in Japan is in a stage of transition. . . . It may in the end eclipse the Western movement in the completeness and rapidity of its development."—FRANCES SWINEY.

VISITORS to Japan are struck by what they see and hear of the quiet progress that Japanese women are now beginning to make towards a freer, more socially useful life than they have led in the past, and in a book on women's organizations in Western lands it occurred to us that some short account of women's achievements in the land of the chrysanthemum might have a particular interest for our countrywomen. The chief point of view from which their history might prove attractive lies in the fact that the Japanese are a nation which, more than any other Oriental people, has adapted foreign principles and methods to meet its own requirements. The Japanese are of such a different culture to ourselves that there can be but few parallels between us; but we, nevertheless, thought it might especially interest our countrywomen to note how far the rising Oriental nation has gone in the adaptation of Western ideas to suit its women's own peculiar circumstances. An important point for the consideration of our countrywomen is this: while the Japanese have borrowed hints and systems from Asia, Europe, and America, have they been able to do so without either sacrificing their own racial independence or casting aside their own religion and traditions in an over-hasty seizing upon the novelties that have presented themselves before them? They have employed Chinese, English, Americans, French, Germans, Italians to teach them educative principles, engineering, naval construction, military methods, law, civil government, agriculture, medicine, art. In their first colony, Formosa, they adopted, after due consideration, the system practised by England throughout British India. The question is, will they, with all this apparent imitation of foreign races, succeed in the assimilation of so many varied methods, and yet preserve their own individuality and ardent nationality. There are many critics who think that they are achieving this difficult task. For these reasons we have felt attracted by the history of the modern Japanese woman, and though she may only now be beginning to shake off the shackles of convention, yet the description of those organizations which she already possesses may, we hope, find a suitable place here.

First of all it may be mentioned that Japanese women, like their sisters in India, held an honourable place in the early records of their country. In ancient Japan women ruled as empresses, and women have always exercised a great influence at the Imperial Court. Ancient Japanese literature owes much to women. The earliest Japanese book extant is the "Kojiki" (Record of Ancient Matters), and the story runs that the Emperor Temnu, who reigned from A.D. 673 to 686, had the histories of the principal noble families collected, with the intention of compiling an account of the Japanese nation. To this end, a lady of the court named Hiyeda no Are, who was noted for her excellent memory, was orally instructed in the whole of these ancient chronicles. Unfortunately, however, the Emperor died before any more lasting record of the chronicles could be made, and for twenty-five years the noble lady retained in her memory the long histories of the ancient families of Japan. Then in A.D. 712, under the auspices of a woman, the Empress Gemmyo, she dictated the whole to a scribe, Yasumaro, and the work at last reached completion. Thus Japan owes her earliest extant literary and historical monument to the talents of one woman and the patronage of another.

Woman's influence on literature continued to show itself; for in A.D. 720, the "Nihongi," or Chronicles of Japan, were written under the patronage of the Empress. It was a woman who wrote the first Japanese novel, the "Gengi Monogatari," by Murasaki no Shikibu, which dates from the early years of the eleventh century; and the "Makura no Zoshi" is a description of social life in Kioto, of the same date, also written by a lady, Sei Shonagon. Both these remarkable works have earned high praise from native and foreign critics, and prove that the intelligence of Japanese women is not a modern product, but has been their possession for centuries. Moreover, the characteristic of Japanese literary women has generally been to preserve the purity of their own language, and to avoid the intermixture of Chinese forms used so freely by the men. In the eleventh century, the Emperor Ichijo had among his circle many other men and women of literary and artistic distinction, yet the works that have survived the lapse of years and become classics are almost entirely the products of the brains of women. Ladies were noted then for their keen intelligence, as well as for their grace and beauty. They seem to have constituted, on a smaller scale, a court literary circle like that of Louis Quatorze in France. But the same thing took place in Japan, which has been already pointed out as occurring in other lands: the loss of feminine prestige, which followed upon a period of great honour paid to women. Japan became a nation of soldiers, none but sons were regarded with favour by their parents, and women's interests were looked upon as unworthy of a warrior's serious attention. Small wonder, then, that the fair sex retired into the background, and gradually came to accept without questioning their secondary position! The "Great Learning of Women," by Kaibara Ekken (1630–1714), was considered the moral text-book to be laid to heart by all young women, and the standard of opinion concerning the female sex may be gathered from a few of its maxims, which, it should be remembered, were written by a famous philosopher and ethical teacher. "The five worst infirmities that afflict the female," he says, "are indocility, discontent, slander, jealousy, and silliness. Without any doubt these five infirmities are found in seven or eight out of every ten women, and it is from these that arises the inferiority of women to men. . . . The worst of them all, and the parent of the other four, is silliness."* Again he writes: "Such is the stupidity of her character that it is incumbent on her in every particular to distrust herself and to obey her husband."†

Alongside these statements there are precepts which the Japanese woman would seem to have specially laid to heart, since in her there shine so brightly the great virtues of unselfishness, obedience, and devotion to duty. "More precious in

* "Women and Wisdom of Japan" (The Wisdom of the East Series), pp. 44, 45.

† *Ibid.*, p. 45.

a woman is a virtuous heart," writes this second Solomon, "than a face of beauty. . . . The only qualities that befit a woman are gentle obedience, chastity, mercy, and quietness. . . .* The great lifelong duty of a woman is obedience."† "In her capacity of wife, she must keep her husband's household in proper order. . . . In everything she must avoid extravagance, and both with regard to food and raiment must act according to her station in life, and never give way to luxury and pride."‡

But although these principles have found an abiding-place in the heart of the true Japanese woman, they must not be taken as embodying the whole ideal of the modern Japanese. For Japan has not escaped the great movement which to-day is assigning to women a more prominent place throughout the world. The most advanced views of the feminist party there, are expressed in a book published in 1899 by Fukuzawa Yukichi, one of Japan's most famous educationalists, who did so much to make Western ideas familiar among his country people. This celebrated book is entitled, in opposition to Kaibara's treatise, "The New Great Learning for Women," and promulgates the theory that woman's sphere, though different to that of man, is nevertheless not inferior, and that she is en-

* "Women and Wisdom of Japan" (The Wisdom of the East Series), pp. 33, 34.

† *Ibid.*, p. 38. ‡ *Ibid.*, p. 41.

titled to the same social rights and privileges as men—in other words, that the older work is entirely behind the times.

The Japanese woman is not an agitator for her own rights, but, nevertheless, she is moving forward on the tide of social progress. The Imperial family and the Government are in favour of women's education, and the result of the efforts made by private individuals and the State is the foundation of a good educational system for girls and women. In 1874 the Tokyo Women's Normal School was opened, to qualify women as teachers, and was the recipient of a grant of 5,000 yen (about £500) from the Empress, as Count Okuma states in "Fifty Years of New Japan." The Empress also showed her keen interest in education by founding the Peeresses' School for daughters of the nobility. There are women's higher normal schools at Tokyo and Nara, at which a four-years' course of study can be taken in literature, science, and arts. In Japan, as in India, good teachers are reported rare; the alleged reason in Japan being the lowness of the salaries offered. The great bulk of the country's education is still in the hands of men. In 1884 Government granted permission to women to enter for the annual examination for the Doctor's Diploma in medicine, and since then Japanese women have devoted themselves to a considerable extent to the study of the healing art. The Tokyo Women's Medical School, started on a small scale, has now several hundreds of women students on its roll, and there are a good many lady doctors practising their profession. The work of urging forward this most important branch of education among their sex is being ardently taken up by several noted Japanese women.

One of the most important educational organizations is, of course, the Women's University of Japan, founded at Tokyo in 1901 by a Japanese Christian, Mr. Naruse, who, after a visit to America to collect information, returned home, and, in spite of opposition, started the scheme for a women's university, which has gained the commendation of various educational authorities. In "Fifty Years of New Japan," compiled by Count Okuma, it is stated that this university "may be said to be built on the principles of equality of the sexes and equal education for men and women. . . . The courses of study . . . are so arranged as to be in full accord with the political and social conditions of the country, as well as with the peculiar characteristics of our women."* One remarkable feature of the university is that the majority of the students after their course is completed eventually marry, and therefore it may be concluded that the future mothers of the nation are availing themselves of the culture imparted by a university course. The greater number are studying, not to take up a professional career but to fit themselves to be

* "Fifty Years of New Japan," vol. ii., p. 220.

better wives and mothers, and better members of the State.

In Chapter VII. we have seen that most Indian women are somewhat ignorant on matters connected with their legal rights. The Japanese have recognized their sex's frequent helplessness in legal affairs, and have made the study of a certain amount of law part of the necessary curriculum in the domestic faculty. There are also children's schools and a kindergarten attached to the university, with the object of familiarizing the students with the education and character of the young. The physical development of the girl students is made a special feature—as it is, in fact, in all schools in Japan. There is, however, little or no study of physiology in its relation to the psychology of the individual, which has been familiar to Hindus of the higher castes for countless centuries. The importance of hygiene and sanitation is impressed on all students of this Japanese university for women.

The aim of the university, as set forth by Kotaro Mochizuki, ex-M.P., in "Japan To-Day" (1910), is to "educate woman, regarding her as a member of State, society, and also as a sex. It is intended to inculcate in her the spirit of self-respect and confidence, and to develop and cultivate her various characteristics as a woman. . . . It is proposed to add to these inherent characteristics those ideas and thoughts imported from abroad, which will enable her to become a useful member of society, apart from being queen of the household. It is to enable Japanese women to assume the duties consequent upon becoming an element and influence in society."*

So Japan's ideal would seem to run parallel with the theories of many English educational scientists, who believe that feminine development should proceed along lines marked out by the inherent differences of the sexes.

This women's university cannot claim to have a woman as its founder, but women in Japan are themselves, nevertheless, now beginning to act as educational pioneers. One of them has founded a school offering a three-years' course of study to girls to equip them for examinations for posts as teachers of English in the Government schools, examinations for which they have hitherto had little facility to prepare. This is a remarkable enterprise, initiated and carried out entirely by a Japanese woman in the interests of her countrywomen. In itself it proves that Japanese women have in them the power of organization, which has hitherto, for various reasons, been left undeveloped.

The great increase which has taken place of recent years in Japan's relations with the rest of the world has led to a certain demand for women in practical callings that were formerly closed doors to them. Moreover, the death of so

* "Japan To-Day" (1910), p. 131.

many men during the wars with China and Russia made it necessary for some women to enter upon a more public life than they had previously led. The loss of the head of the family forced the mother to turn her hand to some definite means in order to support her children, with the result that gradually a change is coming over the general attitude towards women as followers of trade or professional callings. A women's commercial school has been started, a women's sewing and tailoring school, a women's fine arts school, an associated women's technical school, besides art schools and a women's department of the school of photography. In the towns some of the women devote themselves in many practical ways to earning a living. Hair-dressing is reported to be a calling by which a woman may earn a considerable income. In the largest industry in the country—the production and manufacture of silk—women play a most important part. In this trade it is interesting to note that the woman's share in the task of rearing the silkworms and the manufacture of the silk is quite as great as, or greater than the man's, and the result of her ability is shown in the increasing respect in which she is held in that industry, proving that if women took up branches of trade naturally suitable to their sex, they would not fail to distinguish themselves or to co-operate freely with men.

In hotels and restaurants the principles of co-operation between the sexes may clearly be seen at work. Some of the hotels are owned by women, and most of the successful establishments are run by husband and wife. In smaller inns the division of labour is systematically arranged, the wife doing the waiting and the taking of the money, while the man usually turns his attention to the culinary part. The woman's share, as a rule, includes the direction, and she often keeps the accounts. In tea-houses, too, women and girls are generally manageresses. The cleanliness, brightness, and prompt attention which are everywhere met with in hotels and restaurants are a testimony to the Japanese woman's organizing ability and her practical co-operation with the other sex.

A more novel occupation which engages the Japanese woman is bill-collecting, in which she is reported excellent, and it is also said that as circulating library agent she is most enterprising in conveying the books to customers' own houses, a method of booklending which Western librarians have only comparatively recently adopted. Home industries are a feature of the lives of the poorer women, who almost invariably supplement the family income by working in their own homes at weaving, brush and mat making, clog making, etc.

Japan does not exclude women from the printing trade, though the Japanese girl works rather as a compositor's assistant than as actual compositor. In business offices girls are employed as clerks. Literary work engages the energies of a certain number, art occupies a large proportion of women, and women are employed by one railway company as booking-clerks. The Japanese woman's aptitude for landscape gardening is noticed by Lady Lawson in her "Highways and Homes of Japan" (1910), where she reminds her country-people that Japanese women led the way in this profession long before English people dreamt of sending their girls to be trained professionally as Daughters of Ceres at Studley and Swanley Colleges. Art is a subject that is systematically studied to a very large extent, and Japanese lady artists do not confine their enterprise to their own country, for lately one of them held a most interesting exhibition of her own paintings in London, which attracted much attention both from the Press and from visitors who went to see her at work. A Japanese curio shop in London bears the names of two Japanese ladies above its door, showing that the fair sex have discovered an occupation which is both pleasurable and profitable if conducted on business lines. A Japanese lady dentist is also attracting patients in the West End of London. The numbers engaged in these callings in Japan is, however, comparatively small, and scarcely any organizations—such as thrift societies, labour leagues, etc.—exist for their benefit.

The Japanese society in the organization of which women play the greatest part is undoubtedly the Red Cross Society, which trains nurses of both sexes to aid in case of war. The association originated in 1877, but did not receive its present title until 1886, when it was placed under Government control. The patronage and practical support afforded to this society by ladies of high rank, from the Imperial family downwards, have done much to ennoble the nursing profession in the eyes of the general public. The adherence of these ladies does not limit itself to financial aid, for they act on committees, and in many other ways show their keen appreciation of nursing as a calling for women. The Volunteer Lady Nurses Association, formed in 1887, and affiliated with the Red Cross Society, is composed chiefly of ladies of good position, who are taking up the study and practice of nursing, that they may be ready in case of war to help their countrymen. Some of the Imperial Princesses have not hesitated to lead the way and join this association, which has given a great impetus to the nursing profession.

The central hospital of the Red Cross Society is at Tokyo. In times of peace nurses, as well as doctors, are trained there, and after their three-years' course is over, they are free to take up private nursing. They are, however, obliged on leaving to sign a document, declaring their readiness to serve under the society's direction at any time during the next fifteen years in case of war, political troubles, or army manœuvres. At the military manœuvres the nursing staff is dispatched with the army just as it would be in case of war, and the experience thus gained proves of the greatest possible benefit. A pension scheme has been devised for those whose health has suffered through their duties, and in case of death the money passes to their relatives. The pay is good, and the reserve staff are also paid for attendance at manœuvres, etc. It must be stated that, as is to be expected, the head of the Red Cross Hospital is one of the sterner sex, but the great success of the whole scheme and its splendid organization is no doubt attributable to the cordial co-operation between the members of both sexes. Surgeon-General Baron Tadanori Ishiguro, writing on the subject of "The Red Cross in Japan," mentions the services rendered by the nurses on the first occasion of their employment in the field in 1894, during the China-Japan War: "This employment of female nurses met with loud opposition . . . because of antiquated notions regarding the relative status of men and women in Japan. But I stoutly maintained my original position, and employed the Red Cross Hospital nurses in the military hospitals of Hiroshima and elsewhere. The result amply justified my course of action, for all these nurses proved an unqualified success. . . .

"At the close of the war . . . a number of lady head-nurses were decorated with the Order of the Crown, which order had been specially created some years previously, to decorate women for distinguished service."*

This was the trial trip of the Japanese female nurses, and after its successful issue all was plain sailing. When the recent war between Russia and Japan broke out, the efficiency of the splendid staff of the Red Cross Society was a matter of world-wide comment. In connection with the adaptation of foreign institutions in India, it should be noticed that Japan owes the system practised by this organization to Germany. It is not the development of a Japanese idea. Its marked success proves once more the efficacy of adapting Western institutions to suit Eastern environments.

In reflecting upon the associations in which Japanese women are interested for the benefit of their sex, one is struck by the fact that these seem to be few in number, showing that as yet Japanese women do not take a prominent part in such social work. The principal societies that exist are of a patriotic character, such as the two just mentioned. A league which owes its origin to similar motives is the Ladies' Patriotic Association, which has as its object the raising of money to purchase comforts for the soldiers, or funds to be distributed among their widows and

* "Fifty Years of New Japan," by Count Okuma.

orphans. Among its honorary members this society can count several Imperial Princesses. Its headquarters are at Tokyo, and there are branches in various parts of the country. It has a membership of over 750,000, and issues an official journal. As might be expected, its chief functions are exercised in time of war. Testimony to its efficacy is given by Kotaro Mochizuki in his book, entitled "Japan To-Day," where he says: "Those appreciating the objects of the Association, and who made contributions are not limited to the Japanese only. . . . During the Japan-Russian War there were contributions made by individuals and public bodies in Europe and America, proving that the activities of Japanese women exhibited in connection with the work of the Association have been recognized even by the people abroad."*

There are also benevolent societies, in many of which the Empress takes a keen interest, thus setting a splendid example to her countrywomen. One of the most important is the Tokyo Charity Hospital, a free institution for the benefit of the poor, which is maintained by private subscriptions, and has in connection with it a training school for nurses. The work connected with such societies as these is mostly performed by women. There exists also a certain number of women's societies of an educational nature,

* "Japan To-Day," p. 299.

whose members meet at stated times to hear or take part in addresses or discussions.

The problem that lies before India and Japan would seem to be partly of the same nature as far as its women are concerned. Both realize that the nation would be doubly powerful if its women were properly trained; but the difficulty lies in so adapting new ideas as to make them work side by side and in harmony with the best practices of the old régime. A suitable combination of new and old—that is the goal after which to strive. To many Orientals Japan may seem perhaps over-hasty in her grasping after Western systems, but, on the other hand, India and other Eastern countries may appear to the Japanese as too conservative. There can be no actual parallel between India and Japan. India, with countless centuries of culture and philosophic thought behind her, cannot be considered from the same standpoint as the Japanese. The trend of Japanese character is not philosophic: it is industrial and material. Hence it is as far removed from the Indian mind as the East is from the West. The aim of our countrywomen should be to strike the golden mean—to be neither too slow nor too impetuous in their adoption of new ideas. By taking up and applying to their needs certain Western institutions Indian women may perhaps do much to break down the barriers that still divide the Orient from the Occident, and so help to bring nearer that material progress in which the peoples of the earth shall no longer be as strangers, but each nation shall feel itself linked in the bonds of a universal brotherhood.

The type of woman who can promote such organizations for the benefit of humanity as some of those described in the pages of this book must surely be a higher, nobler one than that of her who can only feel concern for her personal comfort or the progress of her own children in life. Sacred as are the duties of motherhood, it is growing every day more apparent that the worthiest mothers are those who take beneath their protecting care, not only their own immediate family but that larger family of the State, and who feel it their duty to act as true parents in endeavouring to redress any wrong they see in the world around them. Just as the true mother in her private family will suffer no injustice to continue that she can remedy, so the mother of that great public family—the nation—should let no abuse exist which she can possibly help to remove. Thus there may arise in time a race of healthy, useful, happy, hopeful human beings, who will each in turn leave the world a little better than they found it. In this sphere of unselfish labour for the good of the community—and especially for their poorer sisters—the keener sympathy, the swifter intuition, the higher moral sense which most women possess, will find their complement in the broader outlook, firmer purpose, and deeper insight of the man, and the co-operation, not antagonism, of the sexes will be enlisted to further that "increasing purpose" which surely runs throughout God's whole creation.

INDEX

THE END